Don't Forget to Cover the Pig

FINDING OURSELVES IN TASMANIA

~ A MEMOIR ~

by

Dick Reese

Published in the USA by RDRR Publishing

Library of Congress Control Number: 2024923547

ISBN: 979-8-9907956-0-0 eBook
ISBN: 979-8-9907956-1-7 Paperback

To the love of my life, Wife #1, Ruth.

CONTENTS

PROLOGUE

Have you ever contemplated escaping, packing it in, and leaving the land of your birth behind? Perhaps you survived a failed relationship, the political landscape has become intolerable, or maybe you are ready for adventure.

In 1988, near the end of Ronald Reagan's reign, before either of the Bush or Clinton presidencies and the advent of the internet and cell phones, for reasons we do not fully fathom, we exchanged American city life for Australian farm life. Far from home, with no farming experience, we bought a sprawling 125-acre farm on the island of Tasmania—Down Under Down Under—where we added Australian citizenship and raised our three children to adulthood along with hundreds of furry, fluffy livestock that we fostered as pets.

From diaper-wearing goat kid and lamb orphans romping through the house to a whiskey-swilling rooster slumbering by the fireplace to launching a sunscreen advertising campaign featuring a 400-pound pig, we fumbled along. Challenged by the cultural divide and the emotional and physical highs and lows, we weathered the tragedies and celebrated the comedies.

I hope that reading about the hurdles we cleared on the path to living our dream, many of which appear too fantastical to believe but are true, will enlighten and entertain.

Also, time and memory may have distorted the telling, so apologies to all our Tasmanian friends and acquaintances, whose names were changed to protect the guilty, for any misrepresentations of you or your fair island paradise.

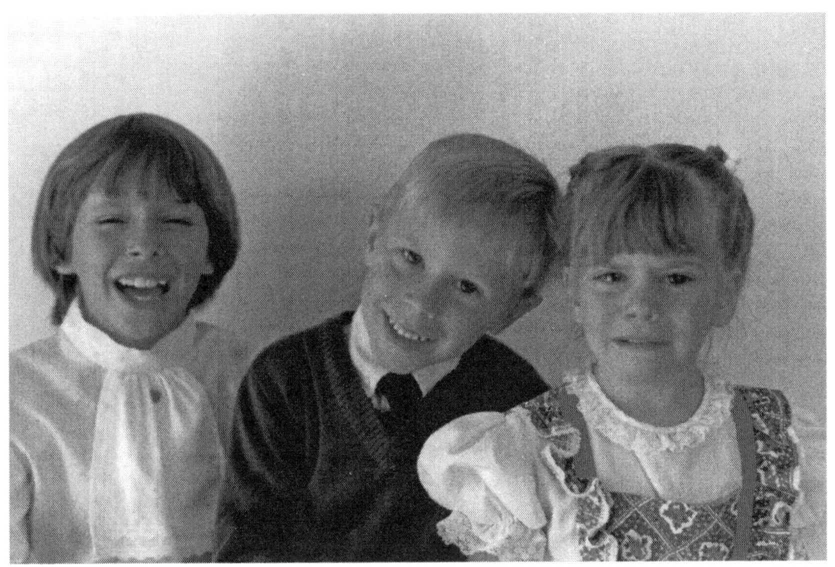

1. COLD FEET

It was a dark and stormy night.

It was the night before Christmas.

It was the night Ruth announced, “I’m not going.”

We faced off in our living room amidst a sea of half-packed moving boxes, rolls of packing tape, and most of the stuff accumulated during twenty years of marriage.

As powdery snow swirled outside the front door of our Nevada home, feelings colder than snow swirled inside me.

I watched her for a sign, hoping she was kidding. But when I gazed into those fiery brown eyes and noted the tight-set jaw, all framed by Scottish-red hair, it pained me to realize that, after two years of planning to migrate to Australia, she had changed her mind.

The holiday spirit vaporized.

We never argued and rarely disagreed because when an issue arose, Ruth resolved it. For example, a few years into our marriage, I criticized how she did my laundry. Two days later, a big-box store van delivered a Maytag washer and matching dryer. We didn't argue, and I learned how to launder my clothes. She continued ironing my clothes until—you think I would have learned—I complained about how she did that. Soon thereafter, an Elna professional clothes press arrived. Again, there was no argument, and I mastered the art of pressing my work attire, professionally. Each gift came with a glittery red-hearts-and-roses card that read: "FOR THE WORLD'S GREATEST HUSBAND."

Although Ruth's argument avoidance technique had worked in the past, this time, a clever solution was not possible.

I shifted my attention to the corner where our tiny Christmas tree stood. The three red-and-green gift-wrapped boxes under the tree painted a miserly Scrooge Christmas scene for our three children.

We had explained to our eldest, nine-year-old Danelle, that when we moved, there wouldn't be enough room in the shipping container for many toys.

Precocious Danelle spoke for herself and her siblings when she laid down the terms of acceptance. They would approve the move if we promised the girls could take their Barbie dolls, Ryan, his Hulk Hogan doll, and the fourteen-foot circular trampoline Santa had delivered the previous Christmas. The latter set the minimum length of the shipping container.

Our children did not look like us. None had Ruth's hair color, freckles, or long legs. Neither did they have my light brown hair, squat body, or oversized feet.

Danelle, like Ryan, has sandy blond hair and blue eyes. She was cute and, with her fiery personality, watched over and protected her siblings like a doting mother hen.

Unlike her big brother and sister, Kristin had glossy dark brown hair and sparkling brown eyes. Coupled with her pearl-skin complexion, she looked like a China doll come to life. Her pleasant disposition usually made her a joy to be around.

***

We realized we were exchanging familiarity and comfort for whatever a foreign culture would throw at us. We may never again see the friends and relatives left behind. Ruth's only close relatives were her sister, Mary, and their elderly mother, Virginia. However, we had discussed this, and Ruth had declared she was on board.

It was 1987. If we were ever going to pursue a major lifestyle change, it was the perfect time. At six- and four-years of age, Ryan and Kristin did not have meaningful ties to other children or their teachers. Danelle, in third grade, had friends, kids she rode the school bus with and neighborhood kids she played with after school, but we had shifted the children around California and Nevada so often that those friendships never lasted more than a year. One positive aspect of the moves, driven by the prospect of better career opportunities and higher pay, was that the children were acclimated to moving.

Based on the information Ruth gleaned from the encyclopedia and news articles, Australia's more agrarian way of life offered the prospect of a healthier environment for both the children and us.

She also discovered that, although Australia ranks slightly below the United States, the country's educational system tilted toward a balanced and practical approach to learning more aligned with our thinking. And if, for some reason, we did not like the schools in Tasmania, the destination we had targeted, we could homeschool our kids.

A week earlier, I had quit my dream job to migrate to Australia. At mid-career, I was no longer Vice President of Engineering. The breadwinner could no longer deliver the bread. If we didn't go, what would I do? Short of going back to my ex-employer with cap in hand, landing a decent job would be a long slog.

Ruth had resigned from a lucrative nursing job. Maybe she reasoned that medical professionals were always in demand, and she could secure a new position with little effort.

***

It was late, and we were exhausted. I wanted to shout, but that might wake the kids. Our black Lab, Molly, curled up in her dog bed by the fireplace, had already perked up her ears at the tone of our voices.

I broke the silence in as steady a voice as I could muster. "What about our dream?"

"My mom and Mary need me. I can't leave. Why can't we live our dream here?"

"You know why."

The move was her idea. She's the idea person in our relationship. I'm the doer, the enabler. It was up to me to make our dream happen.

What was our dream? To own a 20-acre farm

- with rolling pastures and a forest;
- on a river or stream;
- isolated yet near a town;
- at the end of a road;
- where the climate is gentle, the air clean, the soil fertile, and the rainfall abundant;
- where our children would be safe and receive a solid education;
- not too distant from a major metropolitan area with a university and a hospital; and
- where we could sink roots and be happy.

If we could find a place that checked most of those boxes, our dream would come true.

A few nights earlier, Ruth had a vision—more of an out-of-body experience—of our dream farm she shared with me as I was nodding off.

"While I was loading the dishwasher tonight, for one instant, I found myself in a farmhouse. I was looking through a picture window, staring down at a stand of trees beside a sharp bend in a sandy, brown dirt road. Across the road, a stream wove through a flowered meadow. I was there for a blink in time, but it was real. I believe it's the place where we end up."

Maybe she had flashed back to her grandparents' farm in Virginia. Their Victorian farmhouse sat on a hill overlooking a meadow and a gravel road.

I rolled over to face her. "How do you know it was a farmhouse, not a regular house?"

"There was a wooden post-and-rail corral next to the road, and pine trees shaded it."

"Must have been a fluke. Australia has eucalypts. They're called gum trees. No pines."

"I know that, and you're probably right, but it seemed so real. . . It felt like it was our home."

I said, "Maybe it was."

The move had been Ruth's dream in literal and spiritual ways. The Australian and New Zealand wool fiber and textile industries were major draws for her. Both countries are renowned worldwide for producing fine merino wool yarns from Merino sheep and fine mohair yarns from Angora goats. Ruth was a skilled seamstress and weaver. You couldn't walk through the house without bumping into a spinning wheel or a yarn winder. In addition, Ruth loved animals. We first met in Clearwater, Florida, at a pet store where she worked as a cashier. By the end of our first week as husband and wife, Ruth had loaded up the house with pets. Living on a farm in Australia would allow her to indulge all her interests.

***

To prepare for the move to Tasmania, nine months earlier we sold our home in the suburbs of Reno, Nevada, and moved into a rental house in Sparks.

The city of Sparks flanks Reno's eastern border. The saying goes, "Reno is so close to Hell, you can see Sparks." Perhaps that was some of what we were feeling. We enjoyed living in the Reno-Sparks area but had noticed an uptick in crime—or at least that was our perception as the parents of young children. Whatever the reality, we had this overwhelming urge to leave, a compulsion to escape to where we could live our dream and raise our children in a safe and nurturing environment. Ruth claimed some of the impetus stemmed from my childhood upbringing on a farm.

When I was five, my family moved to a 10-acre farmstead in Mecca, Ohio. Though my five older brothers hated the farm, I thrived for four years until the farm went bust, and we retreated to the city. Longing for a return to the life my boyhood memory painted for me, I convinced myself a farm was the only way to satisfy our needs. The big questions: where and for how much?

Ruth and I had lived in the Midwest, South, and West and traveled throughout Europe and the rest of the US. While living in California and Nevada, we vacationed in western Canada and New Zealand. Everywhere we went, we evaluated, and everywhere came up short. Farm prices were a major consideration. Beyond that, something was always missing.

I liked New Zealand and the climate of Christchurch on the South Island, but Ruth felt differently. The weak economy curtailed any desire she had to settle there. However, in Christchurch, we learned of another island across the Tasman Sea in Australia.

Perusing the *New Zealand Herald*, we happened upon a full-page job posting for electrical power engineers to work in

Hobart for the Hydro-Electric Commission, Tasmania's power company. An enticing and touristy description of Hobart and its environs accompanied the ad. Christchurch and Hobart, Tasmania's capital, lie at the same latitude.

Ruth tried to convince me to alter our travel arrangements and spend the last week of our two-week vacation in Tasmania. I refused. I was enjoying a love affair with the South Island's scenery, beer, fish and chips, and cream buns. Why bother with the hassle and extra expense of a side trip to Tasmania?

Upon our return from our New Zealand vacation, Ruth researched Tasmania and found one inadequate tourist brochure and, at the university library, one thin book about Tasmania's Hydro-Electric Commission. Oddly, the lack of information intrigued her. She subscribed to Tasmania's leading newspaper, the *Hobart Mercury*, and I became intrigued.

Australia comprises six states—Queensland, New South Wales, Victoria, South Australia, Western Australia, Tasmania—and the Australian Capital Territory and the Northern Territory. Tasmania is Australia's equivalent of Hawaii, the country's sole island state. About the size of West Virginia, the heart-shaped island lies a couple hundred miles south of mainland Australia across a rough stretch of water known as Bass Strait. Tasmanians refer to mainland Australia, comparable in size to the continental United States, as the "Mainland" or "the Big Island." Mainlanders dub Tasmania "Down Under Down Under" or the "Apple Isle."

Tasmania met some of our dream criteria: temperate and compact, with low murder rates and property values.

Had we ever been there? No (Thanks to me).

Did we know why we were moving halfway around the world? Not really.

Would we be able to make it there? Maybe, maybe not.

Maybe was enough.

***

During the migration process, we discovered that once the government approved our residency application, we, as residents, had all the rights of Australian citizens except voting, which is compulsory for citizens. Two years later, we could become Australian citizens, but to do so, we had to relinquish our US citizenship. We did not plan to take that step unless they lifted the requirement.

The real fun began once we applied to the Australian Consulate in San Francisco and received preliminary approval. While trying to complete a myriad of punch list tasks—sorting what we could and could not take, conducting moving sales, finding a home for Molly (an octogenarian in dog years), finding homes for cars, selecting a moving company, making long-distance travel and rental car arrangements—we suffered through gnawing doubts.

Our relatives thought we were insane. Who in their right mind would leave America?

Our friends lauded us for our sense of adventure but did not offer encouragement.

Ruth's voice snapped me out of my musings. "Didn't you hear me? I've changed my mind. I don't want to go—I am not going!"

I knew that in her heart, she still wanted to go, but her guilt was doing the talking.

"You are going. We are all going."

Tears were welling up in her eyes. Had I pushed too hard? Was it time to negotiate? But with what?

Then it hit me—a compromise.

"How about this? Let's go as planned, and if you find you can't stay, we'll turn right around and come back."

After a painfully long pause, she gave a nearly imperceptible nod.

We're moving to Tasmania!

If I'd had an inkling of what was to come—spider grappling, horse slogging, tractor skiing, goat riding, snake shuffling, pig hoisting—I may not have been so gung ho. And if Ruth had realized she would enjoy the company of all the animals she ever wanted and then some—and that she would run several thriving businesses, including one that involved weaving and another that literally filled our home with nuts—she might have been less reluctant to leave.

2. LEAVING HOME

We planned to depart after New Year's Day 1988, but hit a snag that could nix the move. After six months of sporadic paper battles to qualify for residency in Tasmania, the Australian Institute of Engineers refused to recognize my credentials. The Consulate suggested revising our application to make Ruth, a registered nurse, the primary applicant. Passing a physical exam was all she had to do.

Things were looking up.

Unfortunately, Ruth's chest x-ray showed signs of a past tuberculosis infection. At some point in her career, a patient afflicted with TB had exposed her to the disease. The physician who examined Ruth concluded she could spread the illness, and he would document this in his report to the Consulate. We could not go.

This was Ruth's opportunity to keep the family in the US. To her credit, she told the doctor, "Based on my experience, I can't spread the disease since I don't have an active TB bacterial infection." She demanded a second opinion. The second doctor agreed with her, and the Consulate gave us the greenlight. We were back on track, albeit a month later than planned.

***

At the break of dawn on a freezing February morning, the wheeze and squeak of semi-truck air brakes alerted us to the on-time arrival of our 10 x 20 foot shipping container. Ruth, Kristin, and I bundled up and went outside to find the truck and the trailer-mounted container parked in front of our house. Danelle and Ryan had left for school. We wanted them to experience this momentous day, but felt it was better if they were out of the way. Kristin was old enough to store the memory, yet too young to realize the day's significance. Ruth and I kept her occupied while directing the three-man packing and moving crew.

The men were efficient, wrapping and boxing our delicate items and furniture—the things we did not want to box up. However, their efficiency worked to our detriment. By mid-morning, the crew had loaded most of our belongings and was making noise about getting over Donner Pass before a forecasted snowstorm blew in. They planned to drop the cargo container off at the Port of Oakland and call it an early day.

Upon inspection, I found the container was only half full. Too late, I realized I had pared down our belongings by too much. My poor cargo estimating skill was going to cost us.

I pulled Ruth aside and said, "The container is half full. Can you stall these guys while Kristin and I run out and buy more stuff?"

"Sure."

Ruth plied the crew with coffee and donuts while our youngest and I ran to K-Mart and bought a lawnmower, wheelbarrow, and anything else we could fit into our VW camper van that might be useful on a Tasmanian farm.

I would've purchased large appliances if Australia and America had the same voltage and frequency standards. Australia's 240 volts, fifty Hertz electric supply was incompatible with most US appliances. And even though I did not have a solid grasp on the price of goods in Tasmania, I knew prices would be higher due to freight charges, if nothing else. On that basis, we brought some of our low-power electrical appliances and the stereo and purchased several small voltage converters to power them. We also brought our electrically heated waterbed, and Ruth insisted on bringing her Kirby vacuum cleaner. I had to build converters for those more power-hungry luxuries.

We would regret bringing our TVs and video players since our American TVs were incompatible with Australia's TV transmission format.

Kristin and I rushed home and handed off our purchases to the movers, who promptly loaded and secured our shipment with heavy-duty ratchet straps.

The weather turned to snow as I signed off on the manifest. The movers wished us a bon voyage and left us in a coal-black cloud of diesel exhaust smoke.

We watched the bulk of our worldly goods trundle into a snowy veil and disappear. Would we ever see our goods again, and if so, how damaged would they be from the Pacific Ocean crossing? An idiom from my Navy days came to mind, and I wished our container, "Fair winds and following seas."

***

We camped at the Sparks rental home for several days until the morning of our departure when I wedged Ruth, our three children, fifteen suitcases, and me into our Westfalia camper. Mary, the sister that Ruth was about to leave behind, drove us to the San Francisco International Airport, where the two shared teary goodbyes. We sold Mary the van at a relative's discount, and she planned to put it to use going camping with her two young children.

I got a deal on our one-way Air New Zealand plane fares through one of those enticing classified travel ads claiming, "We can get you fares cheaper than anyone to anywhere." The cheap one-way tickets would get us to Hobart, Tasmania, via New Zealand. The problem arose when we changed planes in Auckland from international to domestic and in Christchurch from domestic back to international. To make those transitions, you hike between terminals with your luggage in tow on a baggage cart and, in our case, two carts. This meant that I, the dad, managed fifteen suitcases while helping Ruth ride herd on three energized children.

After collecting our checked bags and clearing New Zealand Customs in the Auckland International terminal, we lumbered across the tarmac toward the domestic terminal under the heat and glare of the southern summer sun. The cart behind me towed fine, but the one ahead tested my patience when it tipped and rolled, spilling half our luggage.

Guess which suitcase came undone? Yup, the one containing our underwear. During the final move preparation stage, Ruth organized the bags: shirts in one, slacks in two others, underwear in another, etc. Our family and friendly fellow travelers scurried to retrieve our most personal belongings from the blacktop before the wind blew our undergarments to parts unknown or, worse yet, into the intake of a revving jetliner engine.

This after coming off a thirteen-hour flight in which Kristin whined at thirty-second intervals, "I hungy. I hungy." Nothing we, Danelle, Ryan, or the flight attendants tried would appease her. What made matters worse were the stewardesses's attempts to satisfy her hunger pangs with candy. Every time a matronly attendant brought a bowl, all three scooped treats into their laps. Kristin's volume increased by the mile.

The eight-hour layover in Christchurch was worse. We checked in early for the Hobart leg but didn't have any New Zealand currency, and the foreign currency exchange remained closed until right before our flight to Tasmania was due to depart. That meant subduing the pent-up energies of hungry children inside the confines of the terminal after not having had any sleep since leaving San Francisco.

I should mention our children share one strong genetic trait: they like to climb things—any things—curtains, plants, murals, chairs, and Māori cultural displays. If our offspring had a creed to live by, it would be, "Nothing is sacred. Nothing is unclimbable."

Ruth and I spelled each other, watching over our brood. While one of us rested in the standardized discomfort of an airport chair, the other tried to keep our kids from damaging themselves and airport property. They moved like velociraptors.

As annoying as the children were in Christchurch, I recalled a time when their climbing genes were beneficial. To prepare for the move, we sold our Berry Creek, California, vacation cabin. Following the close of escrow, the title company delayed the release of the buyer's money. We were patient until we discovered the company was holding our funds to cream off the interest. That's when Ruth acted. She and the children visited an ice cream shop to make sure the kids were sticky and well-sugared. Next, she turned them loose in the title company office. Business came to a standstill as frazzled agents and clerks removed our kids from atop decorative palms, desktops, and counters. Ruth relaxed in the reception room, reading the firm's magazines, until the manager handed her the check.

I wish I had the same warm memories of the Christchurch layover. The only warm memory of that day came from Ruth while readying to board the jet bound for Hobart.

"You realize you are married to a younger woman."

"We both know I'm three years older than you. You need to get some rest."

"Make that four."

"What?"

"We passed the International Date Line and jumped ahead a day. The lost day was my birthday."

I couldn't believe I had forgotten her birthday. Idiot!

"Honey, I'm so sorry. I'll make it up to you, I swear."

"It's okay. Don't you get it? You don't owe me a present or anything else since my birthday never happened. For once, you're off the hook."

I will forever remember the smile she bestowed upon her sleep-deprived husband.

Birthday or no, I knew I owed her big time. We would celebrate once we settled in, if I remembered.

Boarding the plane for the weekly international flight from Christchurch to Hobart, we sat apart, perhaps because of the cheap tickets. On the last leg of our journey, strangers minded our children during the three-hour flight. I knew our three would be safe. I was not as confident about the fate of the passengers seated next to them.

Ruth ended up a few rows behind me.

I sat next to a coed who was Tasmanian born and raised. Upon telling her our family was moving to her homeland, she asked if I had any questions. I had many questions. I asked the most important one first.

"Are there any sharks in Tasmanian waters, like Great Whites?"

She replied, "You hear of the odd White Pointer in Bass Strait, but the sharks around southern Tasmania are toothless."

I was waiting for the punch line, but it didn't come. She was serious.

Noting my unmistakable look of dismay, she continued.

"They're gummy sharks and only grow to around a meter. Flake on the menu means gummy shark in a fish and chips shop."

As uneducated as I was about sharks, I knew they all have teeth. This young lady's credibility was in doubt. I decided to save my questions for someone I could trust. The remainder of the flight was on the quiet side. I used the time to relax for our arrival in Hobart.

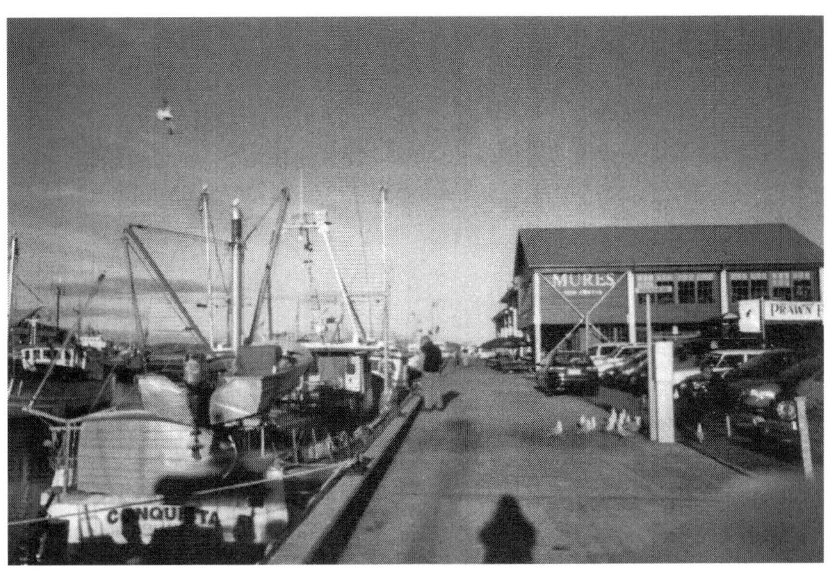

3. A BONUS SUMMER

Planes flying to Hobart sweep in low over Frederick Henry Bay and Seven Mile Beach before touching down on a not-so-long runway. On the afternoon of our arrival, sunlight glinted off the pristine turquoise waters of the bay. As we made the final approach, I had a picture-perfect view along the seven-mile stretch of pine-tree-bordered shoreline. A woman walked a German Shepherd along the deserted beach—a far cry from the crowded beaches we frequented in Florida and California.

The scenery and weather were in stark contrast to our recent Nevada winter. We were about to be treated to a bonus summer. My spirits were high when we disembarked. When Ruth and I met at the bottom of the mobile stairway, doubts about our migration faded in the warm Tasmanian day.

Waiting for the children to exit the plane, we held hands, marveling at the sun-soaked island, and shared our first awestruck impressions of Tasmania.

Ruth assessed the environment, corroborating the inflight magazine's claim that Tasmania has the cleanest air on the planet. "I can't see the air."

I assessed the infrastructure. "The airport control building sits on top of a hill. No tower. And the runway and taxiway are the same. Tasmanians must be the most practical people on earth."

Ruth said, "Did you see the pine trees along the beach? I thought there were only eucalypts here."

"I thought the same. Lots of surprises. The sharks don't have teeth."

She shook her head.

We looked up upon hearing Ryan's voice.

"Hey, Dad! Can we go to the beach?"

He stood at the top of the stairs, his blue eyes squinting from behind thick glasses.

"Maybe tomorrow," I called back.

He shoved aside a lock of blond hair tossed across his glasses by a gust of warm sea air. I watched his impatience grow as he hopped from foot to foot, looking for any opportunity to wriggle past all the slow-moving adults ahead of him and get down those stairs. It was not unusual behavior for a boy about to turn seven.

With Kristin in tow, Danelle spilled out of the plane and slipped around a knot of passengers to join Ryan at the top of the stairs. Danelle, the bossy big sister, smiled and shouted, "Hey, Dad! Can we go to the beach?"

"Okay. Okay. I give up. We'll go."

That brought smiles to the faces of the adults within earshot.

I will forever remember the image of our children standing together on the landing, ready to step into a new world. However, the magic of the memory shattered when Danelle scooped up Kristin and, following Ryan, pushed and shoved each other and anyone in their path to get to us.

Twenty-four hours after leaving San Francisco, with the sun over Tasmania sinking toward the horizon and our journey almost completed, all Ruth and I wanted was sleep. Watching the kids skip and hop toward the international terminal, we knew that would not happen.

***

We entered the cordoned-off arrival area, gathered our luggage for inspection, and presented our passports, residency papers, and customs declaration form to a stern-faced Australian Customs agent. He read over the documents and said, "Show me the oatmeal."

From studying the *Mercury*, Ruth had learned that stores were not open on Sundays in Tasmania. A former Girl Scout, she knew to be prepared; she'd hidden a few oatmeal packets and snacks in our luggage. Brain fog rolled in somewhere over the Tasman Sea when I filled out the customs declaration. I felt obligated to declare oatmeal.

The agent and his crew combed through our luggage, determined to find the breakfast cereal. At that point, I was so exasperated that I felt like offering them Kristin in exchange for letting us into the country. It never came to that. After searching for twenty minutes, the frustrated agent waved us through. We were the last arrivals entering Tasmania on a balmy Saturday evening.

While I searched for the Budget rental car check-in counter, Ruth stayed nearby with the children, attempting to keep them from climbing onto the furniture and counters in the domestic terminal.

The Budget agent's name tag stated: "Anne." She was prim and, to my TV-trained eye, very British-looking.

"Hi. We're here to pick up the station wagon."

As she glanced at my driver's license, credit card, and passport, she replied with a sharp accent, "Good evening, Mr. Reese."

Anne took an imprint of the credit card, returned the documents, and indicated where I needed to sign the car rental agreement. As she placed the car key on the counter, she began speaking in bursts of an unintelligible language I knew could not be English—at least not my version.

Arriving in a foreign country in a depleted condition, I could not interpret what she was saying. I doubted I would have understood her even if I was fully alert. I sensed Anne's exasperation as I stared at her lips, trying to read them. When that didn't work, all I could do was wait for each pause in her speech and ask, "Could you repeat that, please?"

Looking at my family, kids squirming in plastic chairs while Ruth looked on with tired eyes, I shifted my perspective. Science fiction has always been my favorite genre. I spent countless nights lost in the imaginative worlds of Arthur C. Clarke and Robert A. Heinlein. I pictured myself as the first human to encounter an alien life form. She could understand my words, but I could not understand hers.

With my attention fixed on my family and without requesting another repetition from Anne, silence ensued. I don't know how much time passed, but when I turned back to Anne, her eyes locked on mine, and she enunciated in a slow and deliberate manner, "The car is parked straight across the street. Go out through the terminal door. Be careful crossing. Get in the car. Start the engine. Look before you reverse. Back the car up to the curb by the terminal door. If a policeman stops you, tell him Anne said it's okay."

I understood her! I felt like jogging to the car.

With the Reese platoon and the luggage squeezed into the largest station wagon available in Tasmania, a Holden, I returned to the terminal and asked Anne for further assistance.

"Anne. Can you recommend a hotel?"

Following a brief sigh, Anne said in her slow, enunciated voice, "You booked your flights. You arranged for a hire car. But you did not book a room?"

"Well, yeah."

"You realize this is Saturday? You want to book a room for five on a Saturday night in Hobart,"—the way she pronounced it, Hobart rhymed with robot—"the capital city of Tasmania?"

It didn't seem like that big of a deal to me.

"Well, yeah."

Anne exchanged puzzled looks with a nearby agent. Her tongue poked her cheek, and she nodded. Mom used to react the same way when I did something way-out stupid. Then, as now, I couldn't stop myself from grinning.

I suppose my grin was an innate nervous response, much like that of the village idiot. Unfortunately, if I try to suppress it, it grows.

After a half hour of trying, Anne booked us into a comfortable, albeit tiny room at a hotel in the heart of Hobart. I don't know whether she did this out of kindness, pity, or as a desperate attempt to get rid of this stupid, smirking Yank. The latter was the most probable.

***

The next challenge was driving on the opposite side of the road while attempting to navigate. At least I had some experience with right-hand driving because of our New Zealand vacation, plus Anne gave me detailed written directions even this smirking American could follow.

By the time we arrived at the hotel, darkness had fallen, and after rummaging through the luggage to meet everyone's needs for hygiene, clothing, and food, it was almost midnight.

An hour after settling down for the night, jet-lagged and watching Madonna starring in *Desperately Seeking Susan* in black and white on one of the TV's two channels, Ruth said, "I need to get back home to America. I'm leaving tomorrow." Her voice had a strange edge.

The children thought she was joking, but I knew she was deadly serious. Luckily, since I arranged the travel, I was the only one in our family who knew there was only one international flight out of Tasmania each week, and it wouldn't leave until the following weekend.

"Honey, if you feel that strongly, I'll book you a seat on tomorrow's flight," I lied. "For now, get some rest and see how you feel after that."

My deceit bought some time. By late Sunday morning, Ruth had slept for a couple of hours, and we had ventured out and soaked up some summer sun. Mission accomplished. The allure of Hobart helped, too.

Hobart is a nautical town. It looks and feels older than San Francisco and exudes a Parisian charm. The abundant sandstone architecture overlooked by the imposing 4,000-foot-high Mount Wellington adds to its picturesque allure.

We spent most of an enjoyable Sunday morning strolling through the city's heart, observing the place and the people. Tasmanians are more formal in their dress than their American counterparts. Most men wore dark suits with white shirts and narrow ties, while most women dressed in basic black. Some even wore white gloves. I reminded myself that it was Sunday and these were likely churchgoers.

Ruth had followed clothing styles in the *Hobart Mercury* ads before we left the US. She made sure we dressed appropriately, so we did not stand out as we strolled through several downtown parks.

All the parks were impressive, with inviting benches shaded by stately trees grown from saplings and seeds planted by British colonists two centuries earlier. Saint David's Park was particularly enticing. Flowers reminiscent of those growing in any American yard—roses, daffodils, mums, daisies, pansies—bloomed in profusion in manicured beds. Their light, sweet perfume scented the summery air.

If it had been just the two of us, we would have been content to spend the day in the parks, but the children had other plans. After growing tired of climbing trees and statues, they held me to my word to go to Seven Mile Beach.

We were hungry, and restaurants were closed. Divine intervention led us to a Texas-themed diner that would've been closed if it had not been owned by an American. A waitress in a cowgirl outfit greeted us with a phony, "Hi, y'all."

After we enjoyed the Tasmanian version of a Texas BBQ dining experience, we returned to the hotel, but only made it as far as the parking lot. The kids convinced us to skip changing into swimsuits, and we drove straight to Seven Mile Beach with Danelle, Ryan, and Kristin still clad in their Sunday finest, and with solemn promises they would not get wet. They kept their promises for less than five minutes after shedding their shoes. One wave drenched all three. Delighted and giggling, they ran up from the shore and stood before us with wet flower-patterned dresses clinging to the girls and dress slacks and a white shirt plastered to Ryan's body.

The kids thought we were on vacation. Ruth and I knew better. We'd allotted two weeks to tour Tasmania before deciding whether I should search for work in the city of Launceston in the north or Hobart in the south.

We had enough funds in reserve to tide us over for three months. If I didn't have a job after two months in Australia's smallest state, we would try our luck in Perth, Western Australia. If I failed to find work after one month in Australia's largest state, it would be back to Reno.

***

On Monday morning, at the start of our second full day in Tasmania, I went to the Hobart branch of the National Australia Bank to withdraw some of the funds we had transferred from the US.

In the short time since we had left America, the Australian dollar had gained considerable strength against the greenback. The devaluation meant our savings would not stretch as far and the relative price of real estate would be higher. Our finances were at the mercy of the foreign currency market.

I didn't know what to expect on my first trip to a Tasmanian bank. I hoped the transaction wouldn't take long. We were eager to explore the island, and my countdown clock to find employment was ticking. Regrettably, a lone teller was on duty, and because of the complexity of the currency conversion, a queue formed behind me. After she counted the multicolored Australian currency into my hand, I asked her for directions to the medical health insurer. Insurance was a priority since, for the foreseeable future, we would drive on the wrong-to-us side of the road.

"I would be pleased if you would let me show you," she said.

Before I could respond, she locked the cash drawer, placed a CLOSED placard on the teller cage counter, and motioned for me to follow her through a side door.

I attempted to dissuade her. "Look, you don't have to do this. I'll find it if you point me in the right direction."

"Nonsense, Mr. Reese. It will be my pleasure."

I glanced back to see if anyone in the queue was ready to take me out with looks, knife, or gun, but the looks were pleasant, and nobody went for a weapon.

We stepped into an open-air mall.

"Go straight through the mall, cross the street at the end, and turn right. You will see the Medicare sign."

I said, "Ta."

"No worries, Mr. Reese. Have a nice day!"

As the receptionist at our hotel had kindly explained, *Ta* is Australian slang for "thank you." She also said that *Cheers* is another favored expression that denotes "thanks" and "goodbye" all-in-one.

Anne at the rental car desk had not uttered either term, but she'd found us a hotel room, which more than made up for the lack.

4. WELCOME TO THE HUON

After arranging insurance, we left Hobart and our tiny hotel room. Driving south into the Huon (pronounced HUGH-un) Valley, we passed acre after acre of apple orchards interspersed with lush green pastures—*paddocks*—where sheep and cattle grazed under azure skies.

After an hour of leisurely driving, we passed through Huonville, the county seat—the *council*—and followed a winding road alongside the Huon River. Distant peaks in the Hartz Mountain Range made the perfect backdrop to the idyllic rural landscape, beyond which lies the vast and remote Southwest Wilderness.

We arrived at the village of Port Cygnet, short for Port des Cygnes Noir (Port of Black Swans), named by French admiral and explorer Bruni D'Entrecasteaux in the late 1700s. A cygnet is a young swan.

Quaint houses lined Cygnet's two-lane main road, Mary Street.

Staying below the 15 mph speed limit allowed us to gawk at the buildings and businesses coming into view. The first was a single-story structure with white clapboard siding bearing the sign "Cygnet Bowls Club." Cygnet looked like any small farming town you would come across in America. You wouldn't think it could support a bowling alley. I slowed further to get a better look behind the building and spotted men and women in white uniforms, topped with white hats, playing what looked like bocce ball on grassy greens. Ah, "bowls" is not "bowling."

Halfway along Mary Street, Ruth proclaimed, "I want us to live here."

This was not logical. I attempted to placate Ruth, not wanting to tarnish the day, especially in front of the children whose behavior, after they had long sleeps, was better than we could have hoped.

I said, "Honey, remember how you always want to take home the first Christmas tree you find, and later, you acknowledge the one I took my time choosing was the best one, after all?"

"That has nothing to do with Cygnet. I feel good about this place. This is where we're going to live."

Cygnet had an undeniable appeal and no traffic lights. From what I observed, it seemed to have the right number of services. Along the quarter-mile stretch of Mary Street, we saw three banks, three grocery stores, three butchers, three gas stations, and three pubs. My lucky number is three.

I said, "We have a long way to go over the next couple of weeks and lots of towns to see. Why don't we decide where to put down roots after looking around the state?"

She was adamant. "This is where we'll live. Cygnet even has a pharmacy, a newsagent, a hardware store, a laundromat, and a library. It's perfect."

I gave up because I believed that after touring the island, she would discover another town she liked better than Cygnet.

***

Although we didn't need gas, we needed directions—this was before the birth of the GPS—to a place we could use as a base camp from where we could explore the greater southern region of the island. We also had to consider gas station hours. The Budget brochure in the glove compartment cautioned Tasmania does not offer services around the clock. The stations—*servos*—operate on a roster system, whereby one station in each region remains open a few hours after the normal close of business during the week. On the weekend, the on duty station closes on Saturday afternoon and is then on call for the remainder of the weekend. Should you run out of gas, it had better happen during regular business hours; otherwise, you phone the on-call station and hope they'll unlock the pump.

I pulled into Cygnet's middle gas station for a top up.

We were about to have our first encounter with a *bogan*, the Australian version of a redneck.

The attendant, in his mid-twenties and with red hair fashioned in a mullet, sauntered up to my side of the car. I lowered the window, and he stuck his head halfway inside. The embroidered name on his grease-blackened coveralls read, "Bluey."

"What can I do for ya, mate?" he bellowed.

We were unprepared for the intrusion of our personal space. I saw wild-eyed panic in our children's eyes in the rearview mirror.

I said, "Fill up the gas tank, please."

His face moved so near my eyes crossed. Above the stench of old motor oil and gasoline, I detected a hint of last night's grog on his breath.

He shouted, "Now mate, ya sure you're not wantin' petrol 'cause if I'd a known anyone were wantin' gas today, I'd had me red cabbage for breakfast."

Oh, great. I'd asked for gas, not petrol, and that gave Bluey the opening for a fart joke.

He let out a roaring laugh that echoed inside the confines of the station wagon.

When he realized we weren't laughing with him, he pulled back and ambled toward the gas tank, muttering, "Bloody Yanks. Really get up me nose."

Luckily, Ruth and I don't get offended easily. Over a decade earlier, before we had children, we backpacked across Europe, guided by Arthur Frommer's *Europe on $5 a Day*. I knew a few Portuguese words gleaned from a one-year course at the Naval Academy. Ruth had taken French and Spanish in high school. We got by and in the process became experienced flak takers.

Bluey somewhat redeemed himself for his rudeness. After he topped up the tank, he directed us to a quaint motel on the water's edge south of Cygnet. It offered a commanding view of picturesque Huon Island and, beyond that, the D'Entrecasteaux Channel. The setting, views, and proximity to the shore more than made up for the cramped room, rudimentary kitchenette, and lack of a TV.

***

I drove the few kilometers back to the middle shop—not much bigger than a 7-Eleven—for groceries and beer. I wanted to experience the famous Australian beers I had heard about.

My first discovery on this mission: Grocery stores don't sell beer or liquor. "You can get beer at a bottle-o," said the grocery store attendant.

Observing my puzzlement, he said, "At a bottle shop."

"Where can I find a bottle shop?"

"Go to any pub, mate."

Cygnet has a Top Pub, a Middle Pub, and a Bottom Pub. The trick is knowing Top from Bottom. I surmised the Top and Bottom Pubs received their names based on elevation. In

Cygnet, the Top Pub perches on a rise at the northern end of Mary Street, across from the Bowls Club. The Bottom Pub sits on a corner lot close to the bay, at the opposite end of Mary Street. What would happen if a town had four pubs?

I chose the Middle Pub because it had a large sign: "Bottle Shop."

A giant of a man with a nametag that read "Max" greeted me from behind the counter.

"Can I help you, mate?"

Max's bass voice befitted his size.

"I need a beer."

"Gotta go around to the pub for that, mate."

"But I want one to go."

"Oh, you mean you want a takeaway?"

"I guess so."

"Tinnie or Stubbie?"

"In a bottle."

"That'd be a stubbie, mate. You want a slab?"

"Is that a good brand?"

I knew I had made the wrong guess when he studied me for several excruciating seconds before he answered.

"Take it you haven't been in an Australian pub before?"

"Good guess."

"I better help you out, mate. Nothing more humiliating for a bloke than not knowing his way around a pub. Come on through."

The bottle shop occupied a wing in the pub complex. The building also housed a workingman's bar, a gentlemen's bar, a counter meal bar and dining room, a formal dining room, and a two-story hotel. Max explained: "Hotel pubs used to restrict the sale of spirits to travelers only. You sell grog, you need a hotel. No hotel, no travelers, no pub."

Max and his wife owned and operated the Middle Pub, which was dark, like an American dive bar. What stood out was the difference in cleanliness. There was the stale beer odor in the bar areas, but the stringent smell of disinfectant was omnipresent. The couple ran a tight ship.

We lingered in the workingman's bar long enough for Max to draw samples of mainland and local offerings from the draft taps. My accent triggered some questioning stares from patrons, but I didn't care. I was in mission-critical mode.

The samples were strong and tasted like beer should taste. Max sampled right along with me and took the time to explain each brew's brand name, city of origin, popularity, and type: lager, ale, pilsner, stout. He also explained what beers not to ask for in a pub.

"Tasmanians are a parochial lot, and those from the north don't drink beers brewed in the south of the State, and those from the south don't drink beers brewed in the north, at least not in a pub, where asking for the wrong beer could incite a brawl."

Brawls were something I suspected Max had vast experience with.

Sampling every tap took a while. By the last pour, I felt tipsy. I turned my glass upside down on the bar, signaling I was done. Max quickly flipped it upright, brought his face close to mine, and said, "Mate, I don't know about where you come from, but here, turning your glass upside down means you're ready to fight anyone in the bar."

"Thanks," I said. "You just saved my life."

We proceeded to the bottle shop before anyone could take me up on my accidental fight offer.

I wanted a case—the aforementioned *slab*—of each brew I sampled. Considering the jam-packed car, I came away with only one six-pack of a local brew: Cascade Premium Lager, a.k.a.

Tassie Tiger Beer. Even though more expensive than American beer, the smooth and pleasing taste made it worthwhile.

Six-pack tucked under my arm, I offered Max my hand and said, "Thanks for your help and the samples. Out of all of them, this is the best beer I've ever tasted."

As my hand disappeared in his, Max said, "Yeah, she's not a bad drop, that one."

Max had a new and faithful customer, should I ever pass by again. I am forever grateful to him. He was right. Nothing more humiliating for a guy than not knowing his way around a pub. Add to that: Nothing more dangerous than asking for the wrong beer or turning your glass upside down on the bar.

5. SIGNS OF CONFUSION

We stayed a few days in the Huon before heading north. During that time, we learned a lot about Australian culture by deciphering official and unofficial signs.

Ruth pointed to a hand-painted roadside sign advertising "PINKEYES."

"What do you suppose a Pinkeye is?"

"I think it's a bunny rabbit," Danelle called out from the backseat. "A cute little white furry bunny rabbit." She stopped kicking the back of my seat, leaned forward, and peered through the windshield.

Ryan said, "Pinkeye's that gross stuff kids get at school that makes their eyes all red and yucky. Remember when Kristin—"

"I didn't have pinkeye! You're the one who—"

"That's enough," Ruth said. "How many times do I have to tell you to be quiet when your father's driving? Do you want us to have a wreck?"

All went silent, and Danelle returned to kicking my seat.

Spotting another PINKEYE sign, Ruth said, "Let's stop and have a look."

We approached a rickety, wood-framed roadside stand. A beat-up metal coin box with "$1.00 a BAG" inscribed on the cover in black marker sat at one end of the counter. Old burlap potato sacks covered whatever took up the rest of the space. I cautiously lifted one corner of a sack, and we peered beneath. We saw about a dozen clear, gallon-size plastic bags filled with pinkish, golf ball-size potatoes.

The owner of the Pinkeyes appeared.

"G'day. Can I help youse?"

We turned to find a wiry lady wearing a faded gingham dress, frilly apron, and rubber rain boots—*gumboots*. She looked like the archetypal farm granny.

I said, "Hi. We stopped to find out what Pinkeyes are. We're not from here."

She studied us for a moment and said, "Gathered youse must be Canadians."

We noticed Tasmanians presumed we were from Canada. Much later, we discovered Tasmanians make the presumption to avoid offending Canadians because Canadians get hopping mad if you think they're from the US. Once aware, to help avoid prejudice and speed up introductions, we didn't bother clarifying what part of North America we hailed from.

The farm granny went on. "Russet Burbanks or Idaho potatoes, you know about those?"

I said, "We know Idaho potatoes. They're a staple where we come from."

"Idaho or Russet Burbanks. One and the same. Junk. Youse never had a potato till youse had a Pinkeye. Best potato God ever invented."

She clearly pitied these ignorant Canadians who knew nothing about potatoes.

"I was about to pour a cuppa when I saw youse gawkin'. Would youse like to come in?"

We learned that inviting someone in for a cup of tea is a social lubricant in Tasmania. Someone drops by, you put the kettle on to boil, add tea leaves to a teapot, and when the water in the kettle boils, you pour it into the teapot, let it steep until the tea leaves sink to the bottom, and then strain the tea into each cup. You make sure you get the additives right: milk, no milk, and the number of sugars, if any. Within our family, this ritual became known as the Tasmanian tea ceremony. With a lot of practice, we became adept at it.

We also learned, to our embarrassment, there are different types of tea, depending on when it's served. There's the all-purpose *cuppa*, a cup of black tea. But there are also more elaborate types of teas: morning, afternoon, low, high, Devonshire, dinner, or evening. For instance, if a bloke drops by in the late afternoon and you invite him for tea, he thinks: "Blimey! They invited me in for some tucker."

You could tell our hostess was used to children. By the time we removed our shoes to prevent dirtying the polished cork floors and were through the front door and into the coolness of the kitchen, she had produced a cardboard box filled with assorted wooden blocks. She overturned it in the middle of her lounge room.

"Come, children. Youse can play with me grandchildren's toys while your parents and me have a yak."

Not used to toys that didn't have switches and batteries, they hesitated. But it didn't take long for their imaginations to spark, and soon, they were building elaborate block structures that magically fell whenever Ryan came near. No surprise there. At two, Ryan spoke his first word: "broken."

My concern was potential damage to the antiques that overflowed every available piece of horizontal real estate: china vases, glass figurines, and table lamps, all set atop faded lace doilies.

The acrid scent of smoldering fires from bygone winters permeated the air. Ornate moldings and the once-white ceiling roses, now faded to gray, evidenced the house was much older than our newfound friend. It would have been a showplace of Tasmanian craftsmanship in its day.

While she prepared tea for the grown-ups and Kool-Aid in syrup form—*cordial*—for the kids, we learned our hostess's name was Mrs. Von Bibra.

"I was a Huizing in marriage, but went back to me maiden name following me man's passing three years back. Me grandparents on me father's side come here from Holland and fell in love with the Huon and the Tasman Sea. If youse wanna look out from that front window and across the road, youse can see it. The view's why they bought this farm. They passed it to me, and it's still called the Von Bibra Farm. Since I's widowed, the land's gone feral. I've cut back to growing enough veggies to get by and a bit extra to sell at me stall."

She laid out an old carpet square on the lounge room floor and served the cordial to our children. While they chugged the sweet drink, the adults sat at a frilly-topped dining table and sipped tea.

Mrs. Von Bibra explained, "Tasmania grows a quarter of Australia's potatoes and a heap of types—Russets, Desirees, Jersey Royals, Bismarks, Tasmans—and everyone's favorite, the Pinkeye. Each type potato's made for frying, baking, boiling, or mashing. Pinkeyes are best steamed, then coated with butter."

I said, "They're so small. They must be hard to peel?"

Ruth said, "I don't think you peel them, Mrs. Von Bibra?"

"Ya eat the skin with the potato."

Ruth said, "I want to grow these when we buy a farm."

There was a long pause before Ms. Von Bibra spoke again.

"Buy a property in Tassie?"

"Yes," we both said at once.

She looked away in silence, probably thinking: "They don't have a clue about farming" or "We don't need more foreigners here." It may have been both. I was in the early stages of understanding what Tasmanians thought about us.

With the Pinkeyes mystery solved, we finished our tea, had the kids box up the blocks, and paid Mrs. Von Bibra two dollars for two bags of Pinkeyes.

At the stand, I flipped the burlap cover back to grab the bags and saw another section filled with bagged, yellowish-purple, apple-size vegetables beneath a sign that read "SWEDES."

We'd seen roadside signs advertising "SWEDES" and had joked about how great it would be to have a brawny Swede to help around our future farm.

I called out to Mrs. Von Bibra, "What are Swedes?"

She stared at me, slack-jawed. "Rutabagas."

"Oh, and one other thing. Why are farmers giving away chicken eggs? About every other farm has a sign posted out front offering FREE RANGE EGGS."

She shook her head and said, "The eggs aren't *free*. The *chooks* range free, not cooped up."

***

Continuing our exploration of the Huon, we noticed another frequent roadside sign: "DENTAL MECHANIC." Every burgh we passed through had one posted in a front yard along the town's main street.

Danelle's curiosity finally got the best of her. "Mommy, what's a Dental Mechanic?"

"We don't know, sweetheart."

"I think we should stop and ask," Kristin said. "Maybe they'll give us cordial."

I said, “You guys shouldn’t drink too much cordial. The sugar will rot your teeth.”

Ryan said, “And that’s when you have to go to a dental mechanic, and he uses car tools to pull your teeth out.”

Ryan expressed what we were all thinking. We eventually discovered a dental mechanic is a technician who crafts dentures and bridges, not the scary figure we had imagined.

That evening at the motel, we feasted on butter-slathered Pinkeyes and found credence in Mrs. Von Bibra’s claim of Pinkeye superiority.

After evening tea, the main topic of conversation veered from roadside signs to road signs.

In the US, signs warn travelers of the danger of rocks falling onto the roadway with statements like “Danger–Falling Rocks.” In Tasmania, the equivalent sign reads “Beware–Fallen Stones.” American signs warn drivers that rocks may come at you, so be prepared. Australians are more fatalistic. You can’t do anything about what’s coming at you, but watch out for what has happened.

Make of that what you will.

6. BEACHES, BARBIES, BEER, BEWARE!

After getting a taste of the Huon Valley, we drove north, skirting Tasmania's East Coast. Under powder blue skies, the sunniest and most inviting part of the state delivered spectacular views over long, deserted stretches of white sand beaches washed by the rolling turquoise waters of the Tasman Sea.

Like Hawaii, Tasmania has wet and dry sides. The West Coast is notoriously wet, whereas the area we explored was noticeably dry. It's a sparsely populated, undiscovered tourist gem. I would have voted to live along the East Coast, if I could have found work. It remains my favorite part of the island.

Meandering farther and farther north, we swam at the beaches near Orford, Swansea, Coles Bay, Bicheno, and Scamander. We couldn't get enough. Our perception of a crowded beach became a beach where we weren't alone.

We had two crises at Scamander's Steels Beach; one involved Barbie dolls, the other beer.

Ruth and I were foraging for sea shells when Danelle and Kristin ran to us, panting.

Kristin said, "Ryan buried Barbie, and now we can't find her."

Danelle said, "I told him if he doesn't find her, I'm going to steal his Hulk Hogan doll and drown him."

I said, "Whoa, no need for that. We'll help you look for Barbie."

We approached Ryan as he wielded a three-foot length of driftwood, mowing down pampas grass, a tall, feathery invasive species that grew along the dunes. He had already cleared a several-square-meter area. Unbeknownst to him, he had provided a needed service.

"Ryan, do you remember where you buried your sister's Barbie?"

"I didn't bury any Barbie."

Danelle said, "Liar, liar, pants on fire."

"Liar, liar, pants in fire." Kristin mimicked her big sister.

All five of us searched for over an hour, but Barbie was a goner. Thank goodness the girls had packed a spare!

The next evening, following a two-hour drive from Scamander, we checked into a hotel in downtown Launceston—"Launnie" to the locals—the largest city in the north of Tasmania. We discovered we had left three things at the previous motel: my last two southern-brewed beers and Kristin's Barbie. I could replace the beers with northern brews, but the backup Barbie was no more.

If Barbies were available in Tasmania, we could not find them. We drew blank stares when we inquired at several Launceston shops—more evidence that we were in one of the most isolated spots on the planet. Once we established a postal address, we would ask Mary to send replacements. In the meantime, the girls would be Barbie-less.

***

As the family settled for the night, I put my insecurities on hold and relaxed at a nearby pub. There, I discovered James Boag Premium Lager, Cascade's northern competitor, brewed in downtown Launnie. Since I am not in a southern Tasmanian pub as I write this, I can safely declare I enjoyed the Boags.

We looked hard at Launceston. The cosmopolitan business center nestled along the shores of the River Tamar and the South Esk River ticked many of the boxes on our checklist. The Pennyroyal theme park adjacent to the world-renowned Cataract Gorge Reserve added to the city's appeal. However, the place felt too formal.

Had we voted as a family on where to live, the children would have opted for the beach. Unconcerned about life's necessities—employment, medical care, and education—they just wanted to have fun.

I asked Ruth which part of Tasmania she preferred, based on our experiences so far. Her response was predictable: "Cygnet."

Since backpacking across Europe and the US during the early years of our marriage, we had not taken many vacations. We dedicated ourselves to our careers and had only experienced unemployment for short stints between jobs. We seldom quit a job without first securing a new position. And when we had jobs that allowed us to take paid vacations, they were never really vacations. We always devoted a sizable portion of our time to weighing up whether we would want to move to the place we were visiting. Rather than enjoying tourist attractions, we focused on regional job availability, housing, cost of living, climate, and educational opportunities. We even did this when we visited New Zealand—the trip we believed was our vacation of a lifetime. We were restless to the extreme.

***

After a week of leisurely travel exploring Tasmania, I realized we had taken the next step—a challenging leap across the planet.

Doubts about the wisdom of the decision to migrate to a new and distant land had me feeling uneasy and a little queasy. Lounging on the beaches allowed time to think about what we had done. Maybe Ruth's last-minute reluctance to leave our homeland had been well-founded.

I hadn't discussed my increasing disquiet with Ruth, but kids have a sixth sense. Picking up on my angst, they became increasingly agitated, fidgeting and arguing with each other and with us more than usual.

To help ease the stress and celebrate Ryan's seventh birthday, we headed toward Devonport, an hour's drive west of Launceston. With a population of 20,000, it is Tasmania's third-largest city after Hobart and Launceston. I wasn't used to the fact that Tasmania's major metropolitan areas are only an hour or two apart.

Checking out of the Launceston hotel, we asked the receptionist if she could recommend any kid-friendly activities near Devonport. She suggested an amusement park called Serendipity, adding that the caves at Gunns Plains south of Devonport and the Trowunna Wildlife Park in Mole Creek would be worthwhile stops.

Hugging the shores of Bass Strait, Devonport serves as a key shipping hub and the home port for the Bass Strait ferry that sails between Tasmania and mainland Australia, serving passengers with and without vehicles.

Serendipity reminded me of a miniature Disneyland. The rides helped the kids calm down, but made Ruth and me nervous. Unlike Disneyland and other American amusement parks, there were few safety barriers, and no guardrails at the ride entrances.

Children could easily fall onto the ride rails or get their foot stuck between the ride car and the platform. Every ride was a safety nightmare. The kids were having so much fun they didn't want to leave, but we enticed them with the prospect of visiting a cave.

Gunns Plains is a half-hour drive from Devonport. Along the way, we surprised Ryan with a cream-filled chocolate birthday cake we had hidden from prying eyes and hungry bellies.

Stopping at a roadside park next to a fast-flowing stream, we commandeered a picnic table beneath towering gum trees. Ryan blew out seven candles, and we sang the happy birthday ditty, freeing us to indulge in a cake that was equal parts cake and King Island cream. King Island, a small island off the northwest coast, is where Tasmania's tastiest dairy products originate—on par with those I loved in New Zealand years before.

I said, "Happy number seven, Ryan. And to your mother and my wife, happy minus one. Love you all."

Danelle looked at me with concern and said, "Minus one?"

"It's complicated. We crossed the International Date Line and jumped forward on what would have been your mom's birthday. We lost your mother's birthday over the Pacific Ocean. She stays at her previous age until her next birthday."

Ryan was incredulous. "We time traveled?"

"I suppose you could look at it that way."

Danelle and Ryan went back to eating cake. Kristin had not stopped.

A flat-topped barbeque stood next to each picnic table along the stream. Australian barbeques differ from the US variety. Instead of a grate that allows the drippings from whatever you grill to fall onto the coals in the firebox, you grill on a flat steel plate.

Smoke rose skyward from a nearby barbeque in use by a family that looked like ours. I wandered over to the father cooking hot dogs and said, "We're used to barbeques with grates, not griddles. How do the hot dogs turn out the way you're frying them?"

He stared at me in bewilderment and said, "Mate, we call this contraption a *barbie*, and we don't eat hot dogs. You call what I'm cooking *snags* or *bangers*. Never fancied eating a dog, not even a hot one."

I couldn't disagree, but I think you would agree that eating things called snags or bangers is odd. I bit my tongue, gathered the family, and we got back on the road to Gunns Plains.

***

When we arrived, I thought I had made a wrong turn. I couldn't imagine there were caves in this vast, open patchwork of grass- and tree-covered farmland. I expected sheer cliffs and boulders.

Also, we'd been expecting to see the gigantic billboards and flashy signs like those that announce tourist attractions in the US.

As if on cue, a small "Gunns Plains Caves" sign came into view. We parked in the empty lot beside the sign and followed a narrow footpath to a locked rusty iron door planted in a hillside. A square of cardboard tied to the door with twine read: "WAIT HERE — BACK SHORTLY." Who will be back? The answer soon appeared.

"G'day. You kids wanna see stalactites, stalagmites, giant crabs, and worms that glow?"

They all screamed, "Yes!"

The greeter, who appeared to be in my father's age bracket, wore a worn oilskin stockman's coat, gumboots, and the Australian version of a Stetson hat—the *Akubra*.

As I counted out the entry fee, he said, "Ya might wanna *rug up* before we go in." He was suggesting we put on warmer clothing than the shorts, tees, and tennis shoes we were wearing.

I answered for all of us.

"I think we'll be okay. We escaped a snowy North American winter, so we are used to the cold."

"Up to youse."

He unlocked and swung back the door to reveal a pitch-black nothingness.

"Back in a tick," he said as he pulled a flashlight from his coat pocket and stepped through the opening into the void. We heard a click, and several incandescent light bulbs near the door cast a dim glow over a concrete slab entry platform. He beckoned us in.

Once inside, the dank air hit us. It was not too chilly, but it was cool to the point we didn't want to dawdle.

Our host's voice echoed when he explained, "Near a century back, a hunter stumbled on this cave. As time passed, the number of cave discoveries grew. This's the only one open to the public. Inherited the farm sits atop it, and I've spent a lot of time and money making it safe for tourists like youse."

We descended along a series of damp, algae-glazed concrete steps. The rusty pipe handrails looked too weak to prevent a visitor from tumbling into the abyss bordering the stairs. We corralled the children between us and crept forward. Where a bare rock wall was within reach, we stayed close to it. Our tour guide continued ahead and flicked on lights that struggled to penetrate the gloom and cast their glow over gigantic stalactites and stalagmites.

True to our guide's word, we saw giant freshwater crabs in a cascading subterranean stream. However, the best was yet to come.

We reached a circular viewing area atop a bluff in the cave's heart. Rickety handrails blocked further progress. Our guide turned off all the lights. Total blackness engulfed us. The only sounds came from our breathing.

"Look up," our guide instructed.

Hundreds of feet above us, a vast ceiling shimmered with the hues of thousands of glowworms. Green, blue, white, and orange lights twinkled. I forgot about the cold.

We stared at the kaleidoscopic canopy, mesmerized. I knew glowworms are the larval phase of a carnivorous gnat, not worms but maggots, whose luminescence invites insects into their sticky lair. I was glad our guide didn't mention this, although Ryan would have relished the truth.

After a minute of silence, our host said, "Turning the lights on. Takes a bit for the eyes to settle. Ya don't wanna misstep."

The light returned, and my vision came into focus.

The owner yelled, "Crikey!"

I turned to find Kristin doing back hip circles over the iron pipe handrail. She had learned the move in a gymnastics class Ruth had enrolled her in while living in Nevada.

Ruth and I shouted, "STOP!"

I grabbed her and hugged her to my chest.

While we had stared, entranced by the glowworm light show, Kristin completed several loops.

Frozen in stunned silence, hearts pounding, the owner said, "Never had that un happen before."

Even Danelle and Ryan remained silent until our pulse rates slowed.

After partially regaining my composure, I asked, "How deep is the cave?"

"Don't know. But toss a pebble, ya can't hear it hit."

How close we had come to losing our four-year-old, our baby. One of the key reasons for leaving the US was to keep our children safe. In a single day, we'd experienced dangerous conditions at two attractions, both recommended as child-friendly. I was feeling increasingly guilty.

To top off our underground adventure, even though warned by our guide to touch nothing except the handrail, Ryan could not resist. Climbing the stairs toward the light and warmth of the sun, quick as lightning, he knocked the top off a stalagmite. It was a slender adolescent formation, short in cave-years but older than several human generations. Fortunately, our guide was well behind us, flipping off light switches, and did not hear the snap and ping forever embedded in my memory.

This wasn't an isolated incident. You may ask, why would anyone wrap their hand around a cactus when warned not to or place a palm over a car's hot exhaust pipe? Only Ryan has the answers, and now he could add cave desecration to his résumé.

We needed to exit the cave before anything else happened.

It was too late to go to our next planned attraction, the Trowunna Wildlife Park. We overnighted at the nearby Mole Creek Hotel to get an early start.

Staying there had the added benefit of another hotel counter meal ordered and retrieved from the bar, as opposed to full-table service. It's comparable to fast casual meals in the US. I enjoyed the steak and chips. It wasn't Michelin three-stars, but even now, I salivate when I think of the marbled steaks smothered in mushroom peppercorn sauce, sided by French fries, and washed down by a Cascade or Boags premium lager.

Ruth and the kids loved the fish and chips. A week earlier, while exploring in the South, we bought our first fish and chips at a shop in Kingston, a short drive from Hobart. While the dowdy middle-aged woman wrapped our order in plain white newspaper stock (similar to what you have seen in British movies, sans the newsprint), I asked, "What kind of fish?" From her look, I sensed I had asked a stupid question.

"Why flake, of course."

"What kind of fish is flake?"

The look again.

"That'd be gummy shark."

"And they're toothless?"

The look again.

"Yup, and not a bone in a gummy."

Clearly, I needed to be more trusting. I wished I could find and apologize to the coed whose veracity I doubted on the flight to Hobart when she claimed Tasmania's gummy sharks are toothless.

***

The next day at the Trowunna Wildlife Park, we discovered creatures far more dangerous than gummy sharks. The visit provided an eye-opening introduction to Tasmania's odd assortment of animals that are nocturnal in the wild. Those at the park are accustomed to interacting with visitors during the day.

Of the hopping variety, from large to small, we petted kangaroos, wallabies, pademelons, bettongs, and potoroos.

Of the climbing variety, we saw several types of possums: ringtail, brushtail, pygmy, and sugar glider. I learned we should be wary when walking under trees where possums roost because they have excellent aim when they pee on you. The kids found them all cute and cuddly. I favored the endearing, palm-size sugar gliders, similar in looks and actions to flying squirrels.

Bandicoots and quolls come in several varieties. The bandicoot resembles a pointy-nosed rat, while the quoll—a voracious carnivore more commonly known as the native cat—looks like a skunk with spots instead of stripes and minus nasty scent glands.

The attendants let us hold koalas and introduced us to their not-very-friendly cousin, the wombat, whose adorable koala-like face belies its territorial, often aggressive, nature. Wombats have sharp teeth, long claws, and attitude. You wouldn't want to mess with one.

Also, one thing that makes the wombat unique is its cubic scat. It reminded me of toasted coconut marshmallows, which put me off that treat forever.

The aquatic attraction was the duckbill platypus—an egg-laying cross between duck, otter, and beaver with venomous spurs on its hind legs. The echidna, a close and land-bound cousin of the platypus, has backward-facing claws and looks like a plump porcupine with a long, pointy beak.

Many bird species were unfamiliar, like the yellow-tailed black cockatoos and the black swans (swans in the US are more commonly white). Flightless fairy penguins, which are adorable, dwell in coastal dunes. The calls of the lyrebird caught our attention. With vocal cords more flexible than a parrot's, this bird imitated the calls of other birds and manmade sounds in the park.

The infamous Tasmanian Devil was the highlight of the day. The size of a small dog with the body shape of a dwarf bear, it emits raspy growls, bares its teeth, and has a temper several degrees higher than a wombat's. We couldn't get near the creature and didn't want to. Seeing and hearing it, even at a distance, you knew it had bad breath.

The docent clamped the Devil between her leather-gloved hands, paraded the nasty little guy past the park's visitors, and said, "The Devils are highly efficient scavengers and, though perpetually in a hissy fit, are a key element in the native food chain. The jaw clamping power, relative to body size, is greater than any other mammalian carnivore in the world."

True to its reputation, the demonstration Devil snarled, hissed, and wriggled, trying to break free.

"You may have seen the Tasmanian Devil spinning round and round in American cartoons, but did you know that in the Southern Hemisphere, Devils rotate in the opposite direction?" Muffled laughter erupted from the onlookers. "I swear, it's true."

The animals on display resembled the critters I grew up with, but strangely twisted and refashioned. Urinating possums, wombats excreting cubic stools, and what looked like a duck's bill stuck on a beaver's face caused my sense of the island's oddity to notch up another point.

Ruth and the kids loved seeing, petting, and feeding the bizarre creatures, many of which we would encounter on our future farm. I enjoyed watching our family interact, but I couldn't shake my anxiety. Was the Reese family migration a mistake?

7. MY POM PUBMATE

Tasmania had countless other spectacular places to explore, such as the moorlands, Stanley Nut, Edge of the World, Cradle Mountain, Walls of Jerusalem, the remote West Coast, Hartz Mountains National Park, Port Arthur, and Bruny Island. But after one week of touring, I panicked. I needed to know whether this entire venture would succeed.

Also, we were on beauty overload. How much clear air, transparent lakes, and surging turquoise sea could we take? I promised the family we would continue exploring Tasmania when we settled and had time to relax. For now, Ruth and I were saturated, and the kids needed to escape the confines of the car.

We headed south and holed up in a hotel in the Hobart suburb of New Town while I looked for work. While I searched, I needed our rental car. Ruth would need to keep the kids occupied by taking them to parks and shops within walking distance. I felt for her minding three active children in an unfamiliar land.

The *New Zealand Herald* ad for the Hydro-Electric Commission (HEC) lured us to Tasmania, so I made that government-owned utility my first port of call. Much to my chagrin, the HEC had a hiring freeze. My panic increased. The gods were not smiling on us, or so I thought.

In desperation, I looked up "Hobart Consulting Engineers" in the Yellow Pages. I found three listings and chose the first one. I parked and strolled past several multistory buildings until I located my target. Entering the lobby, I encountered a high ceiling, tall windows, and exotic potted shrubs. Stern-faced men in Victorian paintings stared down at me from high above the reception desk. This couldn't be an engineering firm's building—way too classy. The prim-looking, thirtyish, dark-hair-in-a-bun receptionist rounded out the picture. She looked up from her keyboard as I approached.

"May I help you?" she asked in a posh British accent.

"Yes, if this is a consultancy and not a museum. I'm an electrical power engineer looking for work. Do you have any positions open?"

She looked taken aback, nervous, and wide-eyed. "You are in the right place. Please take a seat, and I will check to see whether the General Manager is available."

She bustled into the office behind her and closed the door.

Her actions were odd, but I was getting used to people acting odd whenever I spoke.

It couldn't have been over thirty seconds before the office door opened and the receptionist appeared, followed by a man who introduced himself as Andrew. Tall, middle-aged, balding, dressed in a tailored blue business suit, he said in a strong British accent, "Come in and have a chat, please."

I would learn an expat from Great Britain like Andrew is called a *Pom* or *Pome*. There are many origin stories for that designation. One explanation is that Pom is short for pomegranate since the fruit's red skin reminded the Aussies of the ruddy complexion of the English. Another theory is that Pome is the acronym for Prisoner of Mother England. Neither label is a term of endearment.

Andrew explained he had moved to Tasmania from London after being offered a management position in the far-flung former British penal colony.

After a brief discussion while reviewing my CV, he asked whether I preferred a salaried or a contract position, the latter being the more lucrative but with a limited term. I wasn't familiar with contract positions, but I knew I wanted a secure job. I selected the lower-paying salaried position. He gave me a starting pay figure; we shook hands on it, and that was that.

Andrew explained why the receptionist, Bea, had seemed surprised at my arrival. Minutes before I entered, he had instructed her to place an ad for an electrical engineer in the *Hobart Mercury*. She was typing the ad when I walked in. My qualifications were a perfect match for the position. I felt blessed, as did they. The gods were definitely smiling on me and my family, after all.

***

By mid-afternoon, Andrew and I had concluded our chat, and I had completed the new-hire paperwork. Andrew caught up with me as I was heading out the door. "Do you have time for a stop at the pub?"

"Sure." I wanted to get back to the hotel to give Ruth the news, but I had a couple of hours before she expected me. Bonding with my new boss over a brew was an opportunity not to be missed.

"Do you like Guinness?"

"I don't know, but I'm willing to give it a *bash*."

"Spoken like a true Tasmanian."

I'd learned about "bash" and other colloquialisms by watching Australian TV. I found the news programs to be most informative and entertaining because the newscasters are so direct, confrontational, and quick to tear down anyone, no matter their title or position in society.

Andrew and I walked down a steep street, crossed a major thoroughfare, Davey Street, passed by St. David's Park—the park our family basked in the day after our arrival—and entered Salamanca Place and its wharves. The scene was reminiscent of a nineteenth-century seaport painting, minus the motor vehicles and engine-powered ships.

Andrew led me to the doorway of a building constructed of weathered sandstone blocks. A long row of similar Georgian Colonial structures lined the street, all overlooking the waterfront. Andrew explained. "All were constructed by British prisoners. Convicts cut and set every sandstone block in the façades, and each convict brick carries the thumbprint of the poor soul who cast it."

As we entered the building posted with a sign that read "Knopwood's Retreat," I had the sad thought: "Prisoners never entered the buildings they helped build."

Andrew said, "Patrons call this pub Knoppies. The building dates from the early 1800s. It is among Australia's oldest pubs, founded by the good Reverend Bobby Knopwood as a pub and brothel."

Inside, amber-glazed pub lights cast their glow over polished, dark mahogany-hued woodwork. As Andrew and I bellied up to the bar and he ordered two pints of Guinness Stout, I put aside my sad thoughts about prisoners. The bartender drew the dark brew from a tap into each tilted glass, stopping when the foam was about to spill over the rim. He set the partially filled glasses aside and let the foam settle before topping off, deliberately moving the glass back and forth and side to side under the tap.

With the touch of a seasoned shuffleboard pro, he coasted the glasses down the bar, each slowing to a halt in front of us. I marveled at his skill and the foamy head with the shamrock he had etched into it during the final pour.

Andrew said, "Do you mind if I borrow your pencil?" I pulled a wooden pencil from my jacket pocket protector.

Andrew plunged it point first into the heart of the shamrock in my glass. When he pulled his hand away, my Ticonderoga No. 2 pencil remained embedded in the foam, at attention.

Andrew announced, "Now that is a good Guinness."

I had learned something priceless from this Pom.

I withdrew my pencil and hoisted my pint. Andrew raised his and said, "Now, let's toast to our success. Cheers, mate!" We clinked our glasses and took long pulls.

In the mirror behind the bar, I saw my mustache coated with foam.

Looking at me while licking the foam from his clean-shaven upper lip, Andrew said, "Now that's a real Guinness mustache you've grown there." He added, "The foam acts like a blanket that keeps the brew from oxidizing. To get the most flavor, 'tis best to drink the beer below the foam."

I bought the next round.

Andrew described our employer and the pros and cons of working for the company. On the plus side, they had strong links to the revered British engineering firm where Andrew had worked before accepting the General Manager job in Tasmania; it would be easier for him to climb the corporate ladder in Australia.

On the downside, the Hobart office was a satellite of the high-rise headquarters in Sydney. We were the boots on the ground in mineral-processing-rich little Tasmania—from aluminum to zinc—where the bulk of the larger and more lucrative projects took place. Our small office of less than half a dozen salaried and contract engineers existed to provide field data for the so-called experts at the head office.

Andrew also confided that the Sydney office increased client charges by inflating the billing hours of senior engineers—something Andrew hadn't known when he accepted the posting in Australia.

I appreciated Andrew's openness about the business culture I was entering. His honesty was refreshing. And who was I to judge? Elated at landing a job in my area of expertise, I could overlook just about anything. The job was the first step in rebuilding my confidence. Too, the benefits helped compensate for the lower pay relative to what I earned in the US: thirty-six-hour workweek, four-weeks annual paid vacation and ten days paid sick leave starting on day one, premium medical coverage, employer-paid pension (superannuation), and three-months paid leave after ten years.

"Dick. One other thing you should know. Bea. She's a randy bird."

I was pretty sure I knew what he meant.

"She appears so proper and sophisticated, like Miss Moneypenny in the James Bond movies. Fair warning."

"Taken."

Andrew asked if I was up for a third Guinness. I was out of my drinking league. Andrew had downed two pints, while I'd only taken a few sips of my second.

I shook my head. "I won't be able to walk, let alone drive, if I drink anymore."

Andrew ordered another pint for himself. He downed it like water while I was ready to belt out "Sweet Adeline."

"Andrew, one more thing before I go. What's with the museum vibe at the office?"

"Simple. The firm's British principals assessed the building and determined Hobart direly needed proper culturalization."

Aah. I bade Andrew farewell.

We were off to a great start. I had a spring in my step from the beer, the camaraderie, and because I had a job. Also, Andrew had allayed my fears about the firm's stuffiness. He was relaxed and down to earth, a regular Joe who spoke with a British sitcom lilt.

8. WHEELS AND HOOFBEATS

The touring phase of our quest was over and Ruth was thrilled I had found employment, but now the majority of parenting would fall on her shoulders. Past work experience in the US proved that, at least initially, I would be away each workday for long hours. I doubted the work experience in Tasmania would be any different.

We needed to go car shopping. I would need a car to commute to my new job from wherever we ended up living. Ruth would need one to get herself and the children around.

Except for Subarus, autos in Tasmania are more expensive than in the US. And on an island with few dealerships and limited inventory, forget negotiating. We found a Subaru dealership in Hobart, where we bought two cars in under two hours: a new Subaru Liberty station wagon and a used Volvo DL sedan, both red. We needed a station wagon for family seating and cargo space. All-wheel drive for farm use was a bonus. Ruth wanted a Volvo, a vehicle known for its safety, lest she have a memory lapse and drive on the wrong side of the road. Too, we reckoned the bright red finishes would improve safety by making our cars stand out on roads narrower than we were used to.

The sales process mirrored that of America; the only difference was the salesman's accent.

Two last-minute add-ons to each car were roof racks and *roo* bars. The racks were an easy sell, but would we need roo bars? Would we ever collide with a kangaroo? Recollections of dead wallabies and other wildlife alongside Tasmania's roadways swung the deal.

Our next task proved more challenging—finding a place to live. We opted to lease rather than buy a farm upfront. That would give us time to adapt to country life and culture while checking out farm property prices. We signed a six-month lease on a year-old home on a fully fenced 7 acres in the Hobart suburb of Leslie Vale. The single-story house was roomy and comfortably distant from a relatively busy, paved—*sealed*—country road. About a dozen miles south of Hobart and near the Southern Outlet, first cousin to a freeway, it would make for an easy commute.

Our children would catch the school bus at the neighboring farm where the bus driver lived. Ruth's favorite village, Cygnet, was nearby.

***

Children living in Leslie Vale attend public school in the Hobart suburb of Kingston, a short drive from our rental. Ruth met with the Kingston Primary School principal to enroll Danelle and Ryan—Kristin was too young to start kindergarten—and to learn about a school system that was foreign to us. Our language skills were advancing, but fully understanding the local dialect was years in the future. As best she could, Ruth deciphered the words the principal spouted. Up to that point, everything we knew about Tasmania's educational system we gleaned from articles in the *Hobart Mercury*, the newspaper we pored over weekly when we lived in Nevada.

The 1988 Tasmanian school year began a month earlier while we were still living in Sparks. The delay caused by Ruth's TB scare put Danelle and Ryan at the disadvantage of a late start at a new school in a new land.

Another thing new (to us): school uniforms. Each school in Tasmania requires students to wear the school's plaid uniform, specific in style, pattern, and color to that school—no more jeans, tees, and hoodies for Danelle and Ryan.

The first order of business was a visit to a uniform store for fitting and purchase. Our two eldest came away from the shop looking like the proper Aussie students we had seen playing on school grounds during our travels around the island.

The principal advised we should budget for replacement uniforms annually to accommodate the growth of our children. This would not differ from our US routine, other than avoiding the best-dressed competition endemic in American schools. When a child changed schools or graduated to high school (grades seven through ten) the parents had to spring for a different uniform to comply with the new school's dress code. After year-ten graduation from a public high school, students enrolling at a public college (grades eleven and twelve) were not required to wear uniforms. For those attending private schools, the uniform specific to the school remained the same for all grades through graduation from college.

After touring the Kingston Primary School and peeking into some classrooms, Ruth felt comfortable enrolling Danelle and Ryan. She told me that evening, "With the exception of the students all dressed the same, the classrooms looked like any American grade school."

The long- and short-term risks of forcing our children to receive a non-American education were not lost on us. Ruth had homeschooled Danelle in second grade when we lived in Nevada and planned to do the same for Ryan and Kristin for as long as needed if conditions warranted. We didn't believe that would be necessary, but it was an option.

Beyond that, if Tasmania was still our home after they graduated from college—the equivalent of American high school—we envisioned our children returning to the US to attend university. At that point, Ruth and I would decide whether to follow. In our minds, our children were American to the core, and we would endeavor to instill that in them. Also, influencing our decision whether to stay or go would be the possibility that one of them would opt to attend an Australian university.

Everything was falling into place.

Well, almost everything.

***

Following the lease signing, the rental agent, Nigel, informed us there would be a three-week delay before we could move into the leased home. In the meantime, he had us move into a small, sparsely furnished flat in Kingston, close to the shop where we bought our first order of fish and chips. Still living out of fifteen suitcases and sleeping on the living room floor, we camped indoors.

After getting everyone into bed (pillowed air mattresses bought at a sporting goods store with blankets as linen) for the first night in our temporary home, we woke to a skittering sound followed by the combined shrieks of Danelle and Kristin. The noise was coming from the ceiling. I guessed an attic infested with mice, maybe a rat or something larger. I jumped up and switched on the lights.

As a husband and a father, I cannot show fear in front of my family when faced with sharks, snakes, or spiders—at least when spiders are the size of America's most common species.

The spider clinging to the ceiling above Ruth and the children was the king, or queen, of spiders. I froze in place.

Ruth shouted, "Honey, do something!"

As we would discover, the huntsman spider is all too common in Tasmania. About the size of a man's hand with fingers spread, it looks like a tarantula on steroids. Huntsman spiders reside in shadowy places. Car heater vents are popular abodes. A huntsman emerging from a dashboard vent and scurrying across a windshield, accompanied by passenger screams, creates dangerous distractions.

Our spider galloped across the ceiling, and I swear I heard the hoofbeats. I ran to the kitchen and returned with a broom. By this time, our entire clan huddled in the corner farthest from the creature.

I took careful aim and brought the broom around in a wide arc, intending to send the intruder through the living room doorway and into the hall. The spider, anticipating the approaching broom head, made a beeline for the corner where the family huddled. Ruth and the children moved faster than the spider, leaving me alone with my adversary. It was kill or be killed.

Ruth called from the hallway, "Honey, do you want the vacuum cleaner?"

She was always one step ahead of me, especially when faced with a crisis.

When we lived in Florida, we dealt with many forms of repulsive reptiles and insects, including spiders. Since we adhere to a live and let live credo, we use a vacuum cleaner to eliminate bugs. We suck them in, exit through the nearest door, and empty the vacuum collection bag into foliage or a garbage can.

I doubted the vacuum cleaner hose would be large enough to accommodate this monster.

I tried not to let my family see my quivering hands as I stepped into the hall and took the vacuum cleaner from Ruth.

Everyone followed me as far as the threshold. I force-marched across the room to the corner where the spider remained poised, either ready to make another run for it or launch itself from the ceiling onto my face, where its fangs would clamp around my nose and inject deadly venom.

I took one last look at my beloved family and gave them a false smile before energizing the electric spider trap. As I swung the suction pipe over the spider, it fought to cling to the ceiling. After a brief struggle, the vacuum won and a series of satisfying thunks followed. The spider's body bounced off the inside of the handle as it whisked past my white-knuckled grip.

I called, "Hurry. Open the back door."

Ruth unplugged the vacuum cleaner while Danelle opened the door. Scooping up the vacuum cleaner, I ran through the hall, out the door, and onto the porch. I dropped everything and ran back inside. Slamming the door behind me, I set the deadbolt and, breathless, fell against the wall as I dropped out of the adrenaline rush.

Next came the laughter. Initially, I mistook it for the nervous titter that often follows a hair-raising incident. Then Danelle said, "Dad, why did you lock the door? Did you think the spider could reach the doorknob?"

I had no answer. Perhaps my reaction was a prehistoric survival mechanism, like rolling a boulder in front of the cave mouth.

Although an attack to my face would be unpleasant, I didn't know then that the huntsman is not the deadly spider I had imagined. They are certainly big, hairy, and scary, but they are neither aggressive nor very poisonous.

Our first huntsman encounter ended without injury or loss of life. Another run-in nearly landed me in jail.

9. THE DRUG LORD

We had a perfect March to May Southern Hemisphere autumn with cool nights following warm days. We were settling into a land that was becoming less foreign to us, at least on the surface.

Our rental agent, Nigel, rang in early April to give the all-clear. We could move to the rural Leslie Vale property we had leased. The move was easy since we continued living out of our fifteen suitcases. One-way trips in the Subaru and the Volvo, and the move was over. We still slept on the floor, but each kid had a bedroom while Ruth and I enjoyed the privacy of the master suite. Our container would arrive soon, and with that, the beds would bring our third-world living conditions to an end.

The home was modern, ranch-style rust-red brick with pastoral views. A white post-and-rail fence enclosed a flat, 6-acre paddock between the house and the road. A vacant, three-sided hay shed close to the driveway would be handy for storing garden tools. Behind the house was a small plywood-clad workshop surrounded by a gum tree forest—*bush*. I looked forward to spending time in the workshop with my tools—many of them quality hand-me-downs from my father—in case anything needed fixing. The 7-acre property provided ample room for the kids to play, and the neighbors were far enough away to avoid prying eyes. This was the ideal place to call home until we could find our dream property.

The closest neighbor was the school bus driver, Thomas Jefferson. With his dark beard and ponytail, he looked nothing like his namesake. He came by his first name through his Francophile mother. It was her way of paying tribute to the original Thomas Jefferson who was a fan of France and supported the French Revolution almost two centuries before our neighbor's birth.

Tasmanian Thomas's wife, Marie, came from a long line of Tasmanian farmers. She was cute, bob-haired, with an indomitable spirit and love of children. Together, the Jeffersons helped us acclimatize.

Their farm was over twice the acreage of our rental property. They were farmers in the truest sense, with dairy cows, beef cattle, pigs, sheep, ducks, and chickens. Growing wheat, oats, corn, and many varieties of produce, coupled with a fruit and nut orchard, their farm was sustainable.

Danelle and Ryan were the first to board the school bus each morning. While they waited for Mr. Jefferson to hop aboard and begin his rural route to pick up other children, Marie would deliver snacks and juice cartons to get our kids off to a healthy start.

We couldn't have conjured up better neighbors.

***

Six weeks after landing in Tasmania and two weeks after moving to Leslie Vale, I received a call at the office announcing our shipping container had arrived and that Australian Customs needed to see me immediately. Bowing out of work, I shot over to the Hobart wharf.

I parked at the warehouse loading dock and faced a covey of grim-faced, uniformed men. The greeting committee caught me by surprise. I was more surprised when flanked and escorted inside through an open roll-up door. Everything the movers had packed and loaded with care in Sparks lay strewn around the concrete floor.

The covey encircled me, stood stock-still, and glared.

I broke the silence. "Is something wrong?"

A voice boomed from behind me. "You tell me." I turned to find an imposing, gray-haired agent cradling the large fishing tackle box Ruth had packed as our medical kit. He set it on top of one of the five steamer trunks I had last seen in Sparks, one trunk for each family member. He popped the tackle box latches and, with grand ceremony, slowly lifted the lid.

It revealed the full-blown first aid kit that Ruth had assembled. Unsure of the availability of medical supplies in Australia, she brought all the drugs and medicinal products she could source, including syringes, vials, scalpels, salves, ointments, gauze, antiseptics, anesthetics, and prescription medications.

I said, "My wife's a nurse."

The uniforms waited for the guy standing over the medical kit to say something. A younger guy spoke up first. "Me lady's a nurse too, and this looks like the stuff she keeps in her first aid kit."

That defused the situation. The apparent drug lord was just another Yank. No worries. Within a few minutes, we were chatting like pubmates. They knew we were from America, not Canada, and wanted to know about the region we had come from and what we were doing moving halfway around the world, especially when America is such a wonderful place to live. I couldn't answer the question truthfully because I didn't know myself beyond our desire to fulfill a dream, and I was not about to reveal that to a bunch of strangers. But I did my best to keep the conversation going long enough to get a clean bill of health for our possessions and verification that there would be no need to quarantine anything.

***

After we received clearance, I notified the US-based moving company we had hired. A week later, the movers delivered our repacked container to the front door of the Leslie Vale house. Two guys jumped down from the truck cab. Both wore cargo shorts and the popular pull-on Tasmanian-made leather boots called Blundstones—*Blunnies.* One guy was slim, and the other not-so-slim.

After exchanging pleasantries, they began offloading our belongings using brute strength.

I said, "Why don't you guys use a hand truck?"

The not-so-slim one said, "Our company don't provide them, and why would ya want one, anyways?"

I replied in their native tongue, "So youse backs don't go crick."

I climbed into the container, rummaged until I found my hand truck, and wheeled it out. They reluctantly started using it.

When the container was empty, and they were preparing to depart, the slim one said, "Ta for the trolley, mate."

Before I could respond, the not-so-slim one said, "Won't be needing as much grog to kill me back pain tonight."

Over time, I saw tradesmen use the brute strength approach in many work situations. Typically, two guys in cargo shorts and Blunnies turn up and muscle through whatever manual task has to be done. The practice must be a cultural hand-me-down.

While unpacking, we examined and inventoried our possessions. Nothing was missing, and apart from a broken stereo record player stylus, there was no damage—no chipped china or dinged spinning wheels.

We could now access our clothing by unlatching and swinging open the steamer trunks we'd bought for a pittance at Reno thrift stores. They'd been around the world with other travelers. Plastered with worn and torn shipping labels from exotic destinations, they imparted a musty smell to our clothing, but nothing that a washing wouldn't eliminate. Our better clothes hung from the closet rod in the left half of the trunk, with the rest stowed in cloth-lined drawers in the right half.

The most welcome items were the beds and mattresses. We set up the single beds for the kids before setting up and filling our waterbed. The step-down voltage converter for the waterbed heater did its job, and two days after plug-in, when the water was up to temp, we cocooned in mankind's greatest sleeping invention.

We had inched another step closer to settling.

***

We planned a night on the town to celebrate our successful transition and Ruth's lost birthday. With the kids ensconced at the Jefferson's and Ruth scrubbed up, we headed to the Point, a revolving restaurant perched on Hobart's Wrest Point Hotel Casino tower. Veterans of Reno-Sparks casinos, we looked forward to a nostalgic evening of glitz and fine dining.

Near-silence greeted us when we entered the casino—no raucous laughter, smoky air, or blaring music.

Several men wearing business suits tugged on the handles of slot machines—*pokies*. Rather than the jangling of a win, the payout coins landed with a dull thunk—no ringing bells, rollicking tunes, or flashing lights. Boring.

In place of a cocktail bar, we passed a tea bar where a cluster of elderly ladies lounged on couches. The persistent clickety-click of their knitting needles drowned out the sound of the slot machine wins.

The scene was dystopian.

But the ambiance of the restaurant and the views it afforded of the glittering city and bay countered the ground floor's strange atmosphere.

I toasted Ruth and warned, "No going home, or you will age a year."

At the same time, I wondered if we would ever go back.

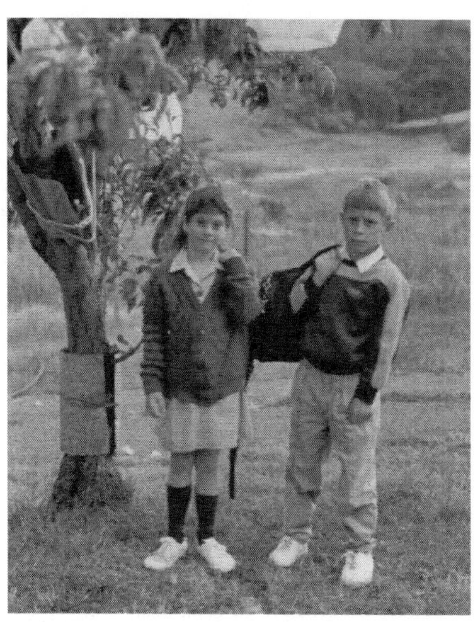

10. MORE LANGUAGE LESSONS

At this point in our adventure, I enjoyed new work challenges while mastering Australian engineering standards and codes. The technical learning was a breeze compared to the language anomalies and the cultural lessons, such as pronouncing "haitch" for the letter "h" and "zed" for the letter "z." Bea corrected me on that and many other things.

I never figured out why my workmates falsely accused me—well, the Yanks—of foisting the metric system on them. America didn't go down that road. The US and Australia traditionally used the British imperial inch-pound measurement system. That changed in Australia when the government shifted its citizens to the metric system in the 1970s. The Australian government used draconian measures to force the change, such as banning inch-scale rulers in schools.

Resentment ran deep, and most folks in my circle still thought and measured in inches and pounds before converting the measurements to metric units.

A British throwback unit for measuring weights was unfamiliar to me: stones. Australians measure weight in pounds, kilograms, and stones.

While checking on a report Bea was typing for me, she said, "What's your weight in stones?"

"What do you mean?"

"A stone is fourteen pounds, so how many stones do you weigh?"

"Are stones a real thing?"

"Yes. Dates from well before we were twinkles in our parents' eyes."

Before continuing, she looked me up and down. "You tell me your stone weight, and I will tell you mine."

Although a proper British lass, Bea was cheeky, and her teasing was challenging for me to untangle.

"You first."

"Seven and a half stone, naked."

I disregarded the "naked" and calculated her weight in pounds—105. That seemed about right for her height.

"I must be around ten stone."

She studied me, then said, "You know, you are not a typical Yank."

"What's a typical Yank?"

"Me Mum told me that, during the war, the saying went that Yanks are overpaid, oversexed, and over here."

I couldn't help but laugh at that one.

"That was likely true in wartime. The sailors and soldiers were far from home and female companionship. Of the three attributes, the only fit for me is the 'over here.'"

"Well, me dear Mum also told me another thing."

Bea had an impish grin when she held up her left hand, waved it in my face, flaunting her diamond wedding ring, and blurted in a Cockney accent, "A ring don't plug a hole."

I didn't get it, so I changed the subject.

"How are you coming along on that report?"

She smiled as she held up my draft copy, pointed to a line, and said, "Is this supposed to be a comma or a full stop?"

"That's a period."

"No, Dick. A period is what I have every month. You mean I should enter a full stop."

"Well, Bea, I'll remember to say full stop from now on."

Halfway home on the Southern Outlet, when the meaning of "A ring don't plug a hole" clicked, I nearly veered off the highway.

I was catching on to the Australian openness about sex and toilet humor. Americans have a Puritan heritage. Australians did not suffer that fate, so their moral compass does not always point in the righteous direction—their needle wobbles.

I didn't see myself as Puritanical. But neither did I want to stray from the path. I also knew that, despite Andrew's warning that she was a "randy bird," Bea was never serious about her overtures.

It struck me that Ruth spent much of her time with our suave real estate agent, Victor, searching for our dream farm in the Cygnet area. I had to trust that some Puritan blood flowed in her veins, too.

Aussie culture was taking some getting used to.

***

We had been on the island long enough to accept we could survive. And apart from the language barrier, the children were breezing through school, or so we thought.

One night, I was in the workshop examining a light switch, questioning the logic of flipping an Australian light switch down to turn a light on when you do the opposite in America. I wanted to see whether I could turn the switch body upside down to make it operate the way it did in our homeland. I was surprised to find Danelle watching me. She wasn't smiling.

"Hi, little buddy. How's my eldest doing?"

"I don't like school here. We have to wear uniforms with hats. The kids make fun of me and Ryan at school, Dad. They call us stupid Yanks and tell us we talk funny."

"Don't let them get you down. Ignore them."

"How do you ignore twenty kids pointing and laughing at you?"

The culture shock to the kids was something we hadn't fully considered. Ruth and I could defend ourselves. We should have done a better job preparing our children for harassment. It was the same difficulty they had to endure each time they started at a new school in the US. However, in Australia, their American accents reminded their classmates they were different whenever they spoke.

"I'll talk with your mom and ask her to speak with your teachers to see what they can do. Other than that, you guys will have to grow thicker skins."

"Yuck, I don't want thick skin."

"What I mean is, you and your brother will have to toughen up. We live in a new country and have to adapt."

"I'm going to have to learn to talk like them?"

"You can't think of Australians as 'them.' Their culture is simply different from what we are used to. I know this will be hard for you both, but if you need to talk and act like the other kids to get along, that's what you gotta do."

That was tough advice to hand out to a nine-year-old. We hoped the experience of adapting to a foreign culture would help our children cope wherever their lives took them.

I let that sink in for a moment, then said, "We love you and moved here so you all would be happy and safe. I'm sorry you're having a tough time, but trust me, it will get easier. If things don't get better, you let me or your mom know."

Ruth's chat with the teachers, in which she made them aware of the situation in American-mom, no-uncertain terms helped. As far as we could tell, the bullying stopped. Ruth would have volunteered at the school to confirm, but she needed to be home with Kristin. Because of my work, I didn't have the time to volunteer or visit the school. Other than feedback from Danelle or Ryan—which they didn't give after the initial complaint—we couldn't know what their school life was really like.

***

One thing that affected our children that we became very aware of was the "hole" in the ozone layer that puts island human and animal residents at greater risk of skin cancer. The closer to Antarctica, the greater the risk. This hole differs from the ozone pollution (smog) we were familiar with in US cities. A few minutes in the clear air under the Tasmanian summer sun without sunscreen or a hat, your skin sears. The risk is so great that primary school children cannot attend unless they wear a hat with a wide brim. We required the kids to lather with sunscreen before stepping outside on a summer day. With her pale complexion, Kristin was the most vulnerable in our family.

That said, we saw many positive changes in our children since coming to Tasmania. Their time playing outdoors had increased, and their manners had improved tenfold. We credited rural living and the emphasis on social skills learned in the early grades—lots of arts and crafts and low-pressure homework compared to what we experienced in our grade school years. Their teachers told Ruth the technical study loads would be heavy once they hit seventh grade and entered high school. At that point, the teaching and the homework would ramp up. Based on Ruth's research, by grade ten, our three would have an education equivalent to American students for that year.

***

Aside from our children's school issues, life flowed smoothly despite a few minor bumps. One of those minor bumps grew into a mountain overnight.

I stepped out of an important client meeting to take a phone call from Nigel.

"Nigel, what's up?"

"I apologize for interrupting your day. I am ringing on behalf of the homeowner's father-in-law. He has some cars he rather urgently needs to put somewhere, and since you have plenty of space on the property, would you mind?"

"Well, we do have more room than we need, but I have been thinking about getting a horse for my wife. Early days, though."

"A horse would fit right in. Can I advise the owner you are fine with the arrangement?"

What did he mean? What was the link between a horse and some cars? Yet another foreign culture enigma. Ruth and I had decided that, at all costs, we would be as friendly as possible with the locals in our quest to fit in. Here's some guy who must have an off-street parking problem—too many cars and not enough spaces in the city—as happens in any big city.

"No problem."

"Thank you so much, Mr. Reese. He will drop them by tomorrow. Have a nice day."

Later, I discovered Aussies hate that American expression, but they offer it to be pleasant—especially when you've granted them a favor.

The next afternoon, Ruth called me at work.

"I thought you said he had an off-street parking problem."

"Well, that's what I assumed."

"Then why did some man unload seven scrawny black Angus calves in our paddock and store a couple dozen hay bales in the shed?"

I called Nigel.

"Nigel. What's with the cows?"

"What do you mean, Mr. Reese?"

"Well, you said the father-in-law was going to drop off some cars."

"No. I distinctly stated cars."

That's when the penny—or, in this case, the "r"—dropped. Australians, much like Bostonians, drop their r's. To my Midwestern-trained ear, when Nigel said "cows," I heard "cars." I now understood why he said, "A horse would fit right in."

If I'd known he planned to dump cows on the property, I would have refused straight away.

What could I do? I had given the owner's father-in-law permission to park his cows on the property we leased. So, I let it go.

I let it go until we learned the wooden fences worked fine to confine horses but did not stop cows. The calves pushed and wriggled between the rails, wandered where they pleased, and consumed what they pleased. Neighboring gardens were easy targets, and soon, we became known as the stupid Yanks with the cows. Our attempt to spread the word that these were not our animals didn't take hold—or didn't matter. It was our problem.

It took three days for Ruth to track down the owner of the cattle, our landlord's father-in-law. He told her to feed out more hay to satisfy their hunger. We had already tried that, and it hadn't worked.

So much for trying to fit in.

11. WATER BUFFALOES AND ABORIGINALS

My work became my escape from cows.

Serendipitously—for me, but not for Ruth—word spread through the office that the mainland headquarters needed an electrical engineer to attend to an emergency at a copper-gold mine in Australia's Northern Territory, somewhere in the outback, beyond Tennant Creek at a place called Warrego on an Aboriginal reservation, a day's drive north of Alice Springs. Alice Springs lies near the center of the Australian continent, but I had to look hard at a map to find Tennant Creek and never found Warrego.

Andrew summoned the engineers to the conference room.

"Are any of you able to take on some work at a mainland mine for a few days? The client's generators intermittently trip and shut the mine down. All qualified field engineers at headquarters have other commitments."

I had relevant experience from working at Nevada mines, so I felt qualified. I had also learned a bit about the Australian way of problem-solving, which I hoped I could put into action.

***

Right after starting my new job, I accompanied a colleague, Rodney, to a privately owned Hobart hospital. Its boiler was having operational problems. From my understanding, it could explode, putting hundreds of lives at risk. For me, it was time to panic, shut the place down, and move all those threatened out of harm's way. To Rodney and the maintenance engineer, it was time for a cuppa, based on the "She'll be right, mate" philosophy.

So, we sat around a conference table sipping tea, reviewing boiler control diagrams, and weighing options. Into our second cuppa, Rodney suggested checking for a faulty relay in the boiler's temperature regulator circuit. We set our cups aside, strolled to the boiler room, and found the relay. Rodney was right. He replaced the relay with a spare from the hospital's inventory. Problem solved.

This approach gave me a new appreciation of the indomitable spirit of a geographically isolated people who had to make do on their own for decades. The Prime Minister of Australia nailed it when he called Australia "The Clever Country." I agree.

While my upbringing would never allow me to fully accept the "She'll be right" philosophy, I at least learned to throttle my initial reaction to a problem or situation.

***

As for the current work challenge, I also rationalized that, as the new guy, I didn't want to make waves. I raised my hand and said, "I'll go if no one else is available in the other branches."

Less than ten minutes later, Bea had booked my early flight to Alice Springs for the following day, Saturday.

I knew I'd screwed up when I called Ruth to tell her I would be away for several days.

"You can't be serious. You're leaving me to deal with cows and kids?"

I was. Did I feel guilty? Yes. Did it stop me from going? No.

Following the five-hour flight, I collected my luggage and loaded it into the trunk of a Holden Commodore rental car parked next to the airport terminal. The heat rising from the pavement produced sweat that Alice Springs' thirsty air gulped down. This helped remind me to load up on water. I pulled a collapsible plastic water container from my bag and returned to the terminal.

While filling the container with tap water from a spigot in the restroom, an old-timer approached. He looked like he was straight out of the *Death Valley Days* TV series, but he spoke Australian.

"Where ya headed, mate?"

"Some place called Warrego."

"River of Sand."

"What?"

"That's what Warrego means in Aboriginal."

"That doesn't sound promising."

"It's all in your perspective, mate. You have to live there, won't seem so bad. If you're visiting, won't seem so good."

Because of a warning I'd received from Andrew, I had to ask, "Hey, you know anything about water buffaloes on the roads at night?"

His nicotine-stained fingers pulled a dented pocket watch from his threadbare jeans. He flipped it open and squinted at the watch face.

"Best you bugger off, mate."

Quite the send-off, but I didn't take offense since I interpreted the "bugger off" as a sign of concern—which only added to my concern.

I heeded his advice, found my way out of Alice Springs, and crossed a bridge that spanned a river of sand—the Todd River. Several all-terrain vehicles raced along the dry riverbed, captained by dark-skinned kids. I later learned that water flows beneath the sand, even when the riverbed appears dry. ATV drivers have to be careful lest they crash through the crust and into the water below.

Keeping an eye on the speedometer and the gas and temperature gauges, I sped north on the Stuart Highway, a two-lane strip of blacktop—*bitumen*—that stretches between Adelaide in the south, Alice Springs in the middle, and Darwin in the far north. I was rushing toward a remote mine in the heart of an Aboriginal reservation where another river of sand flowed.

When Andrew briefed me the day before on the work expected of me, he offered four non-engineering pieces of advice about the drive from Alice Springs to Warrego.

"Carry plenty of water, fill up at every servo, never pass a *road train*, and get to the Warrego Mine before nightfall."

I didn't know what a road train was, but figured I'd know one when I saw one.

"What's important about arriving before nightfall?"

"You reduce the risk of encountering a water buffalo."

Why would water buffaloes roam the outback, and what would happen if I encountered one? Then I remembered Charlie, the water buffalo Mick Dundee hypnotized in the first *Crocodile Dundee* movie. Charlie was huge.

I followed Andrew's first two pieces of advice to carry water and fill up at every gas station. A promise I'd made to Ruth to bring back Aboriginal art caused me to gamble on the last two: passing a road train and driving at night.

Ruth made me pinky-swear to bring her Aboriginal *clap sticks* and a *waterhole map* in penance for leaving her alone with cows and kids. She explained that the clap sticks consist of two short sections of a hardwood tree branch. The Aboriginal artist grinds the ends to dull points and etches each stick with fire-branded symbols that tell a story. When banged together, the sticks create the dance beat for a traditional Aboriginal ceremony—a *corroboree.*

Ruth showed me a picture of a waterhole map to ensure I wouldn't buy a cheap knockoff. Hewn from a wood slab and shaped into a shallow bowl or platter, each map bears a pattern of colored dots that reveal the location of a water hole. Like the music stick messages, you need insider knowledge to decipher the route.

***

Stretches between gas stations were long. At each stop, I glanced at the trinkets in the station but couldn't find Ruth's must-have music sticks or waterhole map.

What I found at the gas stations was segregation—shades of America's old Deep South. Aboriginal men purchased beer at a service window at one end of the building, while whites bought their beer inside. The dark-skinned men congregated under a scorching sun, drinking and chatting, while white guys hung indoors with their mates. I don't know about the Aboriginal language, but the whites' language was on the rougher side. I encountered the same thing at each stop, making each a sad experience.

The terrain for much of the trip alternated between miles-long gradual inclines and miles-long gradual declines. The scrub encroaching on the highway blurred the views on both sides. However, each low-lying crest showcased a sweeping vista of vast plains carpeted with stunted trees and brush. It brought to mind images of Africa's Serengeti Plains pictured in a *National Geographic Magazine.*

The farther north I traveled, the more termite mounds I saw, and the bigger they got. I recognized them—again, thanks to National Geographic—but the photos didn't prepare me for their actual size. Some mounds towered over ten-feet. They looked like gnarled, inverted ice cream cones, similar in hue to the reddish-brown soil. The stunted trees didn't stand a chance against these giant termite colonies.

The constants of the trip were the heat and the dryness, even more than I had anticipated. Fortunately, the air conditioner was up to keeping me cool in a place where temperatures can top 100 degrees.

I was speeding along at above 90 mph, resigned to the fact that I would not be the bearer of the gifts Ruth had requested from the outback, when I spotted a faded "ABORIGINAL ART" sign jutting from the top of a man-high conical termite mound. I barely had time to brake to a stop, kicking up a cloud of red dust over the car and a little shack where a non-Aboriginal woman stood in the doorway.

As I got out of the car, she greeted me. "G'day, mate. In a bit of a hurry, are we?"

I answered as I approached her, dust still hanging heavy in the air. "Yeah. Trying to get to Warrego before dark. I don't want to chance ramming a water buffalo."

"While I'll be *buggered*. A Yank!"

She gave me a sly smile and locked her emerald eyes on me.

I glanced at the woman, the shack, and the surrounding termite mounds. She looked European, petite and quite attractive. She wore a loose-fitting shift of a muslin-like material. Its red-tinged, coffee-brown color matched the color of the shack and her hair.

The shack, built with creosote-laced timber slabs laid one atop the other haphazardly and topped with rusty corrugated sheets of iron, didn't look promising. I hoped the stop was worth my time.

"You're not Aboriginal," I ventured.

The smile again.

"You Yanks are so quick smart."

My cheeks felt hot, and I knew my skin color had become several shades redder than the dust of this place.

"Well, I meant you advertise Aboriginal art, but you don't look Aboriginal."

"Oh, so you want to make sure I'll deliver the authentic goods?"

"Well, yes. I've heard about knockoffs."

The smile again, toying with me.

"Come on in and have a *squiz*."

I stepped from the oppressive heat and bright sunlight into the relative coolness of the dimly lit shack. A tarp strung in front of the back third of the building separated the living quarters from the shop.

"My husband's Aboriginal. He's done some of this." She swept her arm around, drawing my attention to the sagging shelves displaying arts and crafts that even I could tell were high quality. "The rest he sells on consignment for the *mob*," by which she meant tribe.

I saw a profusion of clap sticks and waterhole maps. I recognized other pieces, too. Some Ruth had shown me in a magazine, like the hand-painted *message stones*, but I also saw familiar items like didgeridoos and boomerangs.

I said, "What about you? Where are you from?"

"I'm a Sydney girl. Met and fell in love with my husband at uni."

It was incongruous—a beautiful, well-educated white woman living in the outback selling Aboriginal art. Then again, maybe it's not all that different from American yuppies like me and Ruth giving up modern metropolitan life for farm life on the far side of the planet.

I couldn't help marveling at the shack floor. It appeared to be made from compressed red clay but with deeper tones of red than the soil on which the shack stood.

When I stooped to examine it, she offered, "It's made from termite mounds. Bust 'em up, haul 'em here, tamp 'em down."

Smooth and cool to the touch, the floor had an alien quality.

I explained what I was after, and the shopkeeper helped me select a set of fire-branded clap sticks—she called them *bilma sticks*—and a waterhole map painted by one of the younger, up-and-coming female artists in her husband's mob.

She continued to share her wealth of knowledge about Aboriginal art as she wrapped my purchases in yellowed newsprint. Suddenly, we heard a godawful roar from the highway. I stepped into bright daylight and witnessed my first road train.

A road train comprises a string of two, three, or four semi-trailers towed by a massive, turbocharged tractor rig. They haul freight much as American tractor-trailer rigs do, but on a larger scale and at a faster clip.

I cut the conversation short, stowed Ruth's gifts in the trunk, and kicked up a new cloud of dust as I peeled away.

Testing the limits of that poor Commodore, I discovered why I should have heeded Andrew's warning to never pass a road train.

Road trains move fast, but I was moving faster. While overtaking the road train that had roared past the shack, the last trailer snaked toward me, forcing me onto the unsealed shoulder. As the trailer's side loomed closer with each successive oscillation, I veered farther onto the shoulder. Once all four wheels were no longer in contact with the pavement, it felt like I was driving on ice. Moving along at over 100 mph, I floated more than drove past the road train.

I should mention that if the passing car's driver loses control, there's not much the road train driver can do, if he even notices. Like supertankers at sea, the behemoths require minutes to stop and additional minutes to turn around and return to the scene.

By then, the car's occupants will reside in the afterlife.

The air conditioner wasn't powerful enough to halt the flow of fear-sweat my body produced after I swerved back onto the highway.

I decided to heed Andrew's road train advice for the rest of the trip.

As I closed in on Tenant Creek, I passed by the Devils Marbles, a popular tourist attraction in the middle of nowhere. The fields of massive rounded granite boulders, many impossibly balanced one atop another, tempted me to stop and explore. However, the rays of the sinking sun painting the boulders the fiery orange-red of Hell commanded me to press harder on the accelerator pedal and distance myself from anything Devil-related in this desolate land.

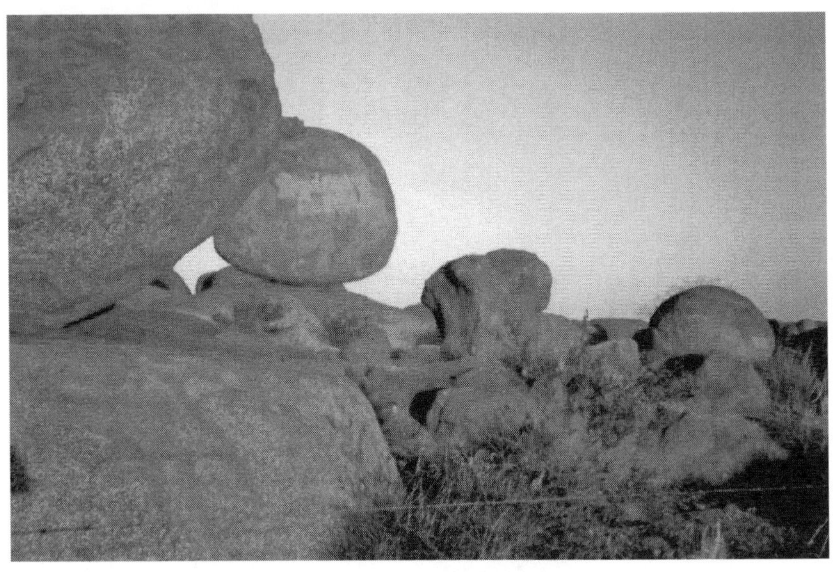

12. SURREAL WARREGO

I was relieved when I rolled into a Tennant Creek gas station at dusk, intact. Thinking Warrego was close to Tennant Creek—it looked close on the map I saw at one of the gas stations—I presumed my day was almost through. I was ready to wash off the road dust, eat, and bed down so I'd be fresh when daylight arrived.

The attendant was locking up as I asked for a tank top up and directions.

"Mate, not knowin' the road, you'll drive west for a long hour."

I would have to drive in the dark.

He acted like he couldn't wait to get rid of me, so he'd be free to do whatever you do in Tennant Creek on a Saturday night—something beer-related, I'm sure.

I attempted to keep my voice steady when I asked about the final threat to my survival.

"What about water buffaloes?"

"What about 'em?"

"Are they around?"

"Sometimes."

I sensed I wasn't about to get a straight answer from this guy, either.

Paid up and buckled up, I left the station behind, shrouded in the familiar cloud of dust.

I drove the narrow, two-lane road west as light faded from the sky. My grip tightened on the steering wheel, and I kept my foot light on the pedal. My eyes grew weary, staring into the night, searching for glowing buffalo eyes.

When I pulled into the mine site at Warrego, full-on night had set in. I felt proud of my achievements. In one day, I had met my commitment to Ruth, survived road trains and elusive water buffaloes, didn't run out of gas, and neither the car nor I had died from overheating.

My elation was short-lived.

I found my Warrego contact, Nelson, inside a massive circus-size canvas tent. The mining town, comprising about one-hundred workers and their families, had turned out to watch a Saturday night movie projected on a large cotton sheet slung from a tent support beam. The heat in the tent was unbearable.

Nelson broke away from *Mad Max Beyond Thunderdome* to show me to my living quarters.

Modular aluminum-clad buildings—*dongas*—occupied a couple acres of coarse rock and powdery sand. Feeble light cast from a Rube Goldberg assortment of pole lights helped guide our way into an empty structure suitable for housing a few dozen workers. A hallway running the length of the spartan building offered access to individual bedrooms, a kitchen, and the industrial-style communal bathroom at the building's center. Each bedroom contained a metal dresser and a twin-size, iron-frame bed with a bare, worn mattress—the metal to better protect against termites. I chose the bedroom at the end of the hallway, farthest from the entry door.

Nelson said, “This is our slow mining season, so there's no need to accommodate contract workers. You have the entire building to yourself.”

I surveyed the modest room that would be my home for the next few days.

“Nelson, where do I find bed linen, a blanket, and a towel?”

“I'll be right back.”

I took the opportunity to move the Commodore closer to the donga. When I re-entered my bedroom, I saw Nelson had laid a folded black wool blanket on the mattress. No sheets, no pillow, no pillow case, and no towels. Who uses wool blankets in the outback? Apparently, me.

Fortunately, I had packed a washcloth—*face washer*—since Australian accommodations, even at high-end hotels, don't provide them.

I was so tired I didn't care what I slept on. I could find a towel later.

***

Somewhere in the night, a door-slam nudged at my subconscious. I was lying on my back atop the wool blanket, naked and perspiring. Hollow echoes of footsteps approached as I woke from a Kodachrome dream filled with romping, multicolored water buffaloes. The hallway lights came to life and shone through the open door of my bedroom. Two silhouettes loomed in the door frame—one tall and slim, the other short and curvy.

A deep-throated voice said, “G'day. Sorry to disturb your blissful rest. I'm Jerry, and this's me partner, Maisie.”

When I realized I was jaybird-naked and not dreaming, I jerked the blanket to cover my essentials.

Maisie added, “We didn't know anyone was bedded down here.”

"Hi. I'm Dick. Nel—"

Maisie's giggles interrupted me.

I continued, "Nelson said I'd be on my own here. Apologies if I shocked you."

Maisie said, "No shock here. Would appreciate some company while Jerry's down in the mine shafting all day."

Jerry said, "Don't pay no attention to her. She's on the piss. I'm the Territory mine inspector. Show up unannounced to catch operators unawares. Forgive Nelson. He had no clue I was coming."

I said, "Okay. Happy to catch up in the morning."

Jerry said, "Understood, mate."

Maisie said, "G'night, *Dick*."

I puzzled over "on the piss" until I recalled from Australian TV that it meant Maisie was drunk. I struggled to remember the meaning of the other piss saying: "take the piss out of someone." Then it hit me. It means to mock someone.

She and Jerry giggled as they trundled down the hall to a nearby bedroom.

The lights went out. It took minutes for me to relax into sleep. A hammering on the walls snapped me back awake. Between bangs, I heard the distant squeak of bedsprings. I pulled the blanket over my head, which did little to drown out the racket. After an interminable amount of time, the noise ended in a grand finale, and I finally fell back into sleep.

***

At the command of my travel alarm clock, I woke to a new day. I didn't know the whereabouts of my new flatmates, but I was eager to get to work, even though it was Sunday. The sooner I got the job done, the sooner I'd be home.

I took a quick shower, had a cuppa in the kitchen, and snacked on the cookies Ruth had packed for me.

Dressed and headed down the hallway, ready to track down Nelson at the mine office, I passed the communal bathroom where a dark-haired woman was showering in full view. It had to be Maisie. I was trying to figure out why she hadn't drawn the shower curtain when she turned my way and smiled. Then I recalled her saying, "Would appreciate some company while Jerry's down in the mine shafting all day."

I sped up, put the episode behind me, and got to work. Nelson said a surprise visit from a mine inspector had disrupted his day. He took a minute to describe the generator issues they were experiencing and handed me a roll of electrical drawings. I let him get on with his day, as I had enough information to make a start.

I returned to the donga's kitchen, took over a dining table, unrolled the drawings, and was busy flattening them when Maisie, barefoot and wearing a man's white tee shirt, strode in.

"G'day, *Dick*."

Oh crap.

"Hello, Maisie. Pleased to meet you in person."

She smiled and said, "I hope we didn't keep you *up* last night, *Dick*. Do you have time for a cuppa?"

"Sorry. I came back to find a quiet place to work and call my wife."

Her smile faded, and her eyes narrowed as she dropped into the chair across from me. She stared, weighing me up, calculating.

I broke the silence. "How's Jerry going?"

"Expect him back in an hour or so. Then we're off to Darwin."

"Oh, do you work there?"

She hesitated and said, "I'm rather flexible. I work wherever and whenever I can."

It took several seconds before it clicked.

When I didn't respond, she said, "That's right. Jerry's a client.

A good one. He takes me with him when he travels. To keep him company, so to speak. I've seen many, many mines."

I did not know how to respond, so I said, "I hope you're happy."

"Me? Of course. With the likes of Jerry's help, plan to retire soon and settle down."

"Sounds like a plan, Maisie. And I hope you don't take it the wrong way, but I have to get a few things done before I make that call."

"Got it." She got up and shuffled down the hall toward her and Jerry's room. The exaggerated sway of her hips under the shirt that almost covered her backside shouted, "LAST CHANCE!"

Her voice reverberated down the hall. "Maybe see ya some other time, *Dick*."

This was unlike similar field assignments in the US, where I stayed in decent on-site housing or a hotel, without being propositioned. I had to remind myself not to complain since I had volunteered. I was the only one to blame for my predicament.

***

Although it was still early, I felt parched and drew a glass of water from the tap before calling Ruth. One thing I puzzled over each time I drank tap water, sipped tea, or took a shower was the hint of fish drifting into my nostrils. I reasoned that living in the outback, the closest fishing hole would be miles away. The smell was a mystery I shoved aside. I needed to focus on my work and get out of this place.

I made the call, eager to tell Ruth about my travel and overnight adventures. She usually sleeps in on Sunday but I didn't think she'd mind hearing from me. She picked up on the first ring. I could hear the girls chattering in the background, and I found it odd they would be up since they usually sleep in on Sundays, too. As I spoke to each one, the reason for their early rise became clear.

“We’ve been up most of the night chasing cows,” Ruth said before sobbing and passing the phone to Danelle.

“Dad, we were up all night trying to keep the cows from getting out,” she whimpered. “Bye, Daddy.”

She passed the phone to Kristin.

Kristin said, “Ryan’s running after this one bad cow. He has a stick he hits it with. It’s a mean one. When are you coming home?”

“It’s going to be a couple of days, sweetheart. Can you put Mommy back on?”

While waiting for Ruth to pick up, I pictured Ryan using a stick to herd a cow several times his size. Thinking back on his attack on the pampas grass, I felt sorry for the cow.

Ruth had recovered enough to talk.

“At four, I ran after a cow.” Her voice choked off.

“It’s okay. Give me the highlights, and don’t say the c-word.”

Ruth went into a rapid-fire explanation.

“I chased and cornered one of the dark monsters in a yard about a mile down the road. It was pitch black. Then all the lights in the house blinked on, and a woman shouted from the back door, ‘What’s going on?’ I thought I was going to get shot.”

Considering she had been awake all night, Ruth was doing a fantastic job holding it together.

“I explained I had a cow cornered. About this time, her husband came out in full jogging gear—and he’s American. It turns out he gets up early and jogs ten kilometers. Today he had a reason to jog as he chased the thing back to our place and into the paddock. And while he did that, the lady invited me in and fixed me a cup of tea.”

The sobbing returned as she continued, “You have to get rid of these. . . these animals.”

I never thought I’d hear Ruth tell me to get rid of anything with fur and four legs.

I called Nigel at his home.

"My apologies for ringing you on Sunday, but we have a problem."

"No worries, Mr. Reese. You caught me as we were leaving for church. How may I be of service on this fine morning?"

"Get the cows gone. "

"What?"

"You heard me. We've been beyond accommodating."

"I understand, and I will see what I can do first thing tomorrow morning."

"No. The cows are a liability. They have ravaged gardens, wandered onto the road at all hours, and have been a general nuisance. They must be off the property today."

"As I told you, I will see what I can do."

"Nigel. Are you familiar with the American propensity for suing? Lawsuits are in my DNA. Don't test me."

There was a long pause.

"I will inform the owner."

"Whatever. Just make sure you pass along my message."

Lawsuit is a term everyone understands, and it takes on an even greater significance when uttered by a Yank.

That afternoon, I knocked off a little early to call Ruth. My call woke her out of a sound sleep. She stayed awake long enough to say, "The owner of the cows came and rounded them up this afternoon. No more cows, ever again."

It wouldn't be long before we'd soften our views.

***

My days in Warrego were busy and flew by. Unfortunately, the job was complex and would take a few weeks and not a few days to complete. Andrew agreed to send relief in the form of a contract power engineer, but it would be two weeks before he arrived.

Ruth would have filed for divorce if the cows remained. However, she understood that the delay in my return was out of my control. We didn't like being separated, but it had happened before when one of us had to go out of town for work, emergency callouts, training, or a conference.

Stranded in the outback, I still couldn't find a towel, pillow, or bed linen. I gave up and air-dried after showering, a process that didn't take long in the stifling heat. I planned to pack a bath towel on future trips.

As fast as the days passed, the nights were long. Nelson had told me that Warrego is an Aboriginal sacred site, which might explain my impressions of the night sky and my visions.

In the skies over Tasmania and Warrego, the moon hangs upside down, the Southern Cross replaces the Big Dipper, and the Milky Way glows brighter than I could ever have imagined. As odd as that view of the heavens struck me in Tasmania, when I stared at the cosmos above Warrego, my mind drifted in an even odder, otherworldly direction.

I'm not one for spirituality, but a bizarre mix of brilliantly colored dreams that felt not of this world filled my nights. Perhaps the dreams weren't spirit related but resulted from sleeping on the coarse multi-purpose blanket, the guilt of abandoning my family during a time of need, or the smothering silence that descended over the mine site at night. Whatever the cause, I expect if I ever have a repeat experience, it will be in the promised land.

***

When the contract engineer spelled me two weeks after my arrival, I was free to go, but not before one last twist.

I returned from the generator plant and prepared to clean up for evening tea. It would be my last supper in Warrego.

An older, rotund fellow wearing khakis appeared in my bedroom doorway and said, "G'day. Dick Reese, is it? Napoleon Thomopoulos here to relieve you."

We shook hands.

"Never have I been so happy to meet anyone."

"If you give me a minute, I'll change," he said, "and perhaps you can give me a debrief."

"Meet you in the kitchen in ten?"

"No worries."

Focused on organizing the plant drawings and my notes, I failed to hear Napoleon enter the kitchen. He plunked down on the plastic chair across the table, generating a disturbing soft plop. To my surprise, Napoleon had debriefed instead of me. He was buck naked, with a body hairier than an ape's.

I attempted to maintain my composure and not run from the room. My parents never taught me how to react when facing a naked man, especially a chubby one cloaked in dark curly wool.

Napoleon spoke first. "I didn't mean to alarm you. Should've told you I'm a nudist."

I finally found my voice and said, "Full time?"

"As much time as I can without getting arrested."

"Okay then. Let's get on with this, and I'll be on my way."

I shortchanged Napoleon on some details, but I felt no guilt.

***

Although itching to return to my family, I felt peculiarly close to the earth and the spirit world in Warrego. Despite the Napoleon episode, the experience with Maisie, and the primitive living conditions, a small part of me resisted leaving—a tiny part, and the feeling didn't last long.

Nelson arranged for a driver to take me to the Tennant Creek Airport in the Commodore. The mining company would return the car to the Alice Springs rental car agency.

The driver, Jack, was a crusty old miner who had worked Northern Territory mines his entire life. We hit it off, chatted, and joked during the ride to the airport. In one of our conversations,

Jack solved the fish mystery for me. In hindsight, I wish he hadn't.

Frogs gave the water its distinctive odor. They live and flourish in the water tanks that collect and store rain runoff from the building roofs, the same tank water system used by Tasmanians, minus the frogs. Frog slime permeated the water I drank and showered in for over two weeks. Yuk!

Jack dropped me at the outdoor gate a few minutes before my flight departed. A twelve-passenger turboprop was revving up its engines as I boarded. I took the remaining seat, buckled in, and looked out the porthole window toward the terminal. Jack, the only person in sight, leaned on the chain-link fence and waved goodbye to me. He kept waving and waving. I thought: "What an excellent mate. We hardly knew each other, yet there he was, wishing me a bon voyage." The passengers seated nearby must have thought I was insane for waving fond goodbyes to some bloke.

The flight to Hobart went well, with a plane change in Melbourne. During the flights, I used a red ink pen to edit the first draft report I created at Warrego. I could spend more time with my family if I finished before landing.

When the plane approached the Hobart Airport, sweeping in over Seven Mile Beach, all the emotions of our arrival from America welled up and washed over me. I did something engineers aren't supposed to do: I cried. Unable to choke off the tears, I avoided eye contact with the other passengers as we deplaned.

My family ran toward me as I approached the terminal, skidding to a stop ten feet away. They began crying too, but their tears were of terror, not joy. They stood, mouths agape, staring at my chest.

Ruth was the first to speak.

"Oh, Honey, does it hurt?"

Her words bewildered me until I looked down and saw the source of their concern. I had forgotten to pack my pocket protector and had not recapped my red pen. Somewhere over northern Tasmania, the ink siphoned into the weave of my chambray shirt and formed an expanding red splotch. The combination of uncharacteristic tears streaming down my cheeks and the apparent blood over my heart gave them the impression I had taken a bullet to the chest.

I feigned a pained expression and said, "Yes. We better get to the Royal"—the Royal Hobart Hospital, the largest in Tasmania.

When I saw their terror turn to panic, I reached into my pocket and pulled out the uncapped pen for them to see. The relief was immediate, and I heard a simultaneous "Oh, *Honey*!" and "Oh, *Dad*!" as we shared a gleeful and overdue group hug.

I added, "Well, it was a rough trip."

Ruth said, "But not wounded rough."

"No, because I didn't come across any water buffaloes. Only a prostitute, a nudist, and me best mate, Jack."

Danelle said, "What's a prostitute, and what's a nudist?"

Ruth said, "Ask your father, dear."

***

Upon my return to the office, I discovered Jack and I weren't as close as I thought. Everyone snickered as I circulated, telling them about Jack, me mate. I couldn't fathom what was so funny.

Finally, Bea took me aside and said, "Jack was giving you the *Aussie salute*."

"The what?"

"Jack was trying to keep the blowflies off his face."

"You mean Jack and me aren't mates?"

"No, Dick."

More culture shock for me—deeply sad and humiliating culture shock.

***

Looking back over my Northern Territory sojourn, other than my Jack faux pas, I reckoned I hadn't screwed up too much. Along the way, I helped the client, learned about Aboriginal art and culture, and got a taste of living in the outback. I could have done without the hooker and nudist encounters, but what an experience.

The whereabouts of the Warrego River of sand and the water buffaloes remain as mysteries.

13. THE GIFT HORSE

Ruth, like many young girls, longed for a pony when she was growing up. In Ruth's case, however, it went beyond longing. A pony was number one on her Christmas and birthday gift wish lists—she had to have a pony.

With each passing Christmas and birthday, she became more desperate, more determined. After several years of trying with no success, she dropped the pony request and instead, each year, asked Santa and her parents for tack—saddle, bridle, stirrups—anything she could use for leverage. Ruth reasoned if she got a harness, for example, she could make a strong case for needing a pony to go with it. Unfortunately, the apartments and houses where she grew up—Washington, D.C.; Roanoke, Virginia; Sunnyvale, California; and Clearwater, Florida—were not conducive to pony ownership.

Ruth had compensated with smaller pets—lots of them.

All the signs of her pet-loving disposition were there well before we married, but I was too smitten to acknowledge them.

Our first date morphed from going to see a movie to going to feed ducks at a nearby lake. Ruth talked a lot about pets but was rather vague about what she envisioned after we married. The acquisition of a Siamese cat, a Spitz-Pekingese dog, two goldfish, and a parakeet—Jo, Sam, Herman-1 & -2, and Bird—in the first week after tying the knot made me acutely aware that marriage had unleashed long-repressed pet acquisition desires she could not appease while living with her family.

I had to intervene when she mentioned bringing another dog and another cat into our animal-overpopulated city home. It finally dawned on me I had married a petaholic, more formally known as a zoophilist. At the risk of destroying nuptial bliss, I put my foot down—well, not exactly.

"This has to stop."

"I love animals, and I thought you did too."

"I do, but enough is enough."

That brought her to tears.

I had only seen Ruth cry that hard when we were at the beach and found a seagull with a fishhook embedded in its neck, which resulted in a mad dash to a bird rescue home. Thankfully, they saved the bird; otherwise Ruth would have remained a basket case for weeks.

I had to stem the incoming pet flow and the outgoing tear flow. That's when I had what I thought was a rare stroke of genius. I remembered my days of youthful joy on my family's farm and told her, promised her, "Someday we'll move to a farm, and when we do, you can have any and as many animals as you want, if you stop collecting now."

Without hesitation, she said, "I agree."

Her swift acquiescence hinted at impending trouble—not for Ruth, but for me.

***

In the meantime, there was Ruth's dream of a pony to fulfill. Now that we lived on property fenced for horses with a 6-acre, cow-free paddock available, I decided I'd surprise Ruth with a horse since a pony was not a fit for an adult.

I asked myself if I was doing this out of love or the guilt I felt over leaving her to deal with the cows? I chose to believe it was love, and, in fairness, I did have the idea in mind before the cars-cows confusion. Whatever the reason, I was unaware that my purchase would alter the course of our lives.

Unlike cars, horses are inexpensive in Tasmania. At least, that was my initial perception.

One Saturday morning, while browsing the *Hobart Mercury*, an ad for a horse caught my attention. It stated: "Ben/15hh/$250."

I was so horse-ignorant I didn't know that "15hh" stood for 15 hands high. Each hand measures four inches, which puts Ben's height at the withers (where the neck meets the front shoulders) at sixty inches. I rang the number in the listing without a clue about what I was doing. The owner came across as a nice enough fellow and did an excellent sales job. He said Ben was gentle, easy to ride, and only fifteen years old. I recalled horses live to around thirty, so I reckoned Ben would be alive long enough for Ruth to get some use out of him. I bought Ben sight unseen and arranged to pick him up the following weekend.

Ben was a bargain at the equivalent of 150 US dollars. I didn't realize the real cost of owning a riding horse is all the extras: bridle, saddle, shoes, shots, feed, trailer—the list goes on.

The horse trailer came first; otherwise, how could I bring Ben home? I went back to the *Mercury* ads. The trailer had to be small, lightweight, and sturdy to tow Ben with the Subaru. I lucked out and found an old single-axle model. Faded blue and marred by patches of rust, it had seen better days. There went $800, over three times Ben's purchase price. I stored the trailer out of Ruth's sight in the Jefferson's barn. I wanted Ben to be the best surprise gift ever.

Ben lived on the far side of Hobart, across the Derwent River in Cambridge, near the Hobart Airport and Seven Mile Beach. That meant I had to cross the river via the Tasman Bridge with the horse trailer in tow. The prospect worried me. A decade earlier, the Tasman Bridge collapsed, and a dozen people died. We'd been unaware of the bridge's infamous history when we crossed it several times during our scouting missions a few months earlier, but once we found out about the collapse, we tried to avoid the crossing. With that in mind, I ventured forth on a Saturday morning alone, leaving the kids at home and safe with Ruth. I told her I had to take care of some urgent business at the office.

I retrieved the trailer and found my way to Ben's owner, Simeon. We walked into a paddock where three horses grazed. Simeon called out, "Ben. Apple." A dappled chestnut left his mates behind and trotted over. As he came to a halt, he began talking. Unlike the human speech of TV's *Mr. Ed*, Ben's utterances sounded like a drunk's slow-fire burps, closer to a human bass voice than a typical horse nicker. And when Ben saw Simeon pull an apple slice from his pocket, he turned up the volume and the tempo. As Ben chomped on the apple, I noticed his teeth looked bigger than I expected. I remembered something about not looking a gift horse in the mouth, but captivated by Ben's voice, I thought no more about it.

After Ben enjoyed a few more apple slices, Simeon turned toward the paddock gate. Ben and I followed in his footsteps. Simeon grabbed a halter and lead rope hanging from the gatepost. He slipped the halter over Ben's head before opening the gate and leading Ben to the old blue trailer. I ran ahead and dropped the ramp. With no hesitation, Ben climbed into the trailer, and Simeon tied the lead to an eye hook at the front. We hoisted the ramp and slid the pins into place. Ben was ready to hit the road.

As I reached for my wallet, Simeon said, "Do you have tack for Ben?"

"What do I need?"

"We have the tack we used for him and no longer need it. English saddle with girth and stirrups, saddle pad, rug, bridle with bit and reins, and a martingale. I can show you. We had to buy them when we bought Ben from the track. I'll make you a good package deal."

I said, "I'll go with your recommendations."

"Give you all of it for a grand. That's a steal, mate."

I knew I should haggle, but without knowing a good deal from a bad one, I had no bargaining power.

Since Ben was a gift horse—the gift above all gifts—for Ruth, I hoped for the best and handed over $1,250. Simeon helped me load the Subaru with the horse tack. I did not know whether Ben would need even half of it. What I did know was that I was out of pocket over two grand. My inner voice whispered: "Your heart was right; your mind was not."

I hadn't considered food for Ben until Simeon said something. I presumed a horse eats pasture grass and hay. Per Simeon, Ben couldn't just graze or munch on hay. He had to have pellets with supplements.

I said, "Simeon, how much will Ben's food cost per month?"

"About the same as your family's food bill."

"You're kidding."

"Sorry, mate."

My inner voice was spot-on.

***

During the ride home, while praying the Subaru had the oomph to get Ben and me over the Tasman Bridge and up the Southern Outlet, the steep highway I traveled to and from work, I realized in our search to fulfill our dream, my ignorance was costing dollars aplenty.

I was worried. I realize I'm frugal, but my worry was justified. The financial unknowns we faced in Tasmania were many times greater than those in America, where we knew the income needed to ensure a desired outcome. In the US, we could live our middle-class lives with a high level of confidence we wouldn't end up on the street. This was the pre-Google era. Except for the information we gleaned from the *Mercury*, we didn't have a good sense of the prices for goods and services or even the tax rates. In Tasmania, we could end up on the street.

One worry resolved: the Subaru had no problem getting us to Leslie Vale. I pulled into the long driveway of our rental property, and as I parked in front of the house next to the paddock gate, I saw three little heads and one bigger one pop up at the living room window. While I walked around to the back of the horse trailer to drop the ramp, the house's front door burst open. Ruth, Danelle, Ryan, and Kristin raced to pull on their gumboots. When I lowered the ramp, untied Ben's lead, and backed him off the trailer, the whole family was screaming with joy and pummeling me with questions.

Danelle said, "Where did you get a horse?"

Ryan said, "How much did it cost?"

Kristin said, "What's the horse's name?"

Ruth said, "Honey! What did you do?"

I said, "I bought you the horse you always wanted."

Ruth cried, gave me a hug I will never forget, and said, "I really, really love you!"

Ben stood there, calm and stoic, unconcerned with human antics.

I led Ben through the gate and into the paddock, where I unhooked the lead rope. He spun around and thundered across the paddock, kicking up clods of earth, whinnying, snorting, and tossing his head.

I said, "He's lonely and looking for his mates."

We watched him race around the paddock, continuing to neigh. Our hearts went out to him. Ben reminded us we missed family and friends, too. We bottled up our feelings. Ben did not.

To lift our spirits, I asked the kids, "Would you like to hear Ben talk?"

Danelle said, "Dad, we know horses can't talk. We're not stupid."

"He doesn't talk like us, but he talks. Run to the pantry and grab an apple."

They were off like a shot.

I turned back to watch Ruth watch Ben.

Ruth gave me another big hug, accompanied by a kiss. She had a lingering tear in one eye. "Ben is exquisite. Thank you."

"You're welcome. And he's all yours."

The kids came clambering back.

Danelle got to us first.

I said, "Give me your apple."

I pulled out my Barlow pocketknife and quartered the apple. Simeon had shown me the right way to do this while we chatted after loading the Subaru with Ben's tack. He explained that giving a horse an entire apple could be fatal if the horse choked on a big chunk.

I handed the sliced apple back to Danelle and quartered the apples Ryan and Kristin had brought.

Ben stood across the paddock. He had stopped, his ears were at attention. He must have heard or got a whiff of another horse.

I hollered, "Ben. Apple."

At that, he turned and ran at full throttle toward the gate where we were standing. We stepped back a few paces.

As he skidded to a stop before us, I said to Ruth, "Honey. Take a piece of Danelle's apple, place it on your palm, and stick your arm over the gate." Again, this treat-giving method was per Simeon's advice.

Ben saw Ruth walking toward him with the apple, and he talked.

The kids cracked up.

All three shouted, "He does talk!"

When Ruth did as I had asked, Ben plucked the apple from her hand, chomped, swallowed, and began the banter again.

We all chuckled as we took turns welcoming Ben to his new home with apple treats. Our lives would never be the same. Ben was now family. He helped ground us to this new land.

As we got to know him, we discovered his unique personality. Simeon told me Ben trained at the racetrack, where he learned to pull a sulky. We figured his trainers treated him poorly because he sometimes acted like a grumpy old man, but he sure looked fine. When his coat glistened in the sun, it matched the color of Ruth's hair. He made you want to be near, stroke, and cuddle with him when he napped. And Ben's lovely scent, especially on a warm day, soothed the soul.

Our neighbor Thomas dropped by. He had grown up on a ranch. After eyeing Ben, he offered some advice that we followed, much to the regret of my wallet.

First, we arranged for a veterinarian to pay Ben a visit, with an emphasis on pay. She examined him and administered a series of shots that would need to be repeated annually. She wormed him and referred us to a farrier. Ben would need to have his hooves trimmed, and he would need to be shod.

The vet's final referral had a sense of urgency to it. If we didn't hire a horse dentist to file down—*float*—Ben's teeth, he wouldn't be able to chew his food and could starve to death.

Whoever heard of a horse dentist? And why the urgency? Ben ate just fine and a lot, mostly the expensive, vitamin-enriched pellets. I thought the vet's advice was overkill. Ruth insisted we follow it.

And when the horse dentist, Helmut, came, and as I watched him put this contraption over Ben's head to hold Ben's mouth open, I made the mistake of mentioning Ben's age.

Helmut said with a snicker, "You think Ben's fifteen? Come and see his teeth."

I peeked into Ben's mouth and said, "I thought his teeth looked rather large."

"You ever hear the phrase 'long in the tooth?' It means old. The older the horse, the longer the teeth."

Helmut looked at me and shook his head, trying to restrain a laugh.

"Ben's at least twenty years old and probably closer to twenty five."

While Helmut filed down Ben's teeth, he told me how much he would charge for the service. Horse dentures would have been cheaper.

The farrier added to Ben's tab. And I learned we would see and pay him for his services every three months.

After the thousands I had spent on Ben, I reckoned his $250 price tag was a gift. But had I been aware of the significance of long teeth and hooves when I first looked at Ruth's gift horse, would my decision to buy him have changed? Probably. However, watching Ruth groom, pet, and spoil Ben made it all worthwhile.

***

I didn't anticipate that Ruth would be afraid to ride Ben. She had read about horses in magazines and books but lacked practical experience. I had neither the studied nor the practical experience, though I was about to gain plenty of the practical.

We were getting into our first Tasmanian winter—June through August—and the sun set long before I arrived home each weeknight. Evening tea would be waiting. We would dig in and, between bites, share our experiences of the day. It was a time for me to catch up with the kids about their school and hear about Ruth's search for a farm in the Cygnet environs.

One evening, when I returned from work, I found Ben saddled up with his lead rope tied to the fence railing.

"You need to ride Ben," Ruth ordered as I exited the car.

"I'm not a horseman."

"It doesn't matter. You have to ride him for half an hour around the paddock."

"But it's dark, it's cold, and I don't know how to ride."

No amount of argument appeased her. Ruth had been doing more horse reading and learned Ben needed to be ridden daily. I would love to find the person who published that sage advice. Until Ruth could take lessons and handle Ben, I had to ride that horse around in circles for half an hour each evening through most of our first Tasmanian winter.

Ben and I slogged around the paddock every day over the next couple of months, come rain or frost. Ruth finally took pity and agreed to take riding lessons. Contrary to her book-learning about riding, Ruth's instructor confirmed horses do not need to be ridden daily. I was relieved of my riding duties. Ruth took a while to apologize to Ben and me.

Ben will always be Ruth's wish-come-true horse and the family's first entry into the world of equine pets. He would be far from the last.

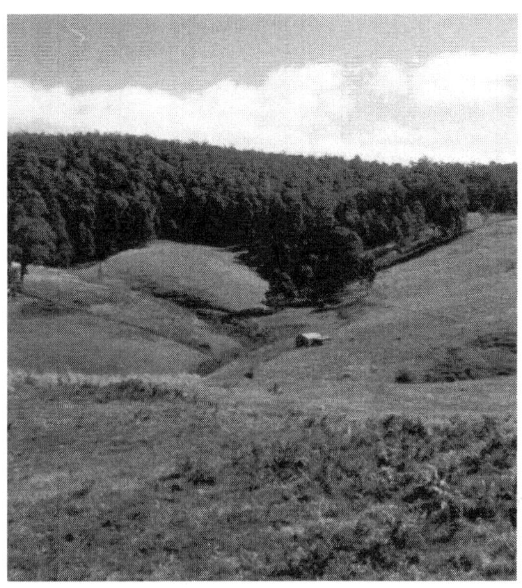

14. BUCKLEY'S CHANCE

Similar to tradition in the US, Tasmanian farmers often bequeath their properties to the next generation. Consequently, and much to our chagrin, few farms came up for sale. As newcomers, we stood little chance of finding the home of our dreams, even though we were prepared to pay cash.

With my engineering workload on the rise, Ruth spent more time with our real estate agent, Victor, than with me. However, her persistence finally paid off when Victor showed her a prospect in, of all places, Cygnet.

On a sunny day near winter's end, Ruth called me at work and said, "You have to meet me in Cygnet within the hour. The end of Woodstock Road. We're going to look at the Whitbread property."

"Cygnet's an hour's drive, and I have to wrap things up here."

"No excuses. You have to see this place. It's perfect."

"I'll do my best, but I'll have to stop for gas."

"Get here, now. At 50 acres, it's more land than the 20 acres we wanted, but everything else about the property ticks the boxes on our list. It's at the end of a road and has two year-round streams, a large shed, a barn, a chicken coop, bush, and a three-bedroom, one-bath house. All that for $100,000."

"Sounds too good to be true. What's the catch?"

"Victor told me the Caulkins, the sellers, said if we want the place, we have to submit an offer today."

"I'm on my way."

I had barely enough gas to get to Bluey's for a fill-up.

He approached, still clad in greasy coveralls. While wiping his hands on what was once a white cloth rag, he said, "Beauty of a day, innit?" Then he remembered me and blessed me with a yellow-toothed grin. "Ya back for more gas, mate?"

"Gas and information. Fill her up, please."

When he finished the job, I paid him and said, "You know anything about the Whitbread property?"

At a volume all of Cygnet could hear, Bluey said, "The Whitbread family bought that land more'n a hundred year back. Were one of the early orchardists helped Tassie earn the name Apple Isle. The Caulkins, who's sellin', bought it from the Whitbreads nigh thirty-year ago, I reckon while I's still soilin' me nappies." He let out a burst of laughter, proud of his clever diaper humor. "Caulkins planned to leave the place to the two daughters, but the birds want no part of it. But mate, ya got Buckley's chance of gettin' that place. Lotta interest."

I said, "*Fair dinkum.*" The phrase means good or true, according to one of my workmates.

Bluey looked shocked and took a step back. "Well, blimey, listen to ya, mate. Startin' to sound like a bloody wannabe *Taswegian.*"

He directed me to the Whitbread property, a five-minute drive from town.

Pulling away, I shouted out the car window, "Good on ya, mate!" I could hear his laugh over the roar of the engine.

Maybe I did wannabe a Taswegian.

"Buckley's chance" puzzled me. I assumed he meant our chances were slim.

***

Per Bluey's advice, I veered off Mary Street and entered a picturesque valley sculpted by a broad serpentine stream millennia before we walked the earth. I turned onto Woodstock Road, where Bluey told me I'd find the Whitbread property up a hill where the road ended. Along the way I saw more than half a dozen farms, a horse ranch, an apple orchard, and a hulking apple-packing shed before the road narrowed and continued across a wooden plank bridge over a stream and past three smaller farms.

I had to downshift to climb the steep grade. The bitumen faded to a sandy brown, compacted-clay surface that leveled to a winding lane. On my right, a tall embankment carved from the rocky hillside blocked my view. The land on my left dropped to a meadow carpeted with wildflowers and early spring grasses. Broom grass, reeds, and intertwined brambles bordered a sparkling stream. The meadow continued up a hillside, where it transitioned to bushland.

I drove past a barn crowded against the left side of the road and stopped short of a closed metal farm gate on the backside of a large, grayed-with-age wooden shed. Woodstock Road continued past the gate as a narrow track over a culvert bridge and uphill past an old, eerie-looking house in desperate need of a paint job. If that's the Whitbread house, forget it.

I turned up a driveway and stopped behind Victor's fancy Peugeot, which was parked in the Whitbread's single-car garage.

The faint scent of eucalyptus and a symphony of buzzing bees and birdsong greeted me when I opened the car door. Under the dome of an intense blue sky, I turned full circle to store the image.

Perched on a rise, a quaint, yellow, single-story house ringed by a lush lawn and flower beds overlooked sprawling paddocks. Trees lined the ridge tops in three directions, leaving the village of Port Cygnet and the bay visible on the fourth side, to the south. I was awestruck. Had Ruth finally found our farm, our home?

I followed a footpath through the backyard lawn, past a honeysuckle-festooned concrete water tank and a cluster of pink and purple fuchsias. The fragrance of the flowers mixed with the camphoraceous scent of the nearby gum trees left me feeling euphoric.

Ruth was waiting for me on the back porch. She glowed with excitement.

Victor appeared and gave us the (almost) complete rundown on the property:

- Nearly 50 acres in fenced and cross-fenced paddocks
- Several acres of bush
- Two year-round streams
- Three-story draft horse barn
- A large apple-packing shed
- 1,100-square-foot house with three bedrooms, one bathroom, and two woodstoves for heating
- Two sources of water—one domestic (house) and one agricultural (yard and livestock)
- Electric water heating for the house
- School bus service to Cygnet Primary three miles away

Victor ushered us through the back door into a narrow hallway that led to the bedrooms and the bathroom, all closer to the house's north side. We followed him back through the hallway and into the kitchen and living areas on the south side of the house. My immediate observations were mainly:

- The house was less than half the size of our Nevada house.

- The bedrooms were small and on the north side of the house.
- The bathroom was compact, with a tub-shower and a single sink. For a family of five, it would prove challenging.
- A pocket door separated the bathroom from the toilet—a clever arrangement, but one loo for a family of five would prove more challenging than one bathroom. The screened window behind the commode could not be closed. This legal ventilation requirement makes for cold visits in winter.
- A laundry room off the kitchen had enough space for a washing machine, but no room for a clothes dryer.
- The kitchen was open to the dining area and reminded me of an old farm-style kitchen—no automatic dishwasher and no provision for one.
- Although the two wood-fired heaters looked in good shape, one in the dining room and the other in the living room, the bedrooms and the bathroom were at the opposite end of the house. Those rooms would be cold in winter and hot in summer. There was no thermostatically controlled central heating and cooling system.
- The squat electric water heater in the crawl space beneath the kitchen floor looked ancient.

Nevertheless, the house would work.

We stepped out and walked around the yard while Victor explained the water supply systems: Rainwater flowed from the house gutters into the concrete holding tank beside the back porch. When the holding tank was full, an electric pump transferred the water uphill to a 5,000-gallon concrete storage tank in the paddock behind the house. Water to the taps in the kitchen, bathroom sink, and shower was courtesy of gravity.

Except for the cost of periodically running the transfer pump, the water was free.

The water for toilet flushing and agricultural use came from a sizable spring-fed pond—*dam*—several hundred yards west of the house, across the stream, and at an elevation several feet higher than the house. A buried polyvinyl pipe carried the water to a galvanized steel holding tank mounted on top of an old concrete block building formerly used for dairy milk storage. From there, the pond water ran in small underground pipes to the toilet for flushing and to several spigots for irrigation and livestock watering. A mechanical float valve shut off the pond water inflow when the holding tank was full. The system was ingenious and did not require any power to operate. It was better than a gray water system, and like the domestic water, it was free.

Six smaller spring-fed ponds, one in each paddock, provided water for the livestock.

Victor emphasized the two streams flowed year-round. Agnes Rivulet—I would have called it a river—was the broad winding stream beside the road I followed through the valley. It coursed through the eastern tip of the Whitbread property. The other stream, the one I noticed weaving through the meadow across Woodstock Road, was smaller and remained unnamed. Victor claimed that naming a watercourse precludes drawing irrigation water from it—yet another Tasmanian quirk.

Victor said, "The Caulkins raise beef cattle. They have a herd of white-face Herefords currently grazing in the upper eastern paddock. The Caulkins want to increase production, thus the need to move to a larger farm."

While trying to soak in what we saw and what Victor was explaining, a pickup truck—*ute*—pulled up the drive and parked behind our Subaru. I saw a flash of worry cross Victor's face. He said, "There's something I need to attend to. Would you mind going back inside and taking another look?"

I said, "No worries."

As we entered the house, I turned and saw Victor approach the pickup truck as the driver lowered his window.

***

Inside the house, Ruth pointed to the large picture window in the dining room. The view was to the south and Port Cygnet, with winding Woodstock Road below us. I could not take my eyes off the distant sea view until Ruth nudged me and gave a slight nod that beckoned me to look down. As in Ruth's déjà vu moment, there was a wooden-fenced corral next to a bend in the road shaded by large pine trees, not gum trees. As I lifted my gaze, I started at the sight of the unnamed stream running through the meadow on the other side of Woodstock Road. It completely matched her out-of-body vision. If we had had any doubts about whether to make an offer, they evaporated. And that was fortunate because our commitment was about to get tested.

I heard the door open as Victor came in. He looked downtrodden when he spoke.

"I had a chat with Mr. Caulkins. That was his ute. The sales price has increased by $55,000, but it's still a deal because the holding grew by 75 acres, bringing the total property size to 125 acres."

The increase in price and property size left us dumbfounded. We were not prepared to pay another $55,000. As Victor went on to inform us, a side deal to sell the 75 acres adjoining the 50 acres on which the house stood had fallen through right before our arrival, and the Caulkins would only entertain an offer for the entire 125 acres—a far cry from the 20 acres on our dream list. As Bluey had predicted, other potential buyers had expressed interest, and they could drive up the sales price. The Caulkins were in a similar situation on a property they wanted to buy on a smaller island, Bruny Island, south of Cygnet and across the D'Entrecasteaux Channel. If we submitted a full price offer today, the farm was ours. I was confident we could get a loan from the bank based on my income. A commitment from us would allow both deals to proceed.

The 75-acre parcel to the northwest was predominantly a bush block with many valuable old-growth trees. Victor said it included a 1940s pickers hut, barebone housing for migrant workers, that was functional but allegedly haunted. This was the rundown house beyond the gate I had feared was the Whitbread house. Was a haunted house good or bad? Since real estate agents never reveal anything negative, a haunted house must be an attribute, and it did pique our curiosity.

The Whitbread property was located right where Ruth determined we were going to live and offered more than we ever dreamed of—75 acres of bush, 50 acres of fenced and cross-fenced paddocks, two year-round streams, seven spring-fed ponds, end-of-the-road privacy, views, and fertile soil. Add to that Ruth's precognition and the months of searching. Losing this farm to someone else was not an option for us. It was time to pony up or rent for who knows how long.

Ruth and I ventured outside. The ute was gone.

Lost in thought, we walked around the yard, neither saying a word.

I broke the silence. "What do you think? Are you ready to be in the poorhouse?"

We put in a full price offer of $155,000, subject to mortgage approval. The Whitbread property became ours and the Bank of Tasmania's.

Before returning to Leslie Vale, we celebrated in the Middle Pub's formal dining room. In a chat with Max and his wife, I suggested they stock up on Tassie Tiger beer for the American bloke who now knows his way around their pub.

15. CYGNET FARM

Following approval of the mortgage, the Bank of Tasmania scheduled an October closing. We would be free to move to the Whitbread property in the spring, a bit over seven months after setting foot on the island.

It felt like forever.

Unlike Mrs. Von Bibra or the Whitbreads, we had no family history that locked us into a name for the farm. We were free to rename the property to our choosing. At long last, after all the searching, we were putting down roots at "Cygnet Farm."

When we heard the Caulkins and their cattle had moved a month before escrow closed, we received permission to move livestock onto the property. Ben was the first inhabitant. He had the run of lush paddocks already awakening to spring, and he could quench his thirst at the large pond whenever he chose. Ruth dropped by on chilly nights to strap on his wool-lined canvas coat—*rug him up*—after which she plied him with apple snacks. The following day, she returned, removed his rug, and gave him a bucket of the expensive pellets.

We were all itching to begin our new lives at Cygnet Farm, but we had to wait for September to end. We passed the time by taking weekend drives to Cygnet Farm and points of interest in the surrounding Huon Valley region.

Each expedition began at Cygnet Farm. After we tired of petting Ben and treating him to apples, we wandered the land. We had owned and sold three properties to finance our migration: the 22-acre vacation property in Berry Creek, California; a 20-acre parcel at Webber Lake near Truckee, California; and our 1-acre Silver Knolls home near Reno. Cygnet Farm dwarfed their combined acreage.

Our scouting visits didn't do the place justice. With its ups and downs, streams, ponds, bush, and meadows, we couldn't view the entire acreage, but what the visits did was impress on us the beauty of our soon-to-be piece of the planet.

Bird life was abundant. A mix of unfamiliar chirps and songs filled the air, some melodious, some less so. The plovers that nested in the meadows bordering the unnamed stream created a ruckus when we got near, squawking and dive bombing.

On one occasion, a giant eagle circled overhead. We learned these large raptors are sea eagles. Much like California turkey vultures, they feast on carrion, but the California birds are lightweights compared to their Tasmanian kin.

The ever-present Tasmanian native hens evoked memories of the cartoon roadrunner from our childhood. Hiking through the meadows, native hens popped out of the grasses, rocketed ahead of us, and vanished into the bush.

One puzzle I could not solve was the near nonstop sound of the to-and-fro of a crosscut saw. It emanated from the bush but stopped whenever we got close. I suspected a couple of thieves, one on each end of a two-man saw, cutting trees soon to be ours. I vowed to find them and seek retribution.

Our short expeditions into the bush were magical and calming. Sea breezes stirred the meadow grasses into waves on both sides of the dirt track as we climbed the steep hillside, past the pickers hut, on our way to the wall of gum trees that graced the hilltops. Yellow-flowering wattle trees demarcated the bush boundary. We trekked past the wattles and through a cattle gate into the woodlands. Above our labored breathing, the only sounds were the quaking leaves high in the gums, the kookaburras—the bird calls heard in jungle movies—and our footsteps, muffled by spongy moss and grass springing from wildlife trails. The children enjoyed the journeys as much if not more than we did.

Thick groves of gums soon obscured the beautiful valley and sea views. Rotting stumps evidenced the work of long-departed loggers. The width of many of the living trees exceeded my outstretched arms. They must have been teenagers when the loggers came through.

Diverse members of the fungi and fern families overlaid the ground between the trees in Cygnet Farm's bushland. Giant tree ferns, known as man ferns, prospered in the gullies. Unlike other flora, they never evolved. Their appearance, broad umbrella crowns topping spiky trunks, is unchanged from the time of the dinosaurs. They thrive in dense groves where gurgling water coughed up by trickling springs feeds their thirsty roots. All that was missing from the scene were leprechauns.

We passed dozens upon dozens of dead gum trees—standing dead. The remnants of the once great giants stood waiting for their time to fall or, fallen, lay crisscrossed in the gullies, stockpiled in disarray. I would never need to cut a living tree. The deadwood could warm our family for countless winters.

Trekking out of the bush along one of the many wildlife tracks, we looked down on the ponds surrounded by scattered gums and cattails—*cumbungi*. The pond placements were strategic because each paddock had plenty of water for livestock. Wherever Ben and his future companions roamed, drinking water would be available.

***

We got a pleasant taste of Cygnet Farm, but while we had the opportunity, we devoted the bulk of our free time to exploring the Huon Valley, which we had just touched on during our first week on the island.

At the Huon Valley Apple Museum, we saw Industrial Revolution-era apple processing machinery. If the Australian version of the Occupational Safety and Health Administration (OSHA) had existed during Tasmania's apple export years, they would have shut down the factories. All the equipment would have been deemed hazardous, from the peeler-corers to sorting conveyors to stacking conveyors.

Empty wooden bins and crates stamped with apple variety names filled the floor space between the vintage equipment. Brightly colored crate labels from long gone orchards adorned the walls.

We learned that, in the late eighteenth century, Admiral Bruni D'Entrecasteaux named the river that flows through today's Huon region after his second-in-command, Huon de Kermadec—also the source name for the Huon Valley, the town of Huonville, and the Huon pine.

The Huon pine is a majestic, long-lived—some over 10,000 years old—and rare softwood tree once abundant in the swampy bushlands of Tasmania. Logged to near extinction by the British for shipbuilding, it is now prized by furniture makers for its golden-yellow hue. Not long after our arrival, ignorant of its true value, I purchased a handcrafted Huon pine kitchen table and chair set for next to nothing. For once, my ignorance worked in our favor.

A bit more relevant history: William Bligh planted a few apple trees on Bruny Island some 200 years ago. It would be another 100 years before the apple industry took root in the Huon Valley. From there, the industry blossomed to produce over 900 apple varieties. In the 1970s, the apple industry in Tasmania lost its exclusivity and crashed after Britain joined the Common Market. With supply dwarfing demand, the government paid orchardists to uproot their apple trees. Some generations-old orchards, like the Whitbread property, fell victim.

The Huon River played a key role in Tasmania's apple industry. At its source, clear water washes down high southwest mountain slopes before seeping through vast moors where buttongrass tannins stain the waters an unappealing golden brown. The darkened waters unite and meander past Huonville and enter the D'Entrecasteaux Channel, where the river blends first with the Tasman Sea and Indian Ocean, then the vast, storm-ridden Southern Ocean before lapping against Antarctica's ice shelves.

By providing passage for wooden ships to dock and load crated apples in Huonville before the vessels set sail for Great Britain, the river was integral to shipping apples off-island. Along the way, the mariners had to skirt several islands and cumbungi-choked swamps where one of the three snake species in Tasmania is rampant: the Tiger snake.

This brings me to share some unsettling facts gleaned from a visit to a snake rescue shelter.

Tiger snakes are long and fat, with venom ranked in the top ten deadliest in the world. When startled, the Tiger rears up, spreads its head like a cobra, hisses, and strikes at a height that is unfortunate for the male of our species. I made a mental note to position my body appropriately in the event of an encounter.

Another native species, the Copperhead—no relation to its American namesake—has venom nearly as toxic as Tiger snake venom. The Whip snake's venom, less poisonous than both, is only deadly if the bite is on tender skin, say on the web between your fingers—not a very comforting fact. However, the one positive, if you can call it that, is that Tasmania's snakes are honest. If bit, unless treated with antivenom, you will kark it.

Cygnet Farm offers the perfect habitat for all three extremely poisonous snake species. Ah, well. Every Garden of Eden has snakes—and, apparently, venomous ants.

Known as the Jack Jumper, this endemic ant is about the size of a paper wasp, with a bite many times more painful than a wasp sting. Multiple bites can prove fatal. Jack Jumpers, who get around by hopping, nest in mounds on the ground and prefer to hang out on gum trees.

Our farm was a habitat for slithering snakes and jumping ants—all poisonous. We would have to tread carefully.

***

Driving deeper into the Huon Valley, we encountered scenery that helped diminish the darker and starker realities of Tasmanian living.

Spring unofficially begins on the first of September in Australia, but winter still reigned in the towering, snow-capped Hartz Mountains that formed the horizon across the Huon River. In the Valley, though, spring was conspicuous in the greening paddocks where sheep, cows, and horses grazed.

Although I was far from as animal crazy as Ruth, I had dreamed of owning a Clydesdale from early childhood. What guy wouldn't want to pal with one of those majestic giants you see pulling a Budweiser wagon during the *Super Bowl* commercials?

The opportunity to make my dream come true presented itself.

As we motored along a country lane near the Huon River, surrounded by blue-gum tree-bordered paddocks, I spotted a hand-painted sign on a gatepost that read "FOR SALE - $200 - CLYDESDALE STALLION - BOYO." On autopilot and without a word to Ruth or the kids, I braked to a stop, reversed, shoved the shifter back into first gear, raced down a rutted driveway, and stopped next to a rundown barn and corral. And in that corral, he stood. Majestic. My dream come true: 16 hands high, bay coat, white mane, and classic white feathers cloaking massive hooves. Boyo was pulling a mouthful of hay from a feed rack.

As I stepped from the car, Boyo raised his striking white face. We locked eyes, his large brown orbs meeting my small blue ones. He let the hay drop from his mouth and snickered, soft and low, "What took you so long?" At least, that's what my brain heard.

The house's front door banging open interrupted my reverie. Boyo and I turned to see a rather stocky lady hobbling our way. Although she looked old, her gait signaled strength. Hard-worn jeans, a faded plaid blouse, and scuffed Blunnies complemented the leathered, sun-wrinkled face. The only hint of softness emanated from her iridescent green eyes.

She said, "Can I help ya?"

Ruth remained in the car with the kids. I knew, even as poor as we were about to become when we closed on Cygnet Farm, bringing home a new pet would thrill her.

"Saw your sign for Boyo, and I'm interested."

She studied me for a moment.

"Ya don't look to be Canadian." She stared at me for a few seconds more. "I'll be buggered. A Yank's interested in my Boyo. Figures. Ya been watching too many commercials for that weak-as-cat-piss Budweiser," she said with a cackle.

I wondered how she knew about Budweiser and their Clydesdales. We'd had limited TV coverage so far.

As if she had read my thoughts, she said, "Saw a wee bit of a *Super Bowl* when I's a younger lass. Quite a show. All 'em pads and helmets. Playin' on a boxy field. And all that startin' and stoppin'. Not much of a contest, really."

I knew what she was getting at. Australian Rules Football, a cross between soccer and rugby and better known as footy, is a fast-paced game played on an oval field with players in shorts and tees—no pads or helmets. I couldn't think of a counterargument.

I stuck out my hand. "My name's Dick."

She shook my office-soft hand with her calloused one and said, "Sarah." Something didn't feel right about her grip. When I looked at her hand, it shocked me to see it was minus a thumb. Much to my shame, my first thought was Tasmanian inbreeding. That's the running joke about generations of Tasmanians confined to an island with a limited population. It's amusing when you tell a Mainlander you're from Tasmania. They demand a peek at your neck to see the scar where they cut off your other head. A prime example of that raw Aussie sense of humor.

I patted Boyo's neck, lifted his upper lip, and saw short teeth. Thank you, God. I had learned my lesson from Ben.

Sarah patted him, too, and said, "He's two years old and blessed with the gentle soul of 'is ancestors."

"How can he be that big and only two years old?"

"He's a *bub*. Give him another year or two, and you'll need a ladder to see over 'is withers. He's a colt, but 'fore long, he'll be a stallion and has to be gelded, right?"

That hadn't crossed my mind, but it didn't deter me. The big guy was going to be mine, regardless.

"Of course. We bought a farm, and so far, we only have one other horse on the property, and he's a gelding. Let's get down to it. How much for Boyo?"

I didn't even bother trying to bargain. Sarah knew she had me, just as Simeon had me when I bought Ben and his tack. At heart, Sarah had the same fond feelings for Boyo as I did. She was down on her luck and forced to sell him. In the end, we struck a fair deal, and she included delivery on the condition that I return and help her load him onto her trailer.

On the drive home to Leslie Vale, when I told Ruth I'd bought a companion for Ben, "Boyo," she didn't say a word. Her only response was a wide smile. The children reacted true to form.

Danelle said, "Boyo's a funny name for a big horse."

Ryan asked, "How much did Boyo cost?"

Kristin said, "I want to ride Boyo."

***

The following day, Ruth dropped me off at Sarah's. I had loaded Ben onto his trailer a few times, and aside from his grumbling, he posed no problem. He was trained to travel in one when transported between racetracks. Boyo, a yearling, was about to learn.

I entered the corral and approached Boyo. Sarah exited the barn and slipped a rope halter over his head. She attached a thick lead rope and handed it off to me.

"Boyo means 'boy' in Welsh. The name won't befit him for long. And remember, ya need to have 'im castrated or no fence in Tasmania will stop 'im from findin' and mountin' a mare in season. And so's ya can't say I didn't warn ya, he'll be able to scent her from more'n a mile away."

I said, "I got it. Castrate Boyo!"

I had already renamed Boyo to Charlie in my mind. It seemed more fitting for a friend, and I suppose, partly stemmed from my memory of the colossal water buffalo, Charlie, in *Crocodile Dundee*.

We left the corral, and I led Boyo/Charlie along a lane toward where Sarah's truck and double-axle trailer waited. Sarah walked behind us.

I jumped when she barked. "Oi! Get the loop outta that damn lead!"

At first, I didn't understand what she meant. Then I realized that walking close to Boyo/Charlie, I had looped the rope around my hand to take up the slack.

I got rid of the loop and turned to look at Sarah. She held her right hand high in the air, waving it.

"How d'ya think I lost me thumb?"

The missing thumb mystery solved.

When I didn't answer, she barked at me again, "Never 'ave a loop in a lead."

Lesson cemented. I made a mental note to pass the lesson along to Ruth and our children.

Getting Charlie onto the trailer was another eye-opener. How can you get one ton of horse onto a trailer he doesn't want to go on?

I watched Sarah in awe. She cajoled, tapped, pulled, patted, yelled, and cursed for the better part of an hour. All the while, Charlie reared, neighed, and pawed at the earth with those huge hooves. Clods of dirt flew, and dust filled the air. I would have given up. Sarah never backed off. Through her sheer willpower, Boyo/Charlie finally got the message and shuffled aboard.

Dust and sweat congealed into a pale clay coating on Sarah's face and hands. She sprayed herself down from a nearby hose, transforming from a living clay figure to her former self.

We arrived at Cygnet Farm, where Charlie/Boyo backstepped out of the trailer with little urging from Sarah. I led him with a loop-free lead rope through a gate and into the lush paddock with the largest pond where Ben roamed. Charlie galloped away in an ungainly gait, hooves pounding down knee-high grasses on his way to meet his new mate, Ben. It would be many years before Charlie saw the inside of a trailer.

We would cross paths with Sarah from time to time, and she always inquired about her Boyo. I always answered her honestly. Except for his escape when he tried to find true love at an elite Arabian horse stud and his unpleasant response to having his hind hooves touched after being gelded, her Boyo did just fine.

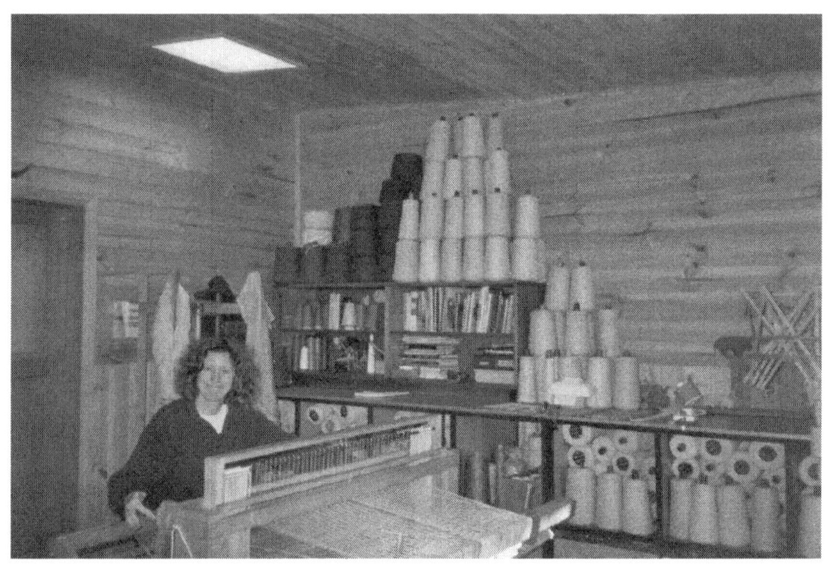

16. MY ENTREPRENEUR

As I've mentioned, when we first discussed where we wanted to follow our dream, the Australian and New Zealand wool fiber and textile industries were major draws for Ruth. She explained to me that both countries are renowned for producing the world's finest merino wool and mohair yarns.

Ruth's interest in fiber and textiles began at an early age. By the time she entered junior high, she was a skilled seamstress, making clothing for herself and her sister. Her interest blossomed, and working with natural fabrics and fibers became her passion. She never strayed far from her sewing machine or spinning wheels in our California and Nevada homes. She even got me involved, maintaining her sewing machines, repairing broken spinning wheels, and building niddy-noddies—a device to form skeins of spun yarn.

As her knowledge and skills advanced, my participation evolved from maintaining her paraphernalia and fashioning yarn production accessories to servicing and fine-tuning looms.

The first looms she bought were compact. I could move them by myself, and the adjustments were simple. Going from woven placemats to blankets to artsy wall hangings, Ruth traded up to larger and more sophisticated looms. Soon, I was moving furniture out of our formal dining room and storing it in the garage to make way for a room-size loom that took days rather than hours to assemble. You couldn't walk through the house without bumping into a spinning wheel or a yarn winder. Baskets overflowing with yarn skeins and roving (picture a thick furry fiber rope fluffed up like cotton candy) of various animal furs—alpaca, camel, cashmere, dog, llama, merino, mohair, and qiviut—cluttered the floors. We could no longer have family and friends over for dinner because there was no place to eat.

In the lead up to moving overseas, I told Ruth, "We can't afford to ship all your spinning and weaving stuff. What can you get rid of?"

"Well, I'll take the big loom."

That wasn't what I wanted to hear. The loom was massive. Ruth had to sit inside the structure to treadle while slinging the shuttle from side to side. Selling the loom in place and buying a replacement in Tasmania made more sense. But Ruth had saved for a long time to buy her loom and had developed an emotional attachment to it.

"I'll take two of my favorite wheels, too, as well as some of the more expensive accessories and those with sentimental value. Everything else, I'll give away or donate."

When I disassembled and packaged the loom, the crates were as big as the fourteen-foot trampoline the kids insisted we take with us.

If I could have gazed into the future and seen what the loom would do for us, I would have been more supportive of her decision. Ruth's fiber passion was about to play a significant role in our fiscal future.

***

The devotion to my day job left little opportunity or energy for me to think about how to turn Cygnet Farm into an investment opportunity. Andrew had ramped up my project management workload. As he spent more time at the Sydney headquarters, I spent more time at the office. I reckoned he was paving the way to transfer from our tiny Tassie office to the big city. I didn't want to make waves, so I didn't complain about extra work for the same pay.

Ruth's schedule was more relaxed, and she spent much of her free time observing, planning, and calculating. Nothing brings out the entrepreneurial spirit like moving to a foreign country—not to mention destitution. Ruth devised a game plan that would guide our lives for years to come.

During a Sunday drive, she said, "We're going to sell wool to Australians."

I tried to humor her. "You mean like selling ice to Eskimos?"

"You catch on quickly. I know we can do this."

"You're not kidding?"

"Nope. Think about it. Cygnet Farm is costing us more than we can afford, but with the fenced paddocks, the place is ready for wool-producing animals to graze and proliferate. That's how the farm can pay for itself."

"So, you want us to go into the sheep business?"

Danelle piped up from the backseat. "I like sheep. I want one for a pet."

Like mother, like daughter.

Ruth continued, "Yes, and Angora goats too."

"How could we compete?"

"By investing in high-quality colored sheep and the best Angora goats we can afford."

"Emphasize *afford*. I don't see how we can be successful. We're going to be down to pocket change."

I had to tread carefully when alluding to our finances since I had recently bought a tractor on a whim.

***

The Caulkins held an auction before fully vacating the property. We purchased several minor items—gardening tools, buckets, troughs—nothing expensive. However, I was keen to bid when the Fiat 152R diesel tractor and a brush hog (a towed, rotary chain mower) came on the block. Ruth squeezed my hand so hard that her nails cut into my palm to keep me from bidding. In the end, my efforts were futile, as the tractor and hog sold for much more than we could afford. But that evening, I got a call from Mr. Caulkins.

"Saw you were itchin' to bid on me tractor and hog today."

"You're very observant."

"Well, the bloke that wanted 'em can't afford 'em, so's if ya want 'em, I'll sell 'em to ya for half the bid."

Before I could stop to weigh up my answer, I said, "I'll get the money to you tomorrow."

Ruth was not happy. However, I think the incident motivated her to reveal her business plan before I could squander any more of our savings.

***

Ruth continued. "We'll succeed because I'll create the market for our products."

I said, "How?"

"Well, remember when we were exploring, we visited that agricultural show and saw women seated behind spinning wheels, treadling and chatting?"

"I recall."

"Those ladies pulled raw, greasy wool from trash bags. Each bag contained the unwashed fleece from one sheep, fouled with weeds, thorns, and the matted dung from beneath the tail—the *dags*."

"I didn't pay much attention."

"I did. They removed as much debris as possible before feeding the dirty wool into the wheel. The result is well-spun, dull, greasy, dirty wool. It still has to be washed, and no matter how meticulous the spinner, the yarns will not be ideal."

"So, how do you plan to change how Australians have produced homespun yarns for centuries?"

"A few ways. First, we provide processed fleeces in different colors. Wool doesn't have to be white, which it predominantly is, based on what I've seen."

"You're talking colored sheep?"

"Yup. It's a matter of finding them and processing their wool properly. And we can dye the white sheep's wool and the Angora's mohair."

"How?"

"First, we'll need a carding machine."

"What would that do?"

"A carder would untangle and comb fleeces, getting rid of debris in the process, and produce roving."

"Where will the money for a carder come from?"

"If we're lucky, it will come after the first shearing."

"Let's talk inside."

***

We had pulled into the parking lot of a hotel with a sign advertising "Devonshire Tea," another roadside mystery sign we'd wanted to investigate.

A hostess led us into the hotel's formal Victorian-style dining room, its tables cloaked in white embroidered linen. Place settings were thick, colorful cloth mats and ornate-pattern silverware set atop lacey napkins. The velvet-cushioned, high-backed mahogany-tone chairs dwarfed Danelle, Ryan, and Kristin.

A teenage waitress wearing a black skirt, white blouse, black bowtie, white apron, and a bonnet—she looked like a throwback to days of old—took our order.

She said, "What can I get for ya?"

I said, "Five Devonshire Teas with cordial in place of tea for the children."

"Oh, Canadians. How exciting! Back in a tick."

Although her accent was Australian, I detected a hint of a Georgia drawl.

While waiting for our order, the kids stayed busy with restaurant-supplied coloring books and crayons. We continued discussing Ruth's business plan.

I said, "Okay. What's the next step?"

"We buy sheep and goats."

She made it sound so simple.

The waitress presented us with a lavish Devonshire Tea service on a silver tray with five demitasse teacups and saucers, a silver teapot, a tea strainer, a pitcher of cherry cordial, a bowl of sugar cubes, and a pitcher of cream. Five plates held two scones each, accompanied by tiny bowls of whipped cream, raspberry jam, and pats of butter.

The waitress served the cordial to the children and the tea to the adults.

I said, "How do we tackle this?"

She took a step back and smiled.

"Ta, for asking. There are several ways, but I'll explain how I take Devonshire Tea."

"First, you open a scone and coat each half with the butter and raspberry preserves. Then, plop a dollop of cream on top. That's it. Enjoy."

We followed the waitress's advice and left, filled and thrilled. Since we were contemplating a business that dated back to before the Industrial Revolution, perhaps it was appropriate that we had enjoyed a dining experience to match.

17. DREAMS DO COME TRUE

On the drive back to Leslie Vale, with the kids sedated in the backseat after crashing from their cordial sugar-rush, I mulled over Ruth's wool scheme. She was correct when she said we needed Cygnet Farm to make money. However, her plan felt like a long shot since our combined farming experience amounted to raising one milk goat and her kid.

Before we moved into the Sparks rental, we lived in the Reno suburb of Silver Knolls on a sagebrush-peppered acre of windswept desert in the shadow of eight-thousand-feet-high Peavine Peak. It was there and then that Ruth decided our children should be raised on goat and not cow milk. I was tasked with building a goat barn, pen, and milking stand.

Returning home from my Reno office one evening, Ruth introduced me to Cicely, a nanny goat. An Alpine-Saanen mix doe, Cicely paced the wire fence pen that bordered the one-stall barn I had built. At the back of the lot and away from our neighbors, her incessant bleating didn't annoy anyone except me.

The next day, I learned why she had been so vocal. Cicely had been in labor. Overnight, she gave birth to a tiny doe—Amy. Our children gained a priceless experience and Cicely produced ample milk for her kid and our kids. Buying a pregnant goat was the closest we'd come to animal husbandry.

On weekend getaways to our Berry Creek cabin, we took our nanny and her kid with us, loading them into the VW van for the four-hour drive. Cicely stood between the front seats with her eyes focused on the road ahead while Amy slept under her mom. To limit the amount of goat berries deposited on the van floor, we stopped at every rest area, attached leashes to their collars, and let them graze and do their business. Many onlookers inquired about the odd breed of our dogs. Their questions pointed to a gaping hole in America's educational curriculum.

Although Cicely produced sweet, creamy milk, she was not a wool producer. She and Amy gave us a farm-lite experience, precursors of how we would raise and transport goats in Tasmania.

***

It was late afternoon by the time we returned to the Leslie Vale house. Thoughts about Ruth's wool scheme continued to tumble in my head like damp clothes in a dryer. I had no clue how much sheep and goats and their fleeces are worth—no basis to gauge the viability of Ruth's plan. I felt compelled to check the classified ads to investigate livestock prices.

Australian newspapers print their premier editions on Saturdays, not Sundays. I plopped down on the couch and pored over the day-old Saturday *Mercury* ads. One stood out: "Moving. Selling out all livestock and sundry items—best small herd wool producers in Tasmania. Trailer, tools, and equipment. Everything a hobby farmer needs."

My voice went up an octave when I called to Ruth, "Honey. Come here. You will not believe this."

Ruth leaned over my shoulder, read the ad, and said, "I can't believe it. How could this be?"

It was like the fortuitous timing when I landed my job. Somebody up there liked us.

I rang the listed number and identified myself. A woman named Tilley invited me to visit Hilltop Farm near the Lea, a ten-minute drive away. I was familiar with the area since I passed the Lea exit on the Southern Outlet during my daily commute.

Fifteen minutes later, with the family reloaded and a checkbook in my back pocket, the Subaru grunted up the winding drive to the top of a ridge and through an open cattle gate. Hilltop Farm's name, spelled out in wrought iron script above the gate, accurately described the property. A fieldstone mansion and barn, surrounded by majestic trees and manicured hedges, reminded me of the English country manors I'd seen in movies. The difference here was the mountaintop setting with views in all directions.

We parked next to the barn.

I told the kids, "Sit tight, and we'll be back shortly."

Kristin said, "Maybe we'll get some cordial."

I said, "You guys need to be on your best behavior. If invited to meet the owner; no asking for cordial or cookies. Got it?"

Three solemn faces nodded in unison.

As Ruth and I climbed out of the car, a woman dressed for a polo match strode toward us: knee-high leather riding boots, tight breeches, a polo top, and a short-billed ball cap. The dark shades of her boots and clothing contrasted with her pale complexion and the flaming red mane her cap could not contain.

We exchanged introductions and traded handshakes.

Tilley asked if we'd like a cuppa.

I said, "Thank you, but we have our children in the car, and it's getting a bit late for them since they have school in the morning."

"I was about to feed the goats and sheep. Do you reckon they would like to help?"

Ruth said, "I certainly would, and I think they would, too."

I turned our three loose, and they sprinted to Tilley and introduced themselves, eldest to youngest. To her credit, Kristin didn't ask for cordial.

Tilley motioned for us to follow her into the barn, which was actually a stable barn. I counted ten stalls. Two fine looking thoroughbreds nickered from behind gates in adjacent stalls.

Tilley said, "Not long ago, I had darlings in every stall. We started selling a month ago when Roger, my husband, decided we should move to Queensland and downsize into the suburbs. These last two, my favorite polo horses, will be gone tomorrow."

She clearly disagreed with the decision, mumbling, "I don't see how I can leave all this behind, 90 acres and the home of my dreams, and move onto a postal-stamp-size lot."

Tilley stepped into an empty stall, returned with two metal pails overflowing with feed pellets, and led us through a man-door on the back wall.

We stepped onto a broad concrete footpath between metal rail enclosed stock pens, one on each side. The one on the right contained half a dozen baaing sheep. Their wool fleeces ranged in color from white to brown to black. The pen on the left contained half a dozen bleating Angora goats. The white locks of their mohair fleeces glowed in the late afternoon sun.

Ruth and I exchanged a look that said, "No way!"

Tilley demonstrated as she spoke. "Grab a handful of pellets, hold your hand out, fingers flat, and slip your hand between the rails. Remember, fingers flat lest you get nipped." The sheep greedily emptied her hand of the pellets.

We followed Tilley's instructions: a handful to the sheep, a handful to the goats. When the novelty wore off, Tilley dumped the remaining pellets into the feeder troughs in each pen. The baaing and bleating chorus melded with the sounds of munching. If we were to become sheep and goat farmers, I would have to resign myself to live with the cacophony.

Kristin was petting a big billy goat through the fence—a billy goat with a long horn spiraling from each side of his head.

I said, "Tilley. Is that goat dangerous?"

"Well, he can be if you threaten his harem. Prince Philip's a prize buck, and if he thinks you might harm one of his does, especially Queen Elizabeth, his favorite and the matriarch, he will have a go at you. And he can do a lot of damage. Luckily, he's a kind bloke, and as you can see, he likes a head scratch."

When I was at the Naval Academy, our mascot, Bill the Goat, stunk. His scent permeated the stadium air at each game. Happily, Prince Philip did not share that condition. I moved closer but still did not detect an offensive odor.

I pointed to the equally large ram in the sheep pen and said, "What about that one?"

"Oh, you mean Prince Edward. He's fine, too. Their former owners told us that Philip and Edward were not coddled or bottle fed when they were young. If they had been, they would be a worry. You can bottle feed a kid doe or ewe lamb, and those girls will grow up to be friendly. Do the same with a buck or a ram, and you will regret it."

That was contradictory. If you show love to the males when they're young, they will be violent when they grow up.

While I was mentally calculating how much we could afford to spend on woolly livestock, Danelle scratched the head of a black sheep and asked, "I thought sheep were white. Maybe that's what 'Baa Baa Black Sheep' is about, but wasn't that a pretend sheep?"

Tilley said, “The song was about taxes on wool in my homeland, long before I was born. Most sheep have white coats, but some sheep come in colors. Sheep farmers like to run a few dark wool sheep with their herds to keep the flocks healthy. The farmers monitor the darker-colored sheep to see if their wool color changes. If their coats fade, that tells the owner his flock is not getting enough copper from grazing, and he needs to supplement their feed to keep them from getting sick. The pellets you fed to the goats and sheep keep them healthy.”

I had a worrying thought: “Oh no. More money for pellets, this time for sheep and goats.” And I wondered: “How much does it cost for shearing? What about hoof trimming?” Sheep and goat upkeep might prove pricier than horse maintenance.

***

I heard the stable’s man-door swing open. We turned to face a giant of a man, ducking to avoid bumping his head on the jamb as he strode toward us.

“Good day. I’m Roger, Tilley’s husband.” His accent was the same as Andrew’s, though several notes lower on the scale.

While introducing ourselves and the children, I could not help admiring the guy. He was formidable yet charming, smiling down at the children. About my age, he was attired in loose dark trousers and a thick cardigan, a herringbone tweed hat, and leather slippers. The only thing missing was the meerschaum pipe; otherwise, he would have fit my image of the British lord of the manor. When we shook hands, I couldn’t help but notice his smooth palm and manicured fingernails. Roger was not a farmer, not even a gentleman farmer.

Ruth said, “Your animals are in such good condition. And their fleeces are amazingly clean.”

Roger said, “That is all on Tilley.”

Tilley said, “Most of my wool-bearing stock Roger bought

this past winter. We didn't know we would be shifting house. I don't know how I can part with them or their wool. Several farmers have been by and made offers. They all have the same goal: Produce a finer, high-quality fiber for sale on the international market. That would mean mixing our lot with their large commercial flocks. I cringe at the thought of my pets mixing with dirty herds."

This was my opportunity to chime in. "So, you want to sell both flocks, the lot, but would you consider selling breeding pairs for a small, non-commercial holding like ours?"

Instead of either of them answering, Roger turned to Tilley and said, "Till, have you invited our guests in for tea and cordial?"

Kristin said, "We like cordial."

Everyone laughed.

Tilley asked Ruth, "Can you spare a few minutes to come to the house? It will give the men time to talk."

I nodded my agreement to Ruth.

Ruth said, "That's so kind. We would love to."

When Tilley, Ruth, and the children were out of earshot, Roger turned to me and said, "We are selling the lot. I accepted a posting in Queensland. Unbeknownst to Tilley, I sold this property. We have to vacate by the end of October. So, to answer your question, we will not sell any breeding pairs."

"We'd be happy to buy the lot, but I suspect our finances won't stretch that far."

Roger responded in a menacing tone. "Are you trying to negotiate? Is this how Yanks do business?"

His entire demeanor had darkened.

Seeing my look of dismay, he continued, but this time more businesslike, minus the menace. "Please, don't try that with me. I make a living negotiating. I could bury you."

"Apologies if I offended you. I wasn't trying to negotiate anything. The simple fact is we spent almost all our savings on a farm that cost more than we expected. Now, in trying to populate it with livestock and get a return, our finances are stretched."

He studied me, then commanded, "Come with me."

I struggled to keep up as I followed Roger through the stable and along a paved driveway.

I had not noticed the three-car garage tucked away on the far side of the mansion. The stately home appeared even larger up close, and the garage was about the size of a four-bedroom American home. Roger punched a code on the keypad mounted beside the nearest roll-up door. It raised to reveal a polished four-door maroon Rolls-Royce. The car looked way too wide and long to be drivable on Tassie's narrow roadways.

When he saw me ogling his Rolls, he said, "Part of my father's estate. I had it shipped from London. I will finally be able to drive it on the wider roads in Queensland and for trips to Sydney."

The middle garage bay contained a dark green MG roadster convertible with a tan leather interior. The model was agonizingly familiar to me. Twenty years earlier, in the euphoric early years of our marriage, I found and bought one at a cut-rate price, owned it for two hours, and never got to drive it.

***

Putting along in Ruth's VW Bug those many years past, I dropped her off at the St. Pete Junior College campus in Clearwater, Florida, where she was taking an evening class. We had low-paying jobs in those days. Our combined income was so meager we had to budget for every expenditure. We scavenged pennies to pay for the VW's gas and even essentials like buying a broom and dustpan. We had some savings, but that was reserved for emergencies.

I must have had a premature midlife crisis. Browsing the classifieds, I found a car identical to the MG in Roger's garage, priced well below Bluebook because of a blown wheel bearing seal. I knew I could fix it for cheap. I met the owner at his home in Clearwater. The car parked in his driveway gleamed under Florida's setting sun. I looked it over, got behind the wheel, started the engine, and revved it a few times. I imagined Ruth and me driving along Florida's coastlines, convertible top down, the breeze ruffling her naturally curly locks, living the carefree life.

It was dark when I picked her up and told her about the deal. She asked for the owner's address, drove there, and convinced him to return the check. I learned the hard way that we should make financial decisions together—a lesson that didn't always stick.

***

With my flashback fading, I lifted my gaze from the MG in Roger's garage and saw him waiting for me in the third garage bay. I wandered over and looked at a green, wooden, drop-side utility trailer packed with neatly arranged equipment, including a chainsaw and string trimmer, hoes, rakes, shovels, feed sacks, hay hooks and forks, rolls of poly electric fence cord, salt lick blocks, and feed troughs. Cardboard boxes took up the remaining space. Most had labels with words I didn't recognize: Banding Tool, Rings, Drench, Ear Punch and Tags, Dagging Shears, Hoof Trimmers, and Mating Crayons. I recognized the labels: Vaccines, Disinfectant, Harness, and Leads.

A horrible question occurred to me: "Do sheep and goat teeth need to be floated?" If so, with flocks this size, we'd be paying Helmut a dozen times Ben's dental bill.

Roger said, "All of this goes with the two herds. It's everything you need to make a go of it."

"Again, and not to be offensive or attempting to negotiate, I doubt we can afford all this. You and Tilley have been more than kind in letting us see and feed the animals and all, but sadly, this is out of our league."

Roger studied me and said, "You hail from the Midwest. Ohio or Indiana?"

I thought: "Who is this guy?"

"Ohio. How'd you know? Most folks think we're from Canada."

"It is part of my job to know who I am dealing with. Though I am a bit disappointed in you."

"And how's that?"

"You are not *up* yourself like most brash Yanks. Not the ego I expected. I believe you are, in your jargon, a nice guy, and I might add, a sound husband and father. In addition, your wife is like Tilley in her love of animals, and to me, that means you would take good care of Tilley's pets."

More shock. After only several minutes in our company, Roger had read us.

He continued. "You would not be aware, but I handpicked and purchased each sheep and goat in those flocks and gifted them to Tilley. On my business travels around the state, if I passed by a grazing sheep or goat that stood out from the herd, I would command my chauffeur to stop. I kept a pair of gumboots at hand to go into the paddock and examine the animal myself. If it passed muster, I paid the owner cash on the spot. My chauffeur and I would cram the poor thing into the limo boot. The livestock you fed today are the cream of the crop from all over Tasmania."

I noted the trace of a smile at my look of awe before he continued.

"You, Ruth, Tilley, and I are kindred spirits. And not to be condescending, but the only difference is that you and Ruth did not have the advantages Tilley and I have had. We came from old money and graduated from prestigious universities."

It kind of was condescending, but I attempted to look at us from Roger's perspective. Although he was from Britain, he had the honest, in-your-face Tasmanian attitude I appreciated more each day.

"I'm not offended, and I get it. To be totally transparent, we ventured far from home for reasons we think we understand but don't. We're under-capitalized yet excited by the adventure and the prospects for our children. At the same time, we're frightened by the consequences our decision may bring down on us in the long run. It was a tremendous risk, and it's on me."

I fumbled around with the stuff in the trailer, opened some boxes, and closed them, none the wiser about their contents. I noticed a couple of plastic jugs with scary-sounding names printed on the labels: Ivermectin and Diazinon. Wool farming was going to be a steep learning curve.

In the spirit of Roger's candid assessment of my family and me, I said, "Roger, since we're going all mano-a-mano, may I ask the real reason you're moving? You've given your all to make Tilley happy, and now you rip that away from her. The estate, horses, sheep, and goats were all for her. And I gather that although you're fond of her pets, you don't appear to be a farmer. You did all of this for her, and now you're taking it away on the premise of a better position. Doesn't add up."

He smirked and said, "Touché. There comes the Yank I was expecting."

He paused before continuing.

"Tilley is unaware of what I am about to tell you, so I insist we keep this between us."

"I can assure you of that. You'll be gone soon, and I don't have any friends I hang with. Ruth wouldn't be interested. Whatever you say won't go beyond these walls."

He looked away from me when he spoke. It reminded me of the behavior of our children when they confessed to a misdeed and couldn't look me in the eye.

"I will not venture into the details. Suffice it to say I made some business decisions to help the Tasmanians. However, I am afraid my adversaries perceive those decisions to be detrimental to Tasmania and beneficial to me. I truly had the best of intentions. Regardless, I find myself in a difficult situation and must find a way to avoid legal consequences, including imprisonment. Thus, the need for uprooting Tilley on the false premise I accepted a more lucrative posting. As you might put it, 'I need to get out of Dodge.'"

"Whoa. I didn't expect that. Our issues are minuscule compared to yours. We're fortunate to be here and feel safe. I trust Queensland can offer you the same."

We didn't speak for a long spell, both unjumbling our thoughts.

Roger broke the silence. "Now that I have completely undermined my bargaining position by telling you my deepest darkest and revealing my short timeline, how much can you afford to pay for the lot: two herds, the trailer, all this equipment and supplies, and some sundry items?"

I wanted to turn tail. The offer I was about to make was a pittance compared to the value of the package. I took a deep breath and named a figure.

Roger studied me, then said, "We have a deal, provided you can clear out everything by next weekend. I am leaving for Queensland. Tilley will schedule with you."

We shook on it.

I still don't understand how it happened. We now had enough money-producing livestock and equipment to make Cygnet Farm a success.

I rounded up the family and gave Tilley a check that would further deplete our ever-shrinking reserves.

On the drive home, I filled Ruth in on the terms of the deal. She was more exhilarated than I had seen her in a long time.

18. BUCKS, RAMS, CHICKENS, OH MY!

Through the good graces of Roger, Tilley, and the Caulkins, we could now populate Cygnet Farm with top-notch, cash-generating livestock before we moved onto the property. However, to do so we had to figure out the logistics of transporting all the Roger and Tilley stuff and the animals. I took a day off, and Ruth arranged for Marie Jefferson to mind the kids after school.

Looking like the Beverly Hillbillies, with tools and boxes strapped to the Subaru roof rack and towing the overloaded drop-side trailer behind, we made the tool and supplies run from Hilltop Farm to Cygnet Farm. We parked the trailer in the apple shed and unpacked the Subaru before hooking up Ben's trailer and returning to Hilltop Farm for the first woolly animal run. Without the benefit of an enclosed stock trailer, we had to make two trips: first with the sheep in the trailer, and another with the goats in the Subaru.

King Philip, master buck of the goatherd, was so impressive that until now we had not given Prince Edward, the master ram of the sheep herd, credit for his attributes. Edward was actually bigger than Philip, but since his horns spiraled down and not out, he gave the illusion of being smaller.

Ruth dug her hands deep into his snowy-white fleece and said, "He's muscled up under his coat. And the fiber is so fine. I can't wait to spin this. Edward was a great find."

Using a bucket of feed pellets, I lured Edward and the sheep herd up the ramp and into the horse trailer. Once inside, Ruth and Tilley raised and pinned the ramp closed, forcing the poor sheep into a baaing woolen rectangle. They were so compressed I had to step on their backs to climb out.

The Subaru had its work cut out as we traversed the winding roads to Cygnet Farm. Sheep are relatively small when compared to horses, but they are solid. The combined weight of the herd outweighed Ben and taxed the single-axle trailer making it unstable.

To avoid fretting over the possibility of veering off the road and plummeting into a ravine, we tossed around a new moniker for Prince Edward. Since he was a striking figure responsible for protecting the vulnerable from predators, we wanted to name him after someone known for their bravery. We thought of James Brady, who took a bullet for President Ronald Reagan. James it would be.

I backed the trailer into the barn paddock where Charlie and Ben grazed. They started when I dropped the trailer ramp, and the sheep herd exploded in reverse into the paddock. The angry baas the sheep emitted subsided after a few minutes as James, formerly Prince Edward, led his ewes around the paddock, exploring the new turf where the herd would dine and live.

We left the trailer at Cygnet Farm since King Philip's rack was too wide for Ben's single-horse trailer. The open drop-side trailer would not work either. We needed to rely on the Subaru as our stock transporter for the second woolly animal run. The process was like transporting our original goats, Cicely and Amy, in the VW van, except the Subaru cab was more compact.

In keeping with his regal name, King Philip would travel in luxury, accompanied by his harem. In addition to the hygiene issue, I was concerned that he would rip the cab ceiling upholstery if he shook or swung his head. He was kind enough to let me wrap the tips of his horns with duct tape, which provided cushioning.

I built a makeshift ramp from a sheet of plywood Tilley had on hand. With the rear seats folded flat, we lined the back section of the car with a plastic tarp. Getting the goats up the ramp into the Subaru was tricky. King Philip wouldn't cooperate until we coaxed Queen Elizabeth inside with feed pellets. Once Philip and Elizabeth were in, we sandwiched in the remaining does.

The hour-long drive from Hill Top Farm to Cygnet Farm felt like ten hours, with our station wagon jam-packed with goats, breathing down our necks, bleating in our ears, peeing, and pooping. The trip was safer without dragging the trailer behind us, but I cringed at the sound of piddling and goat berries ricocheting off the plastic tarp. And each time I looked in the rearview mirror, King Philip's rectangular pupils stared back at me. Following the pattern we set on the previous trip, we renamed goats to take our minds off the desecration happening in the back of our new car. In keeping with the American president theme invoked by James Brady, we re-titled King Philip as Ron and Queen Elizabeth as Nancy.

At Cygnet Farm, I backed the car into the paddock and set the does free to join the menagerie. I crawled into the back to help Ron turn around. Before he could leap out to join the does, I peeled the duct tape off his horns. The does stood nearby, waiting for their man. With Ron in the lead, he and his harem trotted off to explore their new home. I hoped they would like it.

We leaned back against the Subaru, content to take in the pastoral farm scene unfolding before us. The sheep were grazing high on the hill while Ben and Charlie sauntered over to visit the goats, their newest paddock mates.

We owed the Caulkins another round of thanks for letting us put livestock on the property before closing on the farm, although I couldn't imagine what we'd do if the deal for Cygnet Farm fell through at the last minute.

Peeling the tarp out of the Subaru with trepidation, we had to be careful not to spill fresh urine and goat berries on the upholstery and carpet. We were mostly successful, but the fragrances lingered for months.

***

A couple of hours earlier, as we were about to leave Hilltop Farm with the goats on board, Tilley said, "I forgot to ask whether you have a chook coop on your farm?"

I said, "We do, but no chickens."

The paddock behind our farmhouse, the backyard paddock, contained a weathered wooden coop and pen.

"Did Roger mention the chooks and the peafowl?"

"He said there were some sundry items. He wasn't specific."

"Well, you bought a rooster, Pecker, who rules over his five Sussex hens. Besides the prolific egg-layers, you now own a magnificent peacock, Elton, and his three peahen wives."

"How are we ever going to get birds to our farm? We don't have an enclosed trailer or wire cages. They'll fly away at the first opportunity."

"I will show you when you get back. No need to bring a trailer."

The prospect of more animals thrilled Ruth, but not me. Making a third roundtrip for the feathered animals meant finishing late into the night. Too, I was coming around to Ruth's philosophy of making Cygnet Farm pay for itself. You only want livestock that can turn a buck. Would the savings on chicken eggs offset the cost of buying layer mash for the chickens? As evidenced by the myriad of roadside signs advertising free-range eggs, buying eggs might be cheaper than owning an egg source. And how much money could peafowl generate? Sell their feathers? The only positive I could envision from owning chickens and peafowl is they don't need their teeth floated.

I know you're thinking, "What about eating chickens? If we didn't kill and eat them ourselves, we could sell them for the meat value, right?" Wrong. We had discussed animal mortality at great length and long ago decided on the principles that would apply to our future farm. On any other farm, killing animals for consumption or profit makes sense; however, when you partner for life with a vegetarian and a devout animal devotee, the thought of killing a chicken, or any animal, even a predator, is sacrilege. Childhood memories of headless chickens doing the death dance after my father wielded his hatchet helped align my thinking with Ruth's. We agreed that animal deaths on our farm would only be from natural causes.

How naïve we were!

***

When we returned to collect the chickens, the peafowl, and any other sundry items Roger failed to mention, Tilley was waiting beside the stable, wearing shabby clothes. A pile of empty feed sacks lay at her feet.

She said, "Grab a few sacks and come with me."

We did as she bade and followed her down a hill behind the house toward a tall thicket hedge. As we approached an arched opening carved through the hedge, I heard clucks before I saw the chickens in a henhouse on a freshly mowed paddock.

Elton the peacock strolled nearby with three peahens in his wake. As if on cue, Elton's plumes rose into a multicolored fan. He cawed and vibrated his tail feathers as he strutted around the hens. The girls continued pecking for bugs in the grass, seemingly unimpressed and perhaps thinking, "Get over yourself."

With a bag and a short length of twine in hand, Tilley opened the coop door, shut it behind her, and entered the adjacent chicken wire-enclosed pen. The chickens eyed her and continued clucking until she grabbed the legs of the nearest one and held the distressed bird upside down. The entire pen erupted in a whirl of flapping, squawking fowls. They crashed into the pen sides and roof, engulfing Tilley in a cloud of dust and feathers. She deftly shoved the chicken into the feed sack and tied the top closed with baling twine. Beaming like she had just hog-tied a calf in record time at a rodeo, she held the bag up for us to see. The captured chicken was inert, as evidenced by the stillness of the bag.

Tilley said, "They go *tharn* as soon as the bag is closed."

I recalled the term "tharn" from the film *Watership Down* meant deer-in-the-headlights paralysis.

Joining Tilley in the pen, we grabbed and bagged chickens, resulting in a pile of plump feed sacks. Ruth and Tilley removed the bulging sacks and laid them outside the pen as I faced off with the last fowl, Pecker the rooster. It was him or me. I was concerned about his spurs. I remembered the damage roosters did to my dad's forearms when he grabbed them on chopping day. Roosters are sneaky, mean fighters.

Tilley yelled through the chicken wire fabric, "Be careful. Pecker has attitude."

When I grabbed for Pecker, he flew at me instead of away and tried to stab my arm with his spurs. I avoided his jabs, snatched and gripped his feet, stuffing him into a sack. Those spurs would need to be nipped; otherwise, he could injure Ruth or the children.

The peafowl were used to being hand-fed which made them easy to capture, but the long tail feathers meant we had to use larger bags. But Elton and his ladies relaxed and didn't try to escape.

As we were leaving, Ruth said, "Tilley, we hope you and Roger will be happy in Queensland. Don't worry about your pets. We are going to give them a magnificent home. And if you're ever back this way, please come and visit."

"I may do just that."

Tilley stayed in touch with Ruth, but life threw her and Roger a nasty curve ball.

The last time I saw Roger was when we shook hands on the deal. Three months later, Ruth received a call from Tilley informing us that Roger had a heart attack and passed well before his time. Tilley never came to visit.

I'm left with many unanswered questions. How did his family become wealthy? How did he keep his nails manicured on a farm? How did he get so big? What compelled him to leave town so abruptly? What I did know is that he gave us the leg up we needed to stay in Tasmania. Out of respect for Roger, I kept my word and, until this writing, never revealed our conversation to Ruth or anyone else.

By the time we offloaded our feathered flocks at Cygnet Farm, picked up the children from the Jefferson's home and got them into bed, it was close to midnight. We showered, snacked, and fell into bed, worn out yet sated. In one day, we had taken the first real step toward becoming real farmers ready to earn real money.

Again, how naïve we were!

19. YANKS AT THE END OF THE ROAD

On what began as a cloudless October Saturday, we moved to Cygnet Farm. My internal calendar told me the weather should be cool and wet, not warm and dry. We were still adjusting to seasons opposite to those we grew up with. Instead of frost on fall pumpkins, we had dew on spring flowers.

Using the Subaru and Ben's trailer and with the help of Thomas and Marie's brother, Declan, both pickup truck owners, we planned to move all our possessions in one day.

Ryan and I did the early run with the car and horse trailer toting the longer and heavier items—the trampoline, Ruth's loom (still in its shipping crate) and my tools, while Ruth and the girls stayed behind to organize and supervise loading the rest of our belongings by our neighbors.

When we parked by the barn, Charlie and Ben strolled over to say g'day. Ben greeted us with his familiar vocals and Charlie chimed in with a throaty rumble. They leaned over the paddock gate and nuzzled, frisking us for apples. They were friendlier than usual.

Seen side by side, their relative sizes stood out. Charlie's stout body and yard-long head dwarfed Ben. Charlie had grown over the past couple of weeks, feeding on the spring grasses. The last time we saw the horses and the woolly pets was when we stopped by to fill the poultry feeder with enough pellets to tide the chickens over and to connect their float-controlled self-waterer (compliments of Roger and Tilley). We expected to find dozens of eggs incubated by broody hens. That's what chickens do unless you steal their eggs.

While we toured the countryside and packed for the move to Cygnet Farm, both horses had foraged alongside the sheep and goats sans human company. And with the warmer spring weather, Ben did not need to be rugged, so Ruth had not been by to spoil him. The horses were lonely and bored. That would no longer be the case.

We unloaded the Subaru and the trailer in no time. We stored the loom in the barn and my tools in the apple shed. Next came assembling the trampoline in the backyard, all the while with Elton the peacock strutting his stuff for his adoring peafowl ladies and the penned chickens clucking nearby, occasionally interrupted by the crows of Pecker the rooster.

After his umpteenth crow, I looked his way and, for the first time, noticed a redbrick barbecue partially cloaked by bracken ferns. Next to the backyard paddock gate near the chicken pen, a mature golden willow tree shaded the area, making it the perfect spot for cooking outdoors on a hot summer day. The rusty griddle evidenced a lack of use. It would need to be wire-brushed and re-seasoned.

With the trampoline assembled and leveled, Ryan tested it with a few jumps and flips. It had been over a year since the kids had jumped. We'd disassembled the trampoline when we moved from our Silver Knolls home to the rental unit in Sparks; however, at fourteen feet, it was too big for the backyard. Cygnet

Farm provided hundreds of sites to choose from. I chose a spot near the house, visible from the kitchen window so that Ruth could keep an eye on the jumpers.

"Dad. It works just like it did in Reno."

I had no logical reason for tackling the next project. I hung a rope swing. Ryan and I could have taken the time to explore the property further, clean out the barn and the apple shed, collect chicken eggs, nip Pecker's spurs, clean the barbecue, and complete any number of the tasks that lay ahead of us. Reflecting on it now, I wanted our kids to feel like this was home. I had followed a similar pattern when we set up house at our Berry Creek cabin. There, I built a tree house with a swing and fenced the backyard. Danelle and Ryan—Kristin had not come along yet—spent many long days playing in the confines that kept them from wandering into the poison oak-infested forest. And that gave me a happy thought: "poison oak, ivy, or sumac did not plague Tasmania." Poisonous snakes and ants, yes. Itchy poisonous plants, no.

I couldn't have picked a worse day to tackle the swing project. The balmy, westerly breeze that started our day was working itself into a tempest. I was unaware of the Roaring Forties, the fierce winds that pour out of Argentina, stream below Africa's Cape of Good Hope, and race across the Southern Ocean between the latitudes of 40- to 50-degrees during the spring. Bound by Antarctica to the south and unhindered by any land mass, the winds wallop Tasmania.

I gathered the rope I had purchased for the project as sharp wind bursts whistled through the gums and pines near the house. Wagging treetops along the distant ridge, accompanied by the cracks of snapping branches, foretold what was to come.

The largest pine tree, planted at least a century earlier, shaded a gully in the paddock south of the house, near the corral Ruth visioned in Nevada. The tree had sprouted dozens of sturdy limbs. With some trepidation, I slung the long coil of thick hemp rope over my shoulder and climbed limb by limb to the perfect branch. It was two feet in diameter where it sprouted from the trunk. Ryan watched from thirty feet below as his foolish father shinnied out on the branch over the gully. Wind gusts and the swaying limb forced me to clutch with both arms and legs. I prayed the coconut-size pine-cones hanging from nearby limbs wouldn't break free and blow my way.

Ryan's voice reached me between gusts. "Dad. Right there."

I tied off both rope ends about three feet apart, cut off the surplus end, and reverse-shinnied toward the trunk. Halfway there, unearthly screeches erupted from overhead. The sound reminded me of the winged monkeys that captured Dorothy and Toto in *The Wizard of Oz*. I dared a look between the galloping tree limbs and saw the source of the noise. A flock of black cockatoos flew over the house.

Back down on Earth and undamaged, we searched for a swing seat. We found a board in the barn, an antique apple-packing crate remnant that seemed suitable. I tried cutting it to size with my dad's hand saw. That's when I discovered Tasmanian Oak. The saw couldn't dent it. Slicing through steel would have been easier.

Tasmanian Oak is a eucalypt—soft like pine when green, hard like ironwood when dry. When the Whitbreads constructed the buildings on Cygnet Farm, they used Tas Oak for the structural framing and the siding. All of it dried out long ago. Trial and error would teach me that before driving a nail into a two-by-four, I needed to drill a slightly smaller hole and grease the nail shaft before picking up a hammer. Although a hassle to work with, the wood's durability far surpassed pine and Douglas fir, with a lifespan at least twice that of American-grown framing lumber.

For the task at hand, out of desperation I used Roger's chainsaw to slice and notch the plank for the swing seat. We set the swing rope in the notched seat, and Ryan tried it. He soared back and forth, high above the gully. It was perfect.

***

The Jeffersons and Declan began arriving with heavily loaded pickup trucks. Ruth and the girls brought up the rear of the contingent. We spent the rest of the day unloading the beds, trunks, and the dining set. It would take many days to unpack and organize the rest of our boxed goods. At least we could store everything indoors, either in the house, the barn, the garage, or the apple shed. That proved to be a blessing beyond measure.

By mid-afternoon, the wind speed had ratcheted up further. A wall of clouds smudged the horizon above the channel and sailboats bobbed up and down at the Port Cygnet marina, their masts waving at us. The air grew cooler, but nowhere near the type of cold we'd experienced in Nevada in October.

The kids ignored the weather as they tested the limits of the swing and performed flips on the trampoline, reveling in the gusts.

When our Leslie Vale friends had done more than they needed to do for us and tried to leave—we couldn't offer them a cuppa because we couldn't find the kettle—they hit gridlock on Woodstock Road. Traffic on the narrow road forced cars and pickup trucks to back up to the bend where the road was wider to allow arriving vehicles to pass. Every few minutes, another car or pickup crawled past the barn before turning around at the bottom of our driveway and creeping back toward Cygnet.

We could hear decelerating vehicles as they slowed at the bend. We paused unpacking to observe the traffic through the front windows. The faces of strangers, drivers and passengers, looked away when they realized we saw them.

We wanted a home at the end of a road for privacy. We should have been looking for privacy via a security gate.

It threw us off track when a newer model Holden pickup truck didn't turn around, but instead zoomed up the drive and parked behind Ruth's Volvo. Suspicious, I went out to check on the kids and greet this bold stranger. He stood by his pickup truck, looking around, before sauntering toward me, confident, like he owned the place.

He had a few years on me. A rugged, sun-creased, leather-face topped a body honed by hard work—*hard yakka*. He was undoubtedly a farmer.

While about to greet each other, we noticed an old station wagon turning around below.

He said, "Another *stickybeak*. Reckon you folks are today's breaking news on the Cygnet *bush telegraph*. Word must be out: There's Yanks moved in at the end of the road, at the Whitbreads."

I knew a "stickybeak" was a nosey parker or a nibby nose, the terms we used to refer to curious folks in Ohio. "Bush telegraph" is the term for those spreading news and gossip.

I said, "We didn't understand what was going on."

We shook hands, and he said, "It's Cygnet. I'm your neighbor, Bret O'leary. We share the fence line runs atop the hill along your upper eastern paddock." He pointed in the direction his truck faced. His use of the phrase "your upper eastern paddock" brought me great pleasure. We, and not someone else, owned that land.

"Dick Reese. Pleased to meet a neighbor. My wife, Ruth, is in the house unpacking. I'd offer you a cuppa, Bret, but I doubt she's found the kettle."

"No worries. Another time. Just came by to meet ya. Hope ya like the property. It's decent, and the Caulkins cared for the land. Helped them some with my D8 Cat. Dug every dam on the place."

Aah. The one with pond-building expertise was Bret, not the Whitbreads or the Caulkins.

“We’ll do our best caring for the land too, but it’s a bit overwhelming. The size of the place and moving.”

“Let me know if ya need help. Fencing’s always a worry.”

I noticed a barely perceptible smile cross his face.

We stood there, silent. Clumpy gray clouds whisked by, pushed by near-gale-force winds. Staring into the distance at the swaying trees and darkening skies, he said, “Listen, cobber. We’re in for a blow. Some wind and rain tonight and tomorrow. The black cockatoos and me gut are saying, tomorrow night we’re in for a shellacking. May wanna get your animals into the barn.”

“What do you mean about the cockatoos? My son, Ryan, and I saw them flying past and squawking this morning.”

“Many folks don’t believe it, but when ya see black cockatoos flocking together and heading inland, reckon ya better be ready for some real weather.”

“Thanks for the advice. I’ll have to see if I can fit all our stock in the barn.”

“Your horses will be fine. The goats and sheep will need protection.”

I said, “You been farming long?”

“Me whole life. How about you?”

“Call it. . . almost a day.”

He chuckled and said, “Had that feeling when I saw ya loading the place up with livestock before ya moved in. Straight outta *Green Acres*.”

It surprised me he was aware of the Eva Gabor sitcom. God bless Hollywood.

Before I could respond, he said, “Let me guess. Ya name your livestock?”

This bloke was taking the piss out of me.

"Yes, we do. You don't?"

He cracked up. "No. We ear-tag and number them. Run hundreds of White-Faced Herefords. Their time's too short for naming."

I had a thought.

"What about your bull? Does he have a name?"

He smiled and said, "You got me, mate. Two bulls. Festus and Rube."

I felt better.

He said, "Ya wouldn't be aware, but I'm why ya got that extra 75 acres."

"How's that?"

"I was haggling with the Caulkins. We couldn't come to terms. I planned to run some cattle there. We have a gate in the boundary fence to move them onto that block. Not the best grazing land because of the ferns and the bush, but in dry times, it would help. So, if interested in agistment, let me know. I'd give ya a dollar a week per head."

He wanted to rent our land for cow grazing. I had a mental flinch that harked back to our cow misadventures at Leslie Vale. We had sworn off cows—however, money talks.

"We took care of some cows not long ago, and it was far from enjoyable."

"How so?"

I explained the nightmare we had survived.

After he stopped chuckling, he said, "No worries, cobber. Your farm's fenced for cattle, and I'd treat your property like it's me own. I'd even plant it out. Get rid of the native grass and ferns, and plant rye after plowing, disking, and fertilizing."

While he was reeling off his spiel, I was thinking about our farm's no-kill philosophy. Bret was a normal farmer; his livestock were his money-makers. Hiring out our land for short-lived cattle went against our ideology.

"Let me talk it over with Ruth," I said. "When do you need an answer?"

"No rush. Whenever you're ready. And no dramas if it's not on. We'll still be mates and neighbors."

"Thank you."

"And, Dick. Remember. If I can help, give me a ring. I'm in the book."

"There is one thing. Do you know about the bus service to Hobart?"

"Be at the town parking lot at seven sharp Monday. You'll be back at six."

Leslie Vale was an easy commute to Hobart. Cygnet was not—distance and too many hills, dales, and sharp curves to contend with. Taking the bus would allow time to wind up before work and wind down afterward. Too, I would no longer have to pay the high parking fees in Hobart.

Bret gave me a slight nod and a short wave as he backed his pickup truck down the driveway.

His wave was interesting. In every drive around Cygnet, oncoming drivers nodded and waved. The nods and waves we received were unique to each driver. Some were cool, like Bret's, while others were exuberant. I guessed the gesture reflected the driver's personality and wasn't an Aussie blowfly-brushing salute like the one I received in the outback. Whatever the nod and wave types, the practice added to the friendly nature of Cygnet. I would need to develop a technique. Perhaps a peace sign, a thumbs up, or a shaka—the surfer solidarity gesture? The shaka might be meaningless unless the Cygnetites had watched American surfer dude movies. But since Sarah had watched a *Super Bowl* and Bret had watched *Green Acres*, I might have been selling the locals short.

20. DREAMS TO NIGHTMARES

The weather forecast, compliments of Bret and cockatoos, was spot-on. Gale-force gusts blew all day Sunday. Fat raindrops splattered against the windowpanes and hammered down on our corrugated iron roof in a constant, muffled rumble. Between gusts, I could hear the roof runoff splashing into the water tank beside the back porch.

The Caulkins had left some seasoned split wood behind. That allowed us to fire up the two heaters. Warm and snug inside, while sheets of water flew past outside, we experienced a sense of serenity.

We felt for our animals. Ben, rugged up and Charlie not, huddled, backs to the wind under the shelter afforded by a cluster of gum trees. Our woolly pets didn't fare as well. We lured both herds into the barn's lower level, the old draft horse stable, but they weren't happy there and broke through the temporary gate I strung across the doorway. We needed to move them to a more protected area, which was the south paddock next to the house, where I had installed the swing the day before. I tempted them with pellets and they followed me across Woodstock Road. Without a sheepdog, this was the only herding method we had.

The storm was a wake-up call for me. I had been living a pampered life. I worked in Hobart in an air-conditioned office during the week and played on the weekends. My worst outdoor experience in Tasmania was the forced nightly ride on Ben, regardless of Leslie Vale's weather. I was unprepared for the test this storm was about to bring.

While attempting to move the herds, a plump doe from Ron's harem got stuck in the blackberry bushes near the unnamed stream. To cut her free, I had to ford the once trickling brook that now raged.

I thought I was well-outfitted for the task. On the day we signed the Cygnet Farm closing papers, we celebrated by buying the whole family Driazabone stockman's coats, Blunnies, and gumboots. I added an Akubra hat to my farm wardrobe. Okay, I confess. I bought the Akubra because it looked good on the old fella who owned the Gunns Plains Caves.

A stockman's coat and gumboots are necessities for stormy-weather farm chores. The coat, to my mind, is ingenious. The material is heavyweight cotton, as thick as a canvas tarp, coated with a wax compound. Wide gussets repel water and provide flexibility. Strategically located brass snap buttons keep the gussets in place to prevent moisture from finding its way inside, seeping into your clothing, and wicking into your undergarments.

Gumboots are standard garb for farmers and gardeners. Mine ended well below the knee, which I discovered was not high enough when I waded into the creek to rescue the doe.

We enticed the sheep and goat herds through the stock gate and into the south paddock. All the while, they voiced their dislike of the storm. I couldn't blame them. I didn't know whether their wool coats would protect them from the elements. Would our ignorance wipe out both herds? My only optimistic thought was what Ruth had explained to me about wool.

"Wet or dry, wool garments insulate."

So, the sheep wouldn't catch colds and die—*kark it*. Hopefully, the Angora's mohair would act the same way to keep the goats warm.

Ron, master buck of the goatherd, and James, master ram of the sheep herd, took charge and led their wives down by the corral, where the pines helped block the wind. The herds huddled together, their backs to the wind, the same way Ben and Charlie weathered the storm.

We continued unpacking late into the night. Exhausted, we finally had to give it up. The following morning, Monday, I needed to be at the Cygnet public parking lot by seven to catch the commuter bus to start work by eight.

***

A jarring earthquake woke us three hours before the 5:30 a.m. alarm. At least, that was my first thought. We knew what quakes felt like from our California days but didn't think Tasmania was earthquake prone.

Ruth checked on the girls in the bedroom they shared while I checked on Ryan.

I whispered to Ruth. "Ryan's okay and sleeping."

"The girls slept through it."

"Good. Lucky we still have power. Why didn't anyone warn us about earthquakes in Tassie?"

"Maybe it wasn't an earthquake. Thunder?"

Ruth rummaged through some boxes and brought our American radio into the kitchen. Except for the AM/FM bands, almost everything else in Australia felt topsy-turvy—from light switches to the night sky. Our American radio worked in Australia, bringing a sense of normalcy to our strange new world. We could dial past familiar channels that, although populated by broadcasters we had trouble understanding and blasting unfamiliar music, gave us a hint of home.

I plugged the radio into a voltage converter, turned it on, and scrolled through the AM and FM bands. All I got was static. In California, within minutes, dozens of stations would broadcast a quake's location, magnitude, and initial reports of damage. I didn't know how to tune in to public service announcements.

Bret was the only neighbor I knew to call for help. We scrabbled through stacked boxes, searching for the phone book to find his number—no luck. It remained packed away in the apple shed, where we had stashed most of our stuff.

I needed to determine the damage the quake might have caused. Coming down from the quake-induced adrenaline rush, exhausted and in a stupor, I stumbled around the house, looking through the windows into a black void. It was time to don my stockman's coat, which was still damp from earlier missions.

Ruth handed me a flashlight as I went out the back door into the raging storm. The beam barely penetrated the night and sheets of rain that limited my vision to a few feet.

I inspected the house for foundation damage, but about jumped out of my gumboots when I rounded the corner and saw dozens of glowing eyes staring at me. The herds huddled against the lee side of the house. They must have found an opening in the paddock fence. I would deal with the animals later. For now, I had to find and close their escape route.

Finding the opening posed no difficulty. We hadn't experienced an earthquake. A whopper of a blue gum tree had snapped and crash-landed between the chicken pen and the concrete water storage tank in the backyard paddock. If the tree had fallen a couple of feet to either side, it would have been a major disaster: dead chickens in one direction, destroyed domestic water supply in the other.

The fallen tree had taken out a string of barbed wire and ring lock fence. The livestock would have danced across the downed fencing to enter the yard, an easy passage for a sheep or a goat. I had to give them credit for using the house as a wind shield.

From what I could see in the murky night, the fence posts remained intact. To keep Ron, James, and their herds away from neighboring farms, the fence had to be repaired by dawn. If I failed, it would fall on Ruth to spend her day chasing down errant animals. Sound familiar? I shivered at the thought of being served with the divorce papers.

To make the repairs, I would have to cut the trunk into sections where it pinned down the fence wires. Once cleared, I could roll the tree sections aside, pull the fencing upright, and reattach it to the posts.

Although proficient with a chainsaw from years of cutting firewood in Berry Creek and Truckee, I had never used one at night during a storm. I hated to do it, but I asked Ruth to help me by shining a light on the fallen tree.

The storm was relentless, making the job several magnitudes more difficult. Drenched by wind-driven rain and bombarded with pine needles and gum leaves, we persevered. Two hours later, with the repairs completed, we coaxed the nervous herds back into the now-secure paddock.

Mission accomplished, we returned to the warmth of the house. The kids still slept. Ruth dove into bed while I shaved, showered, dressed, and downed a pot of hot tea. My workday awaited after our second night at Cygnet Farm.

The winds had died and the rain had tapered to a drizzle as the morning sun fought to break through the lingering steel-gray storm clouds. I parked the Subaru near the waiting bus.

I felt a slight sense of relief. We had survived our first farm crisis, I would arrive at work on time, and I had not made a fool of myself by calling Bret at an ungodly hour to ask for earthquake advice. That would have established us as not just the Yanks at the end of the road, but the ignorant Yanks at the end of the road.

I boarded the bus, paid the fare to the rotund, uniformed driver, and dropped into a seat at the back, away from other commuters. Bobby McFerrin's song "Don't Worry, Be Happy" blared over the sound system. How appropriate.

As the bus navigated the twists and turns from Cygnet to Hobart, my thoughts followed a similar mental route. Why did the tree have to fall on our shift? Why now? The Caulkins would have been prepared for an event like this. Was it some sort of divine test?

You have to be tough to be a farmer. I was soft and, on top of that, knew next to nothing about farming.

I woke to the bus driver shaking my shoulder. We had arrived in Hobart, close to my office. The bus was empty except for the driver and me.

"Best get to work, mate."

"Don't Worry, Be Happy" played again as I disembarked into a dismal Hobart day.

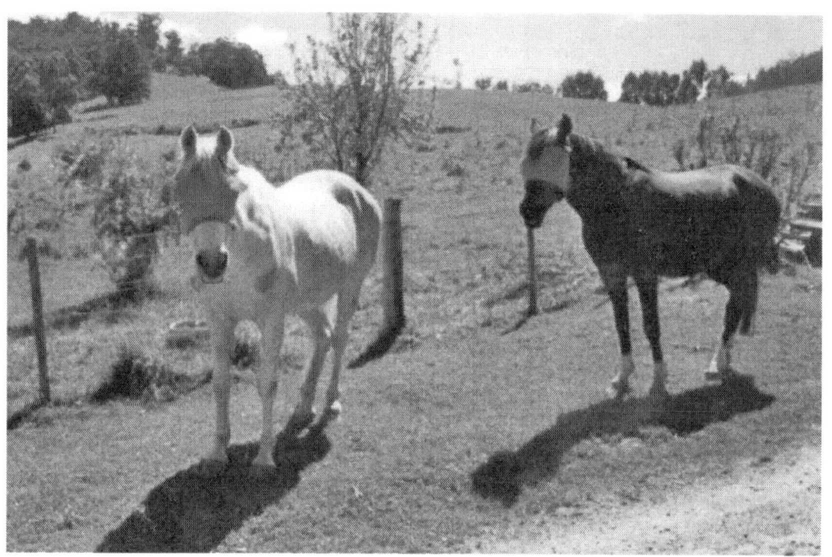

21. WELCOME TO THE NEIGHBORHOOD

Although the gusts of the Roaring Forties continued to roar, the rains departed, leaving behind shoulder-high grass, a boon for the relatively flat hay paddocks north of the house but a problem for the other paddocks, the steep ones where our livestock grazed.

The horses were in good condition but we had to limit their grazing. If they overate the rich spring grass, they could founder. A foundered horse's hooves swell, and if left untreated, the horse will go lame. We all know what happens to a lame horse, even on a no-kill farm.

Much to our chagrin, the sheep and goats would not eat the tall grass and preferred to forage on the short scrub grass we no longer had. The paddocks were chock-a-block with healthy feed they would not eat. We needed a pre-grazed paddock the goats and sheep could share with the horses to prevent the horses from foundering and the flocks from starving.

Our wool producers solved their dining issue. They wandered into the hills by breaching the fences. Calls began coming in from neighbors, some distant, asking whether the goats mowing their lawns belonged to us. Tracking down and herding our runaways home became a new and exhausting chore. Too late, we discovered Cygnet Farm's fences are suitable for confining cattle and horses—not sheep and goats. The fencing on our farm just slowed them down.

Hardening the existing fences by adding expensive, non-climb, ring lock netting was well beyond our means. The only solution was to electrify. We had an electric fence charger and rolls of poly electric fence cord as part of the Roger and Tilley package. I needed post insulators and fastening hardware, which I could buy at the Mitre 10 hardware and farm store in Cygnet. It seemed simple enough.

The rub was getting to Mitre 10 when they were open. During the week, the store was closed by the time I stepped off the bus. Weekend hours were ten to noon on Saturday. Other shops had the same hours. Ruth could shop during the week, but buying the right material was up to me. I had to be at the starting gate by ten come Saturday; otherwise, I had to wait until the following Saturday.

Every Saturday was a race to buy farm and hardware items, an expensive race. Relative to American prices, farm and general hardware prices were shocking, especially if what you sought contained a petroleum or a rubber compound like polyvinyl chloride (PVC) pipe, acrylic and latex paints, or plastic electric fence insulators.

My frustration with prices boiled over when I reached the cash register with hundreds of insulators in the cart. I asked the clerk, "Why are insulators so expensive? A buck each? Come on!"

"Sorry, mate, but since Tassie don't have oil wells, we have all the plastics shipped in. That's expensive."

Fair enough, I suppose, but his explanation didn't improve my mood.

The electrification of the Cygnet Farm paddock fences took me weeks, and during that time, I remained vigilant. No matter how well I strung the electric cord to block the gaps, a full or partial flock would appear on the wrong side of the fence. Their coats were so long they could scoot under the electrified cord and, insulated by their fluffy fleeces, not receive the shocks. Time and my patience were running out.

***

It had been a hard sell, but following several assists from Ruth rounding up wandering sheep and goats, she agreed to Bret grazing his cattle on our land. We didn't know then that, out of necessity (ours), his cows would dine on Cygnet Farm's grasses for many cow generations to come. I suspect Bret knew this all along.

I rang Bret and said, "Dick here. Wonder if you'd mind helping us out by grazing your cattle in the southwest paddock?"

"Ya having trouble keeping the goats where they belong?"

I recalled our pre-storm conversation and his faint smile.

"Both the goats and sheep won't stay put. I suspect you knew the fencing would pose a problem."

"I did, cobber, but didn't want ya to fret. You had enough on your plate, just moving in and all."

"Oh, so true."

"Will run a couple dozen head over in the morning. What say we leave them for a week and then move them to the 75-acre block, the one I almost owned?"

"Sure. Why not?"

"Good on ya, cobber."

The solution wasn't ideal, but it would solve an immediate problem.

A week later, our flocks foraged on the stubble left after Bret's cattle moved onto even greener pastures.

Mother Nature didn't confine the burst of grass growth to the paddocks. Outside the paddock fences, I mowed the lawn and weed-whacked around the apple shed, the garage, and along the road and the driveway. Reserving the weekends for larger projects, I rose by five during the week, wolfed down breakfast, cleared brush by first light, and napped during the bus ride.

***

Knowing how busy we were, our nearest Woodstock Road neighbors, Byron and Harriet—engineer and schoolteacher—threw a "Welcome to the Neighborhood" party in our honor. We could meet our Woodstock Road neighbors in one go.

The days were growing longer, and, thankfully, the Roaring Forties had tapered to a tepid sea breeze. At the Saturday evening party, we experienced our first steak and snags barbie dinner in the shade of Byron's and Harriet's covered patio. Both the neighbors—all about our age—and the meal were superb.

Byron commuted to Hobart on the bus every day. I hadn't noticed him since I was in la-la land, going and coming.

The children on Woodstock Road rode their bikes together to and from the school bus stop at the opposite end of the road. Danelle and Rhonda, Byron and Harriet's daughter, were already friends from school. Simon, their son, and Ryan were in the same grade and were also friends. Kristin, being the youngest, was the odd one out. A key source of entertainment for us and our neighbors was watching her attempts to keep up with the big kids. As they pedaled along on their 26-inch tires, Kristin's legs pumped half again as fast on her 16-inch tires.

Opposite Byron and Harriet lived Isaac and Cath, boat builders and professional photographers. Haley, their daughter, was a year behind Danelle and Rhonda.

Patrick and Arlene, musician and writer, lived one house down.

We had an impressive collection of neighbors on what they termed Upper Woodstock Road.

Seated around the barbie after dinner, Isaac asked, "You flew all the way to Tasmania from America. How did you end up here instead of Tanzania?"

I said, "What do you mean?"

"Some visitors, thinking they are flying to Tasmania, end up in Tanzania. A couple of typos is all it takes. They only notice the mistake when they disembark and see desert instead of greenery."

I thought Isaac was having us on, but later, I saw a news article about a guy that happened to. Given my abysmal travel booking skills, I'm amazed we reached the right destination.

We learned more as the evening went on, mostly farming tips and warnings. Byron told us about the livestock he and Harriet ran on their 60-acre property. They were hobby farmers who raised and butchered cows, sheep, and chickens for food.

Byron said, "Watch out for the ragwort. We lost a cow to it. Causes liver damage. Seeing her die and unable to do anything about it was a horrific experience."

Ruth said, "I don't understand."

"If you don't keep your paddocks free of ragwort, that yellow-flowering weed, your animals may feed on it. If that happens, the animal dies a long and painful death. And even after you rip the bloody weed out of the ground by its roots, it will keep coming back for another eight years."

I recognized the plant he described but did not know its name until now. Cygnet Farm had patches of ragwort aplenty. Eight years of ragwort-pulling appeared in my future.

Harriet said, "The bracken ferns and thistles are worries too, but the livestock won't eat those 'til they're near starving.

However, I noticed you have sheep and Angoras. You're going to want to get shed of the brambles. 'Tis a curse for wool."

I had noticed the goats eating the blackberry bushes along the unnamed stream, but couldn't fathom how they ate the leaves and fruit and left the barbed stems standing. Their grazing left behind tufts of mohair caught on the thorns, waving like wispy flags in the breeze. Broken stems that snagged and broke off in their fleeces provided further evidence of their feeding. How would I ever be able to rid the paddocks of brambles and ragwort? Add these to the worries that kept me awake at night.

Cath said, "I'd like to ask you something. . . two somethings."

She turned to Ruth. "First, what's Thanksgiving really like? We know you serve turkey and stuffing, but what sides do you prepare?"

"Cranberry sauce is mandatory, as are gravy and pumpkin pie. After that, there are options like sweet potatoes, mashed potatoes, salads, breads, fruit pies, and so on. I don't think we could host a Thanksgiving Dinner for Upper Woodstock Road this year, but maybe next. Would that interest you?"

The agreement was unanimous.

Cath continued. "We're all wondering why you have 'Ned Kelly' horses?"

Ruth looked to me for help, but I was as much at a loss as she was.

Cath said, "The masks on your horses make them look like the outlaw Ned Kelly."

Ruth said, "Oh, the fly masks! The mesh keeps flies away from their eyes."

Ruth had seen an ad for fly masks for horses in a California equestrian magazine and asked her sister, Mary, to order and send a couple to our Cygnet Farm address—along with more Barbie dolls.

In the ensuing silence, while I pondered whether to disclose my ignorance about Ned Kelly, I posed the question that had confounded us since our first visit to Cygnet.

"What is 'bowls?'" "We've seen people, usually elderly, dressed in white, rolling balls behind the club."

Isaac said, "That's lawn bowls. Think of it like bocce ball, but more formal and accompanied by heavy drinking."

"Sounds like my kind of sport."

Silence settled over the gathering. Had we run out of things to say, or had we said something to upset them?

Byron broke the spell when he directed the elephant in the room question at me. "What in the bloody hell are Yanks doing in Tasmania?"

At that moment, I heard the crosscut saw. I paused and said, "Who's up there sawing in the bush? I've heard it so many times, but I can never catch the bastards."

All our neighbors, even their children, roared with laughter. Isaac recovered first and said, "Mate, that's not blokes sawing. That's the mating call of a native hen, a turbo chook."

Byron said, "No wonder you never caught the bastards. They run like the *clappers*. Over 50 kph—30 miles per hour."

More laughter as my skin glowed ever brighter. I would never live this down. Oh well, at least I didn't have to come up with an answer to Byron's question about what brought us to Tasmania. How could we explain that a New Zealand vacation, a job ad, and a quest to live on a farm in a safe haven compelled us to leave behind family, friends, and the familiar?

As for Ned Kelly, a few days later, we checked out a library book that revealed Ned was a *bushranger*—an outlaw like Jesse James—who practiced his trade near the end of the nineteenth century. At times, he wore a suit of homemade metal armor topped with a metal helmet that masked his face, thus the mask comparison.

After the party, the Cygnet bush telegraph was abuzz. More folks drove by, wanting a glimpse of the sinister Ned Kelly horses. Soon, Mary was fulfilling multiple orders for local horse owners. Ruth had started a trend.

22. WOOLLY ORPHANS

One weekday morning, as my weed-whacking hour began, I heard a baby cry. Was I imagining it?

Then I heard it again. The cry came from the barn where I discovered babies, two kids, but not human ones. Ron's wife, Nancy, had given birth to twins. She was nursing her newborns. We had our first Cygnet Farm goat kids.

I ran up to the house and roused the family. Fearful of missing the bus, I left it to Ruth to handle the situation. I had no idea what this would entail, but I had faith she would figure it out.

The lambs and kids kept coming. By the weekend, both herds had more than doubled in size.

I learned more about animal husbandry than I wanted to. Except for one ewe-mother, Kelley, and one doe-mother, Louise, rejecting their newborn twins, the new mothers were doing what mothers do. No matter how we enticed coldhearted

Kelley and Louise to tend to their offspring, they refused. The abandoned lambs and kids would not survive the chilly nights without shelter and nourishment. Ruth brought the two sets of twins into our house and set about keeping them alive.

Ruth told Danelle, "Take Kristin with you, rummage through the boxes we got from Roger and Tilley and bring me the dry formula jar, baby bottles, and nipples. If my memory is correct, you'll find them in the same box."

Danelle said, "Okay, Mom."

The girls ran out the door.

Ruth told the boys, "You two get to a shop before closing time. Buy plastic sheeting to cover the floor and a box of disposable diapers. In the meantime, I'll lay down newspapers in the dining room and try to keep the babies hemmed in."

In my last view of Ruth, she was on all fours, attempting to spread newsprint over the cork tile floor while four little ones hopped around her on spring-loaded legs. They didn't have a clue Ruth was saving them. Like human kids, their goal was to play.

We got to the middle store as they were closing. I had bought diapers for our kids, but never for sheep or goats. I had to guestimate butt-size-one would do. We found a painter's plastic tarp and cashed out. The price for each item was ridiculously high.

Since our children were long past the diaper stage, I had not paid attention to how Tasmanians deal with a baby's sanitary needs. I recalled Ruth pointing out cloth diapers hanging from rotating clotheslines—*Hills Hoists*—in our travels. Considering the cost of disposables, cotton diapers seemed like a better long-haul option. I wondered: "How long the long-haul might be?"

When Ryan and I returned, two white-as-snow woolly orphans were hopping around inside a pen constructed of cardboard moving boxes and overturned furniture. Danelle and

Kristin each held a bottle of formula for the other two newborns to nurse from.

We replaced the soiled newsprint, then cleaned and covered the cork floor with plastic sheeting.

The girls loved playing with the live, dancing, diaper-clad babies—much better than playing with plastic, designer-clothed Barbie dolls.

Without mothers to warm them through the spring nights, our young houseguests needed us to light the dining room wood-fire heater. That was a problem since we had burned through the firewood the Caulkins had left behind. My plan, prior to the fostering of the dual twins, was to cut firewood during the approaching summer when the ground would be drier.

***

Did I mention it rains in Tasmania? And not a little rain, real soakers, resulting in swollen streams, boggy tracks, and soggy paddocks. While most of Tasmania's rain falls during winter, the spring storm driven by the Roaring Forties that wreaked so much havoc proved it can rain heavily at any time.

As we learned during our touring phase, the island has wet and dry sides. Cygnet Farm was in between sides, although our microclimate leaned more toward the wet west.

No matter the weather, I had no choice. I had to cut firewood. The first opportunity to access the bush came on my next Sunday off. The rain had dwindled to a sprinkle the previous evening, but the ground remained saturated. Filled with a dull sense of dread, I fired up the Fiat tractor's stuttering diesel engine, hooked up the drop-side trailer, and chugged up the hill toward the smaller eastern bush block. There was not as much deadwood there, but it was closer to home than the 75-acre bush block to the west. With mushy ground ahead, I planned to take my time traversing the 200-foot elevation gain.

I followed the fence lines in an elongated Z-path that made for a more gradual climb. The tractor tires sank to the rims in some spots, but the trusty Fiat kept going. Once I got to the bush and started cutting deadfalls, it began drizzling again. When the trailer was only half full, the rain started coming down in waves, pushed by a powerful southerly. Time to get back to the ranch.

I took the shortest route home to escape the weather, straight down a steep slope, and made two significant discoveries. First, the tractor brakes didn't work, no matter how hard I pressed on the pedals. Second, with the transmission in first gear, the creeper gear, and at idle speed, the tractor tires slowly rotated, and the tractor, the trailer, and I skidded—skied—down the slippery slope. The tractor, with the trailer pushing from behind, accelerated. As if in a dream where time slowed, I watched my white knuckles on the steering wheel jerking back and forth in manic spasms, turning the front wheels from side to side to avoid jackknifing, overturning, or both.

Skiing toward the apple shed at the bottom of the hill, I realized turning off the engine might prevent plowing into the building. I pulled the engine shutdown knob, and the diesel engine choked off. That locked the rear wheels and the tractor, trailer, and I skidded to a stop a yard short of catastrophe.

I sat for several seconds, lost in a daze, oblivious to the downpour. As the shock wore off, I hopped down and looked back. Even through the blur of the blowing rain, I could see the series of S curves carved into the hillside, marking my path. No doubt Ruth would question how that path came to be. I would explain the grooves in the hillside resulted from the need to slow down, like we did on California mountain road switchbacks. I could contend that I custom made the switchbacks for safety's sake.

The justification held a sliver of truth—my maneuvers slowed the tractor. I don't like lying, but being truthful can sometimes lead to severe consequences, like Ruth hiding my tractor keys or, worse yet, selling the tractor. If she found out the tractor brakes didn't work, I knew for certain she would sell or give away my beloved Fiat. I pictured her waiting until I was at work, then helping a local farmer drive it onto a trailer and haul it away, never to be seen by me again. I needed to choose my words carefully. A lot was at stake.

She bought my explanation.

***

The hard-won firewood wouldn't keep the new baby residents and us warm for long. And even I wasn't foolish enough to rely on the brakeless tractor for the steep trips into and out of the bush blocks. So, as much as I disliked using the Subaru to fetch firewood, I had to until I figured out a way to buy a pickup truck. Meanwhile, the Subaru's all-wheel drive was about to face a proper test.

I felt lucky to have a dry weekend when the Subaru, drop-side trailer, chainsaw, and I ventured up the hill, past the haunted pickers hut, past Bret's grazing cattle, and into the larger western bush block. The weather had been kind after my wild ride of the previous week. I reckoned if I kept the car on the track and didn't stop, I wouldn't get stuck in the squishy clay soil.

Continuing uphill toward the ridge that paralleled the west boundary of the farm, the track narrowed. In the bush, the Subaru plowed through tall bracken ferns. I cringed at the rasp of dead, sharp branches raking the sides of our almost-new SUV.

According to what Byron, our neighbor, related to me at the welcoming party, the orchardists built the tracks for apple carts. Charlie's ancestors pulled carts laden with crated fruit from Cygnet Farm's apple-packing shed to the ridge crest, where the track turned downhill toward Cygnet. This circuitous route was necessary in the early days before they widened Woodstock Road from its original width as a riding trail.

The track I followed was steep and rocky. I felt for Charlie's kin, clip-clopping along, coated with sweat and urged forward by a whip-wielding teamster. A top-heavy apple cart could tip over if a wheel bumped over a rock.

I stopped by a gully that bordered the track. I would not have time to waste splitting gum tree rounds, so I cut the smaller-diameter deadwood that had fallen close to the track. When the Subaru and the trailer were full, I faced a problem: where to turn around on the single-lane track. I reached the boundary fence and found just enough room to make a three point turn. Add to my to-do list: Widen the bush track.

As I was driving out of the bush, I felt euphoric. I had harvested the first many tons of firewood from the western bush block. I stopped to gaze over the beauty of Cygnet Farm. The house, sheds, ponds, trees, horses, sheep, and goats were part of a panoramic view of the farm and, beyond that, the port, the moored boats, and the distant Tasman Sea.

However, something wasn't right. Why were little white dots on the opposite side of the fence where the big white dots huddled? My euphoria vanished.

The newborn lambs and kids had slipped under the electric fence, and as I watched, the big dots, the mothers, pushed under the energized cord one-by-one, not to forage on short grass like they did before, but to reach their errant offspring. The mum's wool saved her from getting shocked. All that effort to electrify the fences was for naught as long as the fleeces were long. Once shorn and vulnerable to the shock from the electrified cord, the mums would stay where they belonged, and when hungry enough, the bubs would find their way back to nurse. This also meant we would have to shear on a regular schedule to keep the fleeces short.

We were about to add a lot of "ing" words to our vocabulary: shearing, drenching, backlining, bagging, dagging.

23. THE POOR BASTARD

Sharing our home with orphaned livestock was a new, unanticipated, and, at times, annoying facet of farm life. The entertainment provided by hip-hopping lambs and tap-dancing kids was priceless, but woe to any forgetful soul who switched a light on in the night, setting off dissonant baas and bleats signaling, "We're hungry."

The girls fought over who was going to bottle feed which animal. They even competed to change the diapers.

Next came the naming rights.

Danelle cuddled the two cat-size identical kids and declared, "I name thee Peppy and Poppy."

Ryan surprised us. Holding one lamb in his lap while Kristin clung to the other lamb twin, he said, "Krissy, I want mine to be called Samson. You want to name yours Delilah?"

Kristin nodded, "Okay. This is Delilah, and I love her."

While we tended the baby orphans inside, the woolly adults outside had to be shorn to keep them and the other newborns from wandering—no big deal. We had hand shears that looked like a big, fat pair of spring-loaded scissors. How hard could it be to run them over a sheep or a goat?

We selected the largest doe as our shearing test subject. However, we did not, as they say in Australian with dropped r's, know Arthur from Martha. We presumed all of Ron's goat entourage were females. But when we examined the underside of the one goat that didn't give birth, we discovered the hardware leaned toward male: he had been castrated. We should've noticed he had big horns for a doe. He looked distinguished, so we named him Thomas, after Saint Thomas of Aquinas, the patron saint of scholars.

The discovery prompted us to check out the one ewe that did not reproduce: Harriet. Sure enough, Harriet was a Harry.

Each flock had four, not five, females. While useful for wool production, a castrated sheep or goat would not help the herd grow.

We lured Thomas away from his mates and into the corral below the house.

Sometimes, the things that look the easiest are. . . not. Hand-shearing Thomas was a case in point. He abhorred being tethered to the corral rail. Not long into the shearing, Thomas broke free, ducked and shot between my legs, lifting me onto his back. My boots dangled above the dusty ground as I straddled the big goat, facing backward. He raced around the corral in circles before bucking me off.

As I got up and slapped at the dust coating my jeans and flannel shirt, I saw Thomas had backed into a corner. Great chunks of his coat were missing. He eyed me, probably contemplating revenge. He flicked his head from side to side, flaunting his imposing horns. Had they grown since the start of the day?

Ruth squatted in the opposite corner, facing away from me with her hands covering her face. Keeping a wary eye on Thomas, I hobbled over, fearing Thomas had kicked her.

"Honey. Are you okay?"

When she looked up and pulled her hands away, she clearly wasn't hurt. She was laughing. She laughed so hard that tears streamed down her cheeks, leaving tracks through the dust that powdered her face.

She had trouble finding her voice.

After her laughter finally ebbed, she sputtered, "Next time you ride a goat, I suggest you face forward."

With Thomas tightly secured and with us staying out of the range of his horns, after four hours of wrestling and snipping accompanied by more laughing fits from Ruth, we had a one-gallon plastic bag filled with dribs and drabs of Thomas's once-pristine mohair coat. We were more upset than he was, and bruised and drained. The following day at work, my right hand, which I'd used to squeeze the shears, was too sore and swollen to grip a pencil.

***

I called Bret.

"Bret, you know of any shearers?"

"Yeah. I'll have one of me mates get in touch. He's young."

"As long as he's good, I don't care about his age."

"You'll see why ya want a young one."

A wiry teenager showed up the following Saturday morning and introduced himself as Angus, the shearer.

"Here to clip."

At first glance, he looked too young to do any work, let alone shearing. On closer inspection, I noted he had a tough demeanor about him. To top it off, he had a wad of chew tucked under his lip that occasionally commanded him to spit. That added authenticity.

We cleared accumulated aged manure and straw from the holding pen on the middle level of the tri-level barn. I ran an extension cord so Angus could power his electric shearing machine motor. The drive unit hung from a stand he secured against the pen. An articulated tube connected to the drive ended in a clipper handpiece. These mechanical shears were a vast improvement over the hand shears I used, or I should say, attempted to use.

When he was ready to start, he said, "Mate, where's the backliner, drench, applicators, tags, and bands?"

I stared at him in ignorance. "What?"

Ruth said, "I think we have all of that in the apple shed. Would you mind checking?"

Angus turned away, muttered to himself, before he turned back with a forced smile and said, "Righto."

Thankfully, he found everything he asked for in the Roger and Tilley boxes. We carried them to the barn, and Angus arranged everything to his liking on a folding table next to his shearing machine. He said, "Time to round up your sheep mob, mate. Where's your mongrel?"

"If you mean dog, we don't have one, but I'll get a bucket of pellets, and they'll follow."

Angus didn't look surprised.

Our children sat on the stairs leading to the barn's upper level.

Danelle said, "We can do that."

They were off like a shot, and soon Danelle backed into the empty pen with James, the ram, in the lead following the feed bucket. His harem and Harry followed. Once all the sheep, including five lambs, were inside the pen, I closed the gate and Danelle climbed out. Confinement did not please the sheep, as evidenced by the constant baaing.

Our children returned to their observation posts.

Angus said, "Will take the ram first. Does he have a name?"

I said, "Oh, that's James."

Angus shook his head.

With me tending the gate, Angus wrestled James out of the pen and flipped the big ram onto his butt with ease. "Pleasure to meet ya, James."

Angus sheared under James's belly, then under his tail. He kicked aside the bramble stems and the dags, those nasty clumps from under the tail. As he sheared off the fleece, Ruth scooped it into a clear plastic trash bag with James's name written on it.

Next, Angus shoved a drench gun nozzle—a device that looks like a car grease gun—into James's mouth and pulled the trigger, drawing liquid from the plastic container labeled Ivermectin.

He said, "Drenching will kill the worms in ya, James."

Next, Angus grabbed an ankle, pulled a pair of what looked like rose-pruning shears from a holster, and trimmed a hoof.

"Way overdue for a pedicure, James."

He trimmed the other hooves before rolling the ram back onto all fours. Picking up another gun, this one siphoned from the bottle labeled Diazinon; Angus depressed the trigger while moving the gun nozzle from James's head to his rump along the spine, leaving a blue line on the shaved back.

"That was backlining, James. When those lice ya got circle round, they'll kark it when they cross that line."

Angus pried James's mouth open and examined his teeth.

"James. No cavities. Book with me receptionist, and we'll see ya next year for a haircut, pedicure, and a checkup."

He released James and shooed him out the barn door.

Angus clicked a counter hanging from his machine. "One down. I forgot to ask if ya wanna tag your stock."

Ron, our prize buck, and James already had plastic ear tags stamped with a number. Bret's cows had numbered ear tags, too, but those tags were larger. The colored tags hung from a hole in their ear flaps. I looked at the ear tags in the carton on the table and at the scary-looking applicator. I didn't like what I saw. Each tag has a sharp prong that, when squeezed with the applicator, pierces the animal's ear before the tip locks into a plastic collar. It must be painful. And why did we need to identify them with numbers, anyway? We knew them all by name.

I made eye contact with Ruth and knew we were in lockstep.

I said, "Angus. Think we'll skip it."

"When you have me back in six months, we can do it then."

"Thought we sheared once a year?"

"Mate, spot-on for sheep. Goats, twice a year."

More money going out, but more mohair to sell.

Angus made quick work shearing and treating several more adult sheep and returned each one to the pen. The baaing was worse without James in residence.

Danelle said, "Dad, do Peppy and Poppy need to be sheared? I think it would scare them."

Ryan said, "What about Samson and Delilah?"

Angus looked to me for an explanation.

I said, "Besides the goats in the paddock, we have two lambs and two kids in the house."

"You said 'in.' Inside?" Angus grinned and spit.

"Yes. Their mothers abandoned them."

He shook his head again. "Yanks sure have a funny way of farming."

I thought: "Angus will have a lot to talk about when he makes his rounds."

Angus said, "Bring 'em down and we'll see what ya got."

I turned to Danelle. "Run up and fetch the kids. Oh, and you can remove their nappies."

Angus snorted.

Danelle returned with a kid under each arm and announced, "This is Peppy. He's a boy. And this is Poppy, she's a girl."

Angus said, "Give us a squiz at Peppy."

Danelle handed Peppy to Angus.

Angus checked Peppy's coat and declared, "Not enough fleece on Peppy or Poppy to clip. Same for the lambs—too new in this world."

Our kids returned the orphans to the house while Angus continued working, each sheep shorn faster than the last. He was in the zone. When he finished, we had a pen full of bald sheep half the size they were before the clip.

When he released the shorn and medicated herd, he addressed them. "Thank ya ladies and gents. Now be off."

They ran to James, who patiently waited by the stream. The herd followed him across and up the hillside, where they returned to grazing and making more wool.

***

Next, we had to round up the goats and convince them to enter the pen. They decided they wouldn't fall for the follow-the-feed-bucket trick and scattered. It took our family and Angus yelling, waving hats, and running up, down, and across the paddock to drive them toward the barn. I now understood why Bret stressed the need for a young shearer. Bret knew we were sheepdog-less greenhorns. Angus was lightning fast and didn't break a sweat even though the day was warm.

We got lucky when Ron lost out to temptation and followed the feed bucket into the barn. The goat herd followed, and we penned them in.

Angus looked at my botched job of shearing Thomas and said, "Bloody hell. What happened to this bloke?"

I said, "That's Thomas. He's the reason you're here."

"I'll give him a trim. Not worth keeping what fleece that's left. Can go the way of the dags. The poor bastard."

Angus had quite the vocabulary.

When Angus finished, we had way more than the three-bags-full they had in "Baa, Baa, Black Sheep," but I wasn't confident the fleece sale prices would cover Angus's fee. Well, at least it was a step toward making the farm pay for itself. And more importantly, the flocks, minus their fluffy coats, would respect the electric fence. Or so I hoped.

24. MY COMEUPPANCE AWAITS

As summer approached, Andrew spent more and more time at the Sydney headquarters, leaving me to run the office. I was slipping into his management shoes as he came closer to achieving his goal of taking a position in Sydney. Bea proved to be a reliable support person for day-to-day operations. Even with that, I needed to drive the technical side and oversee admin. I could no longer afford to sleep during the bus commute. I had to work while traveling the winding country roads.

To add to my sleep deprivation, I rose earlier and retired later to keep pace with the expanding daylight. Completing all the chores on weekends was impossible. To come close to keeping up on the main fixes around the farm, I had no choice but to start every day at first light and end at nightfall.

To make matters worse, we were fair game on the weekends for visits from neighbors and an ever-increasing number of acquaintances. No matter the weather, the weekends launched a series of tea ceremonies, some overlapping. Smack in the middle of a project, I would hear the vroom of an engine and the slamming of vehicle doors, signaling it was time to drop tools and turn into the welcoming host. By the time I arrived, Ruth had the visitors seated around our Huon pine table, waiting for the kettle to boil. I would join them for a chat over a cuppa. Once they departed, I picked up where I left off.

Although the visits disrupted my work, they gave us the opportunity to ask questions and keep up on Cygnet news. For example, we learned the dates of the school uniform sale, the library book sale, the Cygnet Footy Club game, and the annual Fishing Carnival.

Bret became our farmer's almanac and mentor, saving us a lot of heartache and grief. And he did so out of kindness, not for reward, and he never criticized our ignorance. We could not have survived farm life without him.

Bret may have viewed the real-time entertainment as adequate compensation for his advice and time. We were a novelty. I ofttimes wondered about us myself. We knew bugger all about farming, yet we persevered and traveled to an island on the opposite end of the world and expected to survive on a farm. What were these Yanks thinking?

***

Until now, the sheep, goats, horses, chickens, and peafowls had satisfied Ruth's passion for pets. But when the adolescent lambs and kids united with the herds, Ruth was left wanting more.

I arrived home on a late-spring evening, exhausted but ready to tackle my evening chores. The whine of a revving jet engine snapped me out of a half-stupor. The ear-piercing squeal came from the backyard paddock where the chickens resided. A chubby pink animal, about the size of a Beagle, zig-zagged through the grass, shrieking.

With all the racket, I didn't realize Ruth had walked up behind me until she shouted, "She's scared and missing her mama."

I shouted back, "Why is a pig here?"

"She's not any pig. She's Matilda."

"Okay. Why is Matilda here?"

"Because I wanted a pig."

"I thought we agreed every animal has to pay for itself. How will Matilda generate income besides pork, ham, and bacon?"

"Not funny. I'll figure out a way. And you don't have to worry about it. Remember our contract? 'You can have any and as many animals as you want—'"

"Okay. Stop. I give up. But who's going to care for all these animals?"

"We will, of course. I'll take care of their emotional needs; you'll take care of their physical needs."

She pecked me on the cheek as we walked toward the house and got away from the squealing. In her normal voice, Ruth said, "I'm so lucky I married an honorable man."

What she meant was she was so lucky she married a man who is easy to manipulate. But two could play the game.

The day before, as the commuter bus approached my office, something caught my eye. We passed a car dealership, one we went by every day. I glimpsed a gray Land Rover ute parked near the front of the lot. It looked like the vehicles you see on African safaris. During lunch, I hiked to the lot and test-drove it. That did it. I had to have it! But how could I get Ruth on board?

The day after Matilda's arrival, I told Ruth, "Why don't you drive the Subaru? It's newer, so it's safer than your Volvo."

She looked at me askance. "Are you up to something? You never offer to let me drive your car."

"I know. I want that to change. You should be able to drive my car, and I should be able to drive yours. End of story."

She took a moment, then said, "Okay."

After digesting Ruth's cheeky comment—I'll take care of their emotional needs; you'll take care of their physical needs—I became emboldened.

The Subaru became Ruth's car. I drove her Volvo DL to the dealer and traded it for my 1971 diesel-powered Land Rover 4WD drop-side pickup. No more scratching up the Subaru in the bush or worrying about getting stuck in the muck. The Land Rover could take me anywhere.

When I returned home that evening, followed all the way from Hobart by a hovering cloud of gray exhaust smoke, I steeled myself for battle.

I parked the Land Rover in the garage, where Ruth usually parks her Volvo.

She came out of the house and strode toward me.

I wanted to get in a few words before she laid into me.

"Honey, I needed a truck for work around the farm. It will be safer than the tractor."

She glanced at the truck, then at me, and said, "The Volvo was safer than the Subaru. I'm going to visit the horses." She turned and stomped off toward the barn paddock.

I knew this wasn't the last I'd hear on the topic.

I wished we could argue, get everything out, then put it back together. No. Ruth left me hanging, waiting for my comeuppance, one that could happen tomorrow, next week, or next decade, but one I knew would happen.

I admit ours was a strange relationship, but it worked for us.

25. BRINGING IN THE HAY

The unpredictable seasonal weather, sometimes all four seasons in under an hour, made dressing for the weather an ongoing challenge. Burning sunshine one minute, wind and rain the next, hail and even snow from time to time, then back to burning sunshine. As I worked around the property, usually on fencing, I bundled up against the cold under a cloudy sky. A few minutes later, the clouds parted to full sunshine, and I was broiling. After that, the heavens might open up, leaving me drenched.

After visitors left following tea ceremonies, I restarted where I had left off, but by then, the weather had changed, and the piece of wardrobe I had hung on a fence post earlier was no longer appropriate. Many times, I would forget where I abandoned my garments. Because of the sprawling property, a sweatshirt, shirt, or jacket might remain on a post for weeks, cloth testaments to where I had worked. All of this to say, the changeable weather posed a challenge for hay baling. We needed dry bales of hay to feed our livestock. Approaching Thanksgiving, balmy, dry days blessed us.

Bret dropped by one evening. After examining our hay paddock, he met with Ruth and me over a cuppa and explained haying.

"Ya heard, make hay while the sun shines?"

Ruth said, "We have."

"Not easy to do in Tassie, but I do me best."

Bret emphasized the importance of completing haying during dry weather when the grasses are at their peak. If mown when wet, tedding (fluffing to dry), raking (into windrows for the baler), or baling, the crop will mold and must be discarded. Finding the right dry weather window is the key.

Bret said, "I get it right most times, but I've had some losers. So's, if ya want me to bale your hay, and whether or not I get it right, ya will owe me fifty cents a bale."

Haying was like playing a game of Vegas craps with the dice loaded by Zeus, the Greek god of weather.

What choice did we have? Ruth gave me a nod.

"Bret, appreciate your helping us and for your honesty. When do you think you'll start?"

"Tomorrow I'll do me own fields. If the weather holds, next week, yours."

***

The weather stayed dry into the following week, and Bret, true to his word, had prepped our hay field for baling. When I arrived home in the Land Rover after work, I found someone had attached a low-slung, flatbed trailer to my Fiat tractor.

Bret passed by on his tractor with his baler in tow, stopped in our hay paddock, and lined up with the first windrow. Half a dozen young guys stood chatting nearby, hands in their pockets. Bret strode over to me.

"We're in for rain later. Ya need to follow me baler with your tractor so's these blokes can load up the cart."

As you are aware, tractor driving is not my forte—especially when driving a tractor without brakes. What else could I do?

I said, "Do I have time to change clothes?"

His look answered my question. I peeled off my necktie and suit coat and tossed them into the cab.

As I climbed onto the tractor, Ruth walked down the driveway and said, "Bret asked if I could drive the Land Rover to haul bales. Since it's your truck, is that all right with you?"

I detected some irony in her voice.

I nodded my okay and fired up the tractor. This would be a night to remember, but not in a good way.

Since the tractor was in creeper gear following Bret or stopped on level ground at the apple shed to unload bales, the lack of brakes made no difference. The problem came around midnight when it began sprinkling. With the baler, Fiat, and Land Rover running nonstop, we had just over 900 dry bales stowed. By 1 a.m., we had stacked the remaining 100 damp bales in the barn.

Bret and his helpers joined Ruth and me at our Huon pine table, exhausted. Everyone cracked open and knocked back a well-deserved beer. Outside, the rain fell in buckets. We had hay, most of it dry.

Focused on getting the hay in, I had not seen Ruth up close until she sat across from me. Her cheeks were pale, ashen—not the rosy cheeks of a redhead. I planned to take a sick day—a *sickie*—to recover and be around to check on her. After paying everyone the amount owed and some extra for the last hour's sprint, we collapsed into bed.

***

The rain had stopped, and the sun was peeking over the horizon when I woke to Bret pounding on the back door. How could he be up and going so early?

I shuffled down the hall in my pajamas.

He said, "Good morning, mate. Ya got a diggin' bar?"

"What?"

"A diggin' bar."

"Oh, you mean a spud bar? I've got one of those." He meant a six-foot, one-inch diameter steel bar, pointed at one end and wedge shaped at the other.

"Bring it to the barn."

"Okay. I'll throw on some clothes."

I met Bret at the barn and handed off the spud bar. He rammed it point first into the haystack, embedding it between the damp bales.

"Don't move it and check it tomorrow morning. If it's too hot to touch, ya need to pull all the bales outta here before they catch fire."

"Thanks, Bret. Spontaneous combustion. What an ingenious way to check."

"Remember to feed out this hay first, so's ya don't give sick hay to your livestock."

I checked the spud bar the following morning, per Bret's direction. The bar was hot, but I could grip it. I checked it every morning over the next week and found it cooler to the touch each day.

We could have lost the barn and the hay to fire if he hadn't helped us. And we wouldn't have had a two-year supply of quality hay. If he weren't older than me, I would have adopted Bret.

26. HOT HOLIDAYS

Ruth was not doing well, no doubt the result of haying—she had hooked and slung bales onto the Land Rover bed along with the young blokes—and the accumulated stress of the move, farm life, parenting, and putting up with me. Her visits to a general practitioner and then a specialist (addressed as Mr. or Ms. and not Dr.) were our introductions to socialized medicine. We liked it. Tasmania's medical care system and its practitioners were top-notch.

The specialist diagnosed and treated Ruth for a thyroid condition. She was back to herself within the week. That was the first time and the last time Ruth helped bring in the hay.

Around the same time, I had some minor health issues I had to seek GP advice on. I got an appointment with Lou, who preferred being called by his first name. It felt like I was talking to an old friend. Lou encouraged me to take my time. He delved into every aspect of my health history and current condition. He fixed me then and on many other occasions, all for zero dollars out of pocket.

We were both back to good health and ready for the next mission: the wool business.

Since the business would be hers, Ruth applied for an account in her name at the Bank of Tasmania's Cygnet branch. The cashier was happy to help her complete the paperwork, but there was a catch. A husband had to sign the application; otherwise, the bank would not open the account. If you want to get Ruth fired up, tell her she needs her husband's permission to do something. It took several days communing with her pets for her to calm down to the point she could return the application to the bank—the one I signed.

Although Ruth had a Master of Science degree in Nursing, she did not have a formal degree and credentials in the Fine Arts. To help legitimize the wool business, she enrolled in a Fiber Arts program in Hobart. The classes convened in a convict-era sandstone building on picturesque Macquarie Wharf, Hobart's main deepwater pier. The two-year degree program would allow her to extend her creative arts skills, network with peers, and give her a break from farm life for a few days each week.

Still adjusting to our new life in Tasmania and the rigors of balancing farm work and engineering work for me and farm work and schooling for Ruth and our children, the American winter holidays caught us off guard by arriving in Tasmania's summer.

I took the kids with me on a quest to find our Thanksgiving turkey. The grocery store clerk looked at me as if I was mentally unfit to be a parent when I asked, "Where do you keep the turkeys?"

"We don't sell turkeys. If ya want a turkey, have to order it from the butcher."

I failed to consider where we were living. In Australia, the whole Pilgrim schtick is "As Seen on TV."

Given my soft spot for Max's Middle Pub and Bluey's middle gas station, I chose the middle butcher shop. When we entered, a middle-aged chap, Janus per the nametag on his apron, reached over the counter. He held out three finger-size sausages.

"G'day. You kids want a *saveloy*?" He was referring to a small English pork sausage.

Giving a saveloy to children is a common practice at butcher shops, like hooking a kid on drugs.

Janus asked me, "What can I get for ya today?"

"I was told I could buy a turkey here?"

"Ya wanna a turkey? Ya need to order it at least three months 'fore ya cook it. But it's your lucky day, mate, 'cause I ordered one for another Yank and he never came by, so's ya can take it off me hands."

He entered the meat locker and returned with a turkey the size of a Costco chicken.

"That's a turkey?"

"Does look a wee bit underweight, don't it?"

It was. The price was not. Our Thanksgiving turkey tasted like chicken, but we figured maybe that was normal for turkeys in Australia.

By Christmas, the media was cautioning folks that slaughterhouses—*abattoirs*—were passing off large chickens as turkeys. American transplants, beware.

***

We found the Christmas experience different, too. The commercialization of the holidays had not caught on in Tasmania. Celebrating, decorating, gifting, and caroling were subdued. I believe the summer heat squelched the spirit.

Danelle helped change that when she created the Teenyboppers. First, she nailed a rusted out mailbox to the railing of the Upper Woodstock Road bridge, the span at the lower end of our property and next to Danelle's neighbor-friends and schoolmates, Rhonda and Haley. The girls dropped off notes and Crayola artwork for each other. Soon, the threesome grew to a fivesome as two other Woodstock Road girls joined. Kristin took part as a junior member, making the total number of members five-and-a-half. They met regularly and converted the cavity at the base of a fallen hundred-year-old pine into their club's girl cave—no boys allowed—leaving Ryan and Simon to their own devices, which became harassing the Teenyboppers. Unless Danelle invited the boys to participate, it was war. This was how the Woodstock Road children spent their summers until the preteens aged into teens.

The Teenyboppers made that first Christmas at Cygnet Farm, and many more, feel more like Christmas by caroling up and down Woodstock Road, even delighting the Lower Woodstock Road residents. Danelle allowed Ryan and Simon to join in. They practiced for hours, and at sunset on Christmas Eve, each kid carried a lit candle and sang their heart out.

We couldn't do much about other holiday traditions. Canned pumpkin was one. When Ruth went to the shop to buy a can of pumpkin pie filling, the clerk explained pumpkins don't come in cans. You harvest an orange pumpkin, as opposed to a green one, and carve out the innards to make a pie. Even worse, we discovered that cake making requires starting from scratch. There's no such thing as cake mix in a box.

On their first Christmas in Tasmania, the kids endured another round of miserly gifts.

Danelle and Kristin received the latest fashion-themed Barbie dolls, courtesy of their Aunt Mary. Ryan got the Australian equivalent of the American erector set—a *Meccano Set*. We did what we could with what we had and vowed Santa would up his game next time. That carried little weight; however, it helped when our three saw the Christmas gifts the neighbor kids received were even less stellar than those Santa delivered to our home. We hoped the lack of commercialization would temper their expectations for next Christmas and beyond.

Not an hour after they unwrapped their gifts, I peeked into the girls' bedroom. They were busy playing dress-up Barbies.

Ryan's bedroom door was closed—never a good sign. As I was about to enter, I heard a loud pop, and the hallway lights went out. I opened his door and entered a smoke-filled room. Squatting on the floor, clad in jockeys, Ryan's complexion had turned pasty white. In front of him were the charred remnants of a six volt Meccano Set motor designed to power the toys depicted in the instruction booklet. The room smelled like melted copper and charred wire insulation.

"What did you do?"

Ryan looked at me wide-eyed and lied, "Nothing."

For safety, general-purpose outlets (GPO) in Australia have on-off switches. I looked at the black-smudged GPO on the wall Ryan faced. The switch was in the "down" or "on" position.

"You pushed the motor wires into the outlet?"

He nodded and said, "I wanted to see what would happen."

Remember, this is the kid whose first word was "broken."

"Never, ever shove anything into an outlet. The voltage is lethal, much higher than in America. That could've killed you."

Ruth called from the living room. "Honey, why is the power out?"

"You don't want to know."

I found the electrical panel inside a wood cabinet on the front porch—no circuit breakers, only porcelain fuse-wire holders and three small coils of bare fuse-wire stored on a shelf with labels that read 15 amps, 20 amps, and 50 amps. The fuse wires on two of the panel's antique holders had burned open. I removed those holders, replaced the wires with those of the same gauge and plugged them back into their sockets. We had power.

I had never encountered a system like it in my engineering career. While the panel and fuse system would have been an impressive addition to a museum, right next to Edison's first light bulb, I acknowledged its practical design—right up there with the gravity-flow water supply systems.

Although an engineer and not a farmer, I patted my back. I had some practical knowledge that was helpful on the farm.

And "practical" pretty well defines farm living in Tasmania.

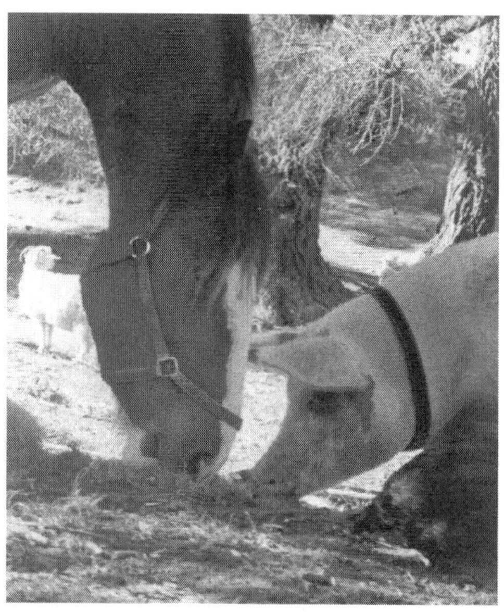

27. THE FAMOUS PIG

The late summer-into-fall weather was glorious, with warm, cloudless days followed by crisp, clear nights. During the chilly mornings, we marveled at the band of fog rising from Port Cygnet. Nudged by a gentle breeze, the silent mist crept along the valley floor and slowly rose through our farm before blanketing the bush and vanishing under the sun's glare.

The Land Rover, my chainsaw, and I were spending more of my not-so-free time in the bush gathering enough firewood to keep us warm through the coming winter. Many times, stacking the rounds to overflowing on the flat tray bed, I continued working until daylight faded to twilight. In the approaching darkness, standing still with my back resting against the bed, a magical world came alive before me.

In the remote hollows, I witnessed the silhouettes of possums creeping down from the treetops. Wallabies zigzagged through the bush on wallaby missions, rustling the bracken fern fronds. Unknown creatures scurried through the underbrush, invisible in the deepening shadows. Distant calls of miniature owls—*mopokes*—brought back childhood memories of the hourly reports from my mother's German cuckoo clock. But no matter how motionless I stayed, kookaburras would find me and break the spell with their raucous calls, scolding me, telling me to go home. And when I heeded their advice, the only light guiding me out of the bush and onto the track that led back to our home came from the stars and the pickup's weak headlight beams. Far below, the golden glow from windows beckoned me to a hot shower, a warm meal, and a waterbed shared with my wife.

With the hay stored, the holidays over, and the children returning to school, we looked back on our first year in Tasmania. For half of that year, we lived on the farm where all our pets were moving, growing, and begetting. The explosive growth of those pets crept up on us.

Distinguishing the former diaper-wearing lambs and kids from the adults in the flocks was becoming more difficult. Tiny chicks and peafowl babies chirped and followed their mum's clucking orders, pecking at bugs and worms. Sheep and goats were gettin' it on. Elton, the peacock, was struttin' his stuff. His caws and Pecker the rooster's crows echoed off the gum trees and carried into the valley.

Matilda the pig, nearly full-grown, roamed the yard and paddocks, snorting and rooting. Sometimes, a goat kid hopped aboard. Although I'm sure the tiny hooves provided a pleasant back massage, that wasn't the company Matilda sought. Lonely and searching for one of her kind, she'd hang out with the goats, then the sheep, and then the horses—the same routine every day with the same results. She wandered home each evening and squealed her demand for pig pellets, which Ruth gave her after commanding her to sit. Ruth had trained her like a dog. Matilda would sit, stay, open, fetch, roll over, or lie down at Ruth's command, but no sitting pretty.

The grasses in the paddocks dwindled as the year drifted into fall. We began feeding out hay to the horses, sheep, and goats. The chickens and peafowl dined on mash and seeds. Matilda lived on pellets and family meal leftovers.

The wool business turned into a Catch-22. We needed to differentiate our product—make it stand out from the crowd—to market and sell our first shearing so we could buy a carding machine we couldn't afford until we sold the fleeces. We needed a gimmick. Matilda turned out to be our great pink hope.

Matilda had napped away a chunk of her days under the summer sun. When I found Ruth on her hands and knees on the lawn, lathering sunscreen on Matilda's exposed flank, I had to ask, "What are you doing?"

"Protecting Matilda's skin. I don't want her to get cancer."

"You don't think smearing sunscreen on a pig is odd?"

"It's not. Matilda doesn't have fur like other animals. She has a thin coat of wiry hair to cover her pink-and-white skin. She needs protection, just like we do, against the UV rays the hole in the ozone layer lets through."

Ruth was right, but the practice was, to put it mildly, unconventional. It was also the catalyst for a marketing campaign.

Ruth said, "Have you ever seen the little girl's bared butt cheek in Coppertone ads? A dog tugs at her swimsuit, exposing her tan line."

"Sure, I recall the ad."

"I envision a similar sunscreen ad using Matilda as a model. I can give her a tan line. Crazy, right?"

"Yup."

"You're probably right, but all summer I've been buying sunscreen by the gallon, so maybe Matilda can make us enough money to recoup the sunscreen cost and help offset the price of a carder."

I doubted anything would come of Ruth's quest, but to my surprise, when she pitched the idea to a Sydney advertising agency, they expressed interest.

***

Word of a crazy, pig-loving Yank lady caught fire on the Cygnet bush telegraph. That generated a great deal of interest and visitors. Matilda's favorite callers were those of Mediterranean heritage because she enjoyed the massaging of her hams. In a trance-like state, while massaging, Matilda groupies looked heavenward and chanted, "Sausage, ham, pork."

All brought treats, like stale bread, apples, or shucked corn. So long as the treat wasn't meat or a meat byproduct, we accommodated Matilda's visitors, but avoided letting the visits turn into tea ceremonies.

Matilda grasped that the sound of an approaching vehicle translated to food. She greeted each car and truck that turned around or came up the driveway. While waiting, she napped under the peach tree next to Ryan's bedroom to ensure a better success rate. The driveway was a quick jaunt from there. She became the Cygnet Farm greeter and watch pig, and a noisy one at that. She accompanied her jog down the driveway with a squeal even distant neighbors could hear.

Matilda did me most proud when she attempted to greet religion peddlers. The dressed-up folk with the glossy brochures were quick to return to their cars and race back down Woodstock Road to avoid a clash with the gigantic, wailing pig trotting toward them.

Falling peaches were an added benefit of napping under the tree. At the thud of a ripe peach hitting the ground, Matilda snapped awake, jumped to her feet, sniffed, and snorted around until she found and scarfed down the peach before spitting out the pit. Afterward, she returned to napping, waiting for the next visitor or peach.

A *Hobart Mercury* reporter rang to request an interview with Ruth and Matilda. Ruth reckoned that would contribute to the success of her ad campaign and agreed.

The day after the interview, a photo of Ruth and Matilda dominated the front page of the *Mercury*. The image captured Matilda sitting while Ruth offered her pellets from an open palm. It must have been a slow news day because Ruth and Matilda became famous overnight—so famous that the Tasmanian Department of Agriculture sent out an inspector.

Even though we had one pig, the Tasmanian Government viewed the farm as a piggery. By law, we had to comply with mandated living conditions and food sources for Matilda. During the *Mercury* interview, when the journalist asked what Matilda ate, Ruth said, "Pig pellets and table scraps." The latter opened a Pandora's box of questions from the inspector. Table scraps were verboten. Consider the possibility of her eating an Italian sausage and contracting a transmissible disease that might eradicate Tasmania's pig population. Ruth explained to the inspector, "We serve only the best table scraps to Matilda and never any meat. That would be cannibalism."

The inspector pressed Ruth to complete a piggery compliance questionnaire, but the questions did not apply to Matilda or her living conditions. Next came a tour of Matilda's living quarters in the backyard paddock near the chicken pen and a willow tree. An aged galvanized steel water tank resting on its side with one end missing served as her bedroom. We lined the curved floor with fresh straw daily and covered Matilda with a heavy wool blanket at night. During the day, the willow tree shaded her home from the summer sun.

The inspector examined the pellets we fed Matilda and agreed they met the Department's standards.

Unable to find fault, the inspector departed, confused, and doubtless wondering what he would report to his boss. He must have spun a convincing tale because we never heard from the Tasmanian Department of Agriculture again.

Matilda had to be the oldest and most pampered pig on the island. Oblivious of her status and good fortune, Matilda went on with her life, eating, growing, and searching for a mate. Except for my Clydesdale stallion, Charlie, our four-legged livestock ignored her. In Charlie, she found a friend. They spent hours together, grazing side by side.

When not napping under the peach tree, she roamed the farm with Charlie, ducking under fence rails, wires and electrified cords to be with him. Matilda even learned how to avoid the shocks posed by the cords. She waited, sensing the rhythm of the electric pulses, and scooted under the cords during the second or two when they were dead. Like most members of her species, Matilda was very intelligent.

Charlie would break away from grazing to nuzzle Matilda's back. Matilda would tug on his tail or stand under him, rubbing her flank against his leg. And when it suited her, Matilda would lie next to Charlie when he laid down to nap in a paddock. They were an odd couple.

The pig-loving Yank lady became commonly known as "Pig Lady". I was "Pig Man" through marriage. The titles didn't bother us much, but our children caught a lot of flak at school, and that was before Matilda went national.

***

A Tasmanian TV station news crew filmed a ten-minute special segment on Matilda. It had to be one of their strangest assignments. As they wrapped up and headed back to their van, I overheard the newscaster ask the cameraman, "What did we just do?"

What they did was attract the attention of the Australian Broadcasting Corporation (ABC), the equivalent of America's National Public Radio. A show host, Renée, contacted Ruth, and they arranged a weekly segment entitled *A Chat with Matilda the Pig*.

Renée and Ruth spoke each week pre-show and outlined a topic of the day. They used Matilda as a ploy to cover current events. Ruth would carry a portable phone out to Matilda, and Renée would bombard the pig with questions. Matilda answered with humphs, grunts, snorts, and squeals that Ruth interpreted for the listeners. Renée was at the top of her game with the questions, and Ruth is a natural, quick-witted entertainer. The hilarious show drew a sizable following of regular listeners that grew into a Matilda fan club.

Over time, the program content shifted to relationships. The discussion of Matilda's and Charlie's interspecies relationship became the jumping-off point for a discussion of human relationship issues when Renée was having some love drama in her life. Were Charlie and Matilda in love? Were they on rocky ground? How could they consummate their relationship?

The last question led to the program's most popular episode.

Ruth said, "Well, Renée, there are some compatibility issues. One is Matilda's height. She stands about two-feet at the shoulder, whereas Charlie towers over her. A sizable gap."

"Well, Ruth, have you thought about building a ramp or some other contraption that will allow them to get together?"

"That leads us to the second compatibility issue."

"And what is that?"

"Charlie's size."

"You already mentioned that."

"Not that size. You know, his *size*."

There was a long pause before Renée responded.

"Oh, you mean that size? How big a size are we talking?"

There was a long pause before Ruth responded.

"Have you ever seen an American baseball bat?"

"Oh, my God! Then size does make a difference."

"In this case, more of a difficulty than a difference."

"Well, that is a difficulty to be reckoned with. If any of our listeners can offer advice, call our toll-free number from anywhere in Australia, including Down Under Down Under."

The discussions became more bizarre by the week. Coincidentally, truffles were in season on the hillside above Agnes Rivulet, the remote patch of bush at the south end of the property. Matilda abandoned Charlie for several days to root up the shady hillside in search of her favorite snack. Instead of Waltzing Matilda, we had Walkabout Matilda.

Her vanishing act was a perfect fit for a breakup narrative. Renée announced a phone-in request, asking listeners to give Matilda comforting advice. The most disgruntled response was "a quarter ounce of lead behind her ear."

Matilda's continuing rise to stardom prompted the *Hobart Mercury* to post a new article updating her successes and ongoing quest for fame. This time Matilda's coverage dropped from the front page to page thirty five. The change reflected Matilda's dying star.

The ABC show went by the wayside not long after that, along with the advertising agency. Matilda never knew that she had once been famous. She only cared about the treats and massages from visitors and, of course, Charlie.

The Yanks at the end of Woodstock Road were more well-known than ever in Cygnet, but for the wrong reasons. The only real financial gain generated by Matilda came from a magazine contest win for an article I wrote about our life with Matilda. It didn't earn enough of a reward to buy a carding machine, but it was enough to cover sunscreen costs and propel us into our next—feel free to call it crazy—business endeavor.

28. THE WHITE RABBIT

Before revealing our next enterprise, I'll introduce some other pets that influenced our lives for worse and for better.

Happily, our livestock did not develop a taste for ragwort when the paddocks were flush with rich green grasses. With the seasonal grasses and weeds dying or dead going into winter, the concern was that our pets might satisfy their hunger by eating the weed that causes a slow and tortured death.

Thistles and blackberry bushes were not poisonous but were a nuisance. The goats nibbled on the blackberry bushes and ate thistle flowers; however, the dried stems and stocks that remained and caught in their coats devalued the wool and mohair fleeces.

Conventional farmers rid their properties of noxious weeds by spraying herbicides. We did not want to contaminate our land, the animals, or ourselves with toxic chemicals. The backlining and drenching of the flocks during shearing stretched our tolerance for the use of poisons to the limit. I had cut down some ragwort, but as Byron had pointed out, the weeds needed to be pulled. The safest option, ripping the ragwort and thistles out of the ground by their roots and bagging them for disposal, would be too much work for one person. I needed help: the Teenyboppers.

I hired the club and Ryan and Simon to rid our paddocks of the noxious weeds. Outfitted with gloves and plastic garbage bags, the kids undertook the job with enthusiasm. I paid them piecemeal by the weed with a promise to treat them to a movie of their choice in Hobart as a bonus. Two Saturdays and the paddocks were clear. The third Saturday would be movie day.

The movie *Celia* was playing. Neither our neighbors nor we knew anything about the film, but the girls were keen to see it.

Since *Celia* was about a young girl, the boys opted to stay and play on the farm. Ryan and Simon had discovered several adventurous ways to enjoy country life.

At the top of the list: getting inside a discarded galvanized steel rain barrel and rolling down our southeast paddock's steep slope, aiming for the creek more than the length of a football field below. They struggled to push the rusted out, six-foot diameter tube up the hill. At the top, they hopped inside and jogged, trying to keep up as the barrel rolled and picked up speed. Unable to keep pace, the force sent them tumbling and bouncing out of the open ends. Sprawled in the grass, sometimes atop manure, laughing, they reconnoitered and did it all over again. The winner of the game was the one who stayed inside the longest. Aside from the occasional scratch or bruise, they survived. I don't believe either of them ever remained inside long enough to get a dunking in the creek.

Another popular game for the boys, and sometimes the girls, involved Wrinkles, the most vicious male sheep in the herd. True to Tilley's warning, one of the cute, bottle-fed lambs grew into a clunky headbutter. The game participants perched on the split rail fence and waited for the bravest soul to scoot into the paddock where Wrinkles grazed. That child then crept as close to Wrinkles as they dared before shouting and waving to draw the ram's attention. Wrinkles charged, and the onlookers cheered the runner on. The winner reached the fence's safety; the loser copped a bruise. A Wrinkle headbutt left a purple bruise of honor on the backside of many a Woodstock Road child.

There was another reason for Ryan's interest in avoiding activities with the girls. Danelle had talked us into hosting a sleepover for the Teenyboppers and several of her girlfriends from school. This provided the perfect opportunity for Ryan to show off—something he excelled at.

Taking turns seeing who could swing the highest on the tree swing I hung on our first day on the farm, Ryan pulled the seat high into the pine tree, hopped aboard standing, and soared far out over the gully. No one had ever swung that far, and that was just as well. As he reached the zenith of the arc, the g-force sent his trousers to his ankles. Unable to release his grip on the rope to pull them up, he swung back, pants down, his back destined to slam into the unforgiving tree trunk. Fortunately, his big sister caught him. I'm certain that pulling up his trousers before an audience of tittering girls scarred Ryan forever.

***

Keeping my promise to treat the girls to a movie, we headed to Hobart with five and one-half Teenyboppers wedged into the Subaru on an unseasonably sultry April afternoon.

While stopped at a red light on Macquarie Street, the main drag, with all the windows down, the girls began shrieking and squealing. I had no idea what was happening. Drivers and passengers in the surrounding autos gawked at me. Their stares screamed: "What are you doing to those poor little girls?"

Danelle yelled, "Huntsman!"

A monstrous spider clung to the ceiling in the backseat, hovering over the Teenyboppers. I switched off the engine and hopped out, pulling a red bandanna—a proper farmer has to carry a bandanna—from my pocket on the way. I heard car doors opening, and out of the corner of my eye, I saw two men headed our way. Ignoring them, I opened the rear driver's side door, reached over the girls, and snatched the huntsman into my hanky. I backed out, grasping a handful of spider, hoping it would not bite through the fabric. I flung the insect and my handkerchief to the pavement at the feet of two rather large men. They jumped back in fear when the huntsman emerged. The supersize arachnid scurried between the stopped cars and disappeared.

The men chuckled as they returned to their cars. One turned and said, "Mate, best get your car fumigated. Chances are that Sheila hatched bubs." It was not a reassuring message.

During the huntsman event, the traffic light turned green, and vehicles at the back of the pack, not having witnessed the cause of the delay, began honking. The deafening blast of a log-laden semi behind us dwarfed the car horn honks and shook me to my core.

Did I mention how much I despise logging trucks? They raced along winding byroads and through downtown Hobart day and night. They were the Grim Reapers of the highways.

Tasmania was ripe for plucking old-growth trees, but at what cost? Ruth and I understood commerce and the need to use resources to the optimum advantage. Timber is the backbone of the building industry throughout the world. Stop logging and many families will lose their livelihoods. But in the bigger picture, the practice of downing old-growth trees and using poison to kill wildlife that threatens the planting of new saplings in their place amounted to quick gains in exchange for shortchanging future generations. Tasmania hosts one of the last temperate rainforests on the planet, one of the last traces of the primal world. Profiting from its destruction affirms the greed and shortsightedness of corporate shareholders.

I hope this digression helps explain why, standing in the center of Macquarie Street in the capital city of Tasmania, facing a logging truck, I looked up over the Kenworth hood ornament, through the windshield, and locked eyes with the burly driver. I so wanted to flip him off, but I held back in deference to the Teenyboppers—not to mention the size of the man and the truck relative to me and my car.

Farther back in the huntsman-caused traffic jam, the flashing red and blue lights of a police cruiser lit up. I retrieved my soon-to-be-discarded handkerchief. Everyone got back into their cars, and the traffic moved on.

I pulled into a nearby parking space and leaned my head on the steering wheel. While waiting for the police to arrive, the girls giggled and poked fun at me until I turned and glared. Silence filled the car. The police cruiser shot by, lights flashing and siren wailing. They were pursuing someone else. Phew!

***

Celia proved to be a horror flick unsuitable for humans of any age. It featured imaginary monsters, voodoo, and a cute pet rabbit, Murgatroyd, who was rabbit-napped and died at a zoo. I did not understand why the adults in the audience cheered at the rabbit's demise, though later I discovered the reason.

On the walk to the car, the girls couldn't stop crying over Murgatroyd's death. Treating the Teenyboppers to *Celia* turned out to be more punishment than reward. The only solution was a round of ice cream, the fix for everything.

Witnessing the movie's emotional impact on the Teenyboppers gave Ruth the perfect excuse to adopt a pure white baby bunny she named Hector. The Teenyboppers loved him. My guilt over the girls' damaged psyches compelled me to build a cage, buy pellets, and welcome Hector into the fold. I received absolution from the neighboring Teenyboppers over

Celia, but their parents' silence signaled they held a grudge. Or so I assumed.

A few months passed before Bret noticed we had a rabbit, a rather large one by then. After looking Hector over, Bret said, "Dick, ya gotta get rid of that buck. Glad to do it for ya."

"I don't understand. We grew up with rabbits and like them."

"Rabbits are a scourge. Wipe out any plant that grows. Get rid of him 'fore he can spread his seed."

Through subsequent research, I learned that over a century earlier, a Pom—one of Andrew's and Roger's countrymen—who loved hunting, had turned a couple of dozen rabbits loose into the wild. Without natural predators and with their drive to procreate, the cute bunnies multiplied to hundreds of millions. In the process, they destroyed millions of acres of Australian flora and drove some fauna into extinction. The reason for the cheering by the adult theatergoers and the silence of the neighbors was now clear to me. Australians despise rabbits.

Living on rabbit pellets and confined to the cage, Hector had grown into an obese white critter—picture Jabba the Hutt cloaked in downy white fur. He had also grown mean. Cute and cuddly in his infancy, now an adult, he lashed out if anyone tried to touch him, kicking with his hind feet in rapid-fire rabbit punches. Since his toenails were long and sharp, those who dared open his cage came away with bloody, scratched forearms.

Recalling Tilley's admonition about handling young rams and bucks, I wondered whether Hector's monstrous behavior was our fault. Regardless, we did not look for him when he dislodged the cage wire and escaped.

After Hector's jailbreak, we noticed next-generation wild rabbits sported white splotches in their native gray-brown fur. That told us Hector was thriving. As usual, Bret was right. I just hoped the rabbits that populated our farm and the surrounding ones didn't inherit Hector's temper.

29. A TALE OF TWO ROOSTERS

Besides Hector, we had another pet that did not fit the Cygnet Farm mold: Pecker the rooster. Much like some human males I've known, the older, the meaner.

One afternoon when Ruth was gardening in the backyard, Pecker sidled over to her, helicoptered into the air, and came down spurs first into Ruth's left gumboot, puncturing the boot and her calf. I had meant to trim his spurs, but it had fallen down my task list, along with replacing the tractor and Land Rover brake shoes. The latter jobs would test my mechanical skills, but nipping spurs did not. When I got home from work and heard what had happened, I tackled Pecker and nipped off the tips of his spurs with goat hoof trimmers. That would put an end to his dirty tricks, or so I thought.

A few weeks later, Pecker lunged at Kristin. Ryan was close by and kept him at bay by jumping in front of Kristin and giving the big bird the boot.

When I got home, I grabbed Pecker and held him upside down to examine his spurs. I couldn't believe what I saw. His spurs had grown back longer and sharper.

I couldn't let any animal harm my family. Ruth intervened as I was about to make an exception to our no-kill policy.

"There has to be another way to deal with Pecker."

"I could take him to the *tip*," I said, referring to the dump.

With no garbage collection service in Cygnet, the residents deposited their trash at the Cygnet tip. Situated atop a hill with views of the port and rolling hills, it may have been the world's most beautiful dump site.

Twice each month, we hauled and dumped our trash onto the years-old mounds of accumulated garbage and junk. Dozens of roosters greeted us, squawking and scrambling to avoid getting run over before returning to their search for food scraps. During the whole dumping process, roosters serenaded us with their boastful crows. In Cygnet, the sentence for a problem rooster is life without parole at the tip.

Ruth said, "As mean as he is, he doesn't deserve the tip. Could you drop him off in the bush?"

"Hadn't thought of that. I'll give it a go."

I bagged Pecker like Tilley had taught us, tossed him onto the Land Rover flatbed, and turned him loose at the top of the 75-acre bush block. He strutted in circles, showing not a glimmer of submission, only a soft clucking I interpreted as Pecker cussing me out under his breath.

I felt sad leaving him alone in the wild, surrounded by thick brush and towering trees. Pecker's life had revolved around coop-living, protecting and mating with the hens, and gorging on the calcium-rich feed intended for the laying hens. Inexperienced in the bush, he'd be an easy meal for quolls, eagles, or other predators.

"So long, Pecker. Watch your back."

I guess he did. Ten days later, Ruth heard a rooster crowing high in the bush. The next day, Pecker emerged and strolled down the track. The following day, he was back with his long spurs and attitude, hitting on his ladies.

To avoid wringing Pecker's neck and facing Ruth's wrath, I returned him to the bush. He was back in three days this time, but worse for wear. We were into a wet and chilly winter that was sapping the energy out of all the animals.

Our rooster disposal method was not working. While reconsidering whether to deposit him at the tip, we noticed Pecker's attitude had softened. He no longer foraged or lived with the hens, and his appetite dwindled. Between the weather and old age, Pecker had mellowed. The Teenyboppers began tending to him, preparing cooked, rolled oats and barley. They salvaged a wooden crate and placed it in the garage, where the reformed rooster slept on a bed of straw. In his final days, Pecker redeemed himself. When he died, I dug a hole near the chicken coop, and we laid Pecker to rest. Our girls painted "Here Lies Pecker" on a flat rock and placed it over his grave, along with a bouquet of wildflowers.

Our naivete about death on a farm continued to confound me. Cygnet Farm's idealistic no-kill ideology could only stretch so far. Like all mortals, animals die by accident, disease, or old age, but as any pet lover can attest, we condone the act of putting animals out of their misery.

To my distress, the killing of a mortally wounded—usually from getting hung up in barbed wire—diseased or elderly sheep, goat, or chicken fell on my shoulders. Death from the crushing blow of my bullnose shovel blade sent many of our pets to the beyond and filled me with remorse. I was relieved when livestock exited this world on their own. Pecker's natural passing had done me a favor. And his burial required a lot less labor than digging a grave for a deceased sheep or goat.

As mean as he had been, Pecker protected and serviced the hens. We needed a rooster if we were going to have an egg supply and grow the flock. The older Sussex hens from Roger and Tilley continued to lay eggs, but in smaller quantities. We needed younger hens, and the kids demanded a Pecker replacement.

Kristin solved the issue rather craftily.

***

Our second winter in Tasmania topped the first in terms of storms, or so it seemed. Feeding and tending to our pets forced us to be outdoors, be it warm and dry or cold and wet. The march of back-to-back storms was relentless.

Returning home in the darkness from another day at work, the Land Rover's wipers fought to clear the windshield of a heavy deluge. Driving past the Duloe Arabian horse stud at the bottom of Woodstock Road, I saw a tiny figure huddled by the roadside. Nobody should have been out in such weather. I stopped and backed up.

Rolling down the window, I called over the roar of the diesel and the storm, "Are you okay?"

A tiny figure in a stockman's coat trudged to the pickup. Six-year-old Kristin looked up at me. She cradled a small chicken to her chest.

"Dad. This chicken was stuck in the ditch, drowning. I saved him."

"You should be at home. Get in."

She came around, opened the passenger door, and passed the sopping wet creature to me. I reached over with my free hand and pulled Kristin up into the cab.

I handed the bird back to her and said, "What were you thinking? You have no business being out in a storm."

"I was helping Becky feed the horses. When she left, I was supposed to go home, but I didn't want to leave. Some earthworms were drowning, and while I was saving them, I heard a peep from the ditch. Sunny was drowning."

"Sunny?"

"That's what Becky named him. Because he glows when the sun shines on him."

"Him?"

"Dad, he's a rooster."

Becky was the resident trainer at the Duloe Arabians horse stud. She and the stud's owners, Peter and Lois Wright, proved instrumental in Kristin's development into an avid rider.

The Wrights had moved onto their property more than a decade before our arrival. However, we weren't aware of Peter's celebrity status until we learned that his memoir, *Spycatcher*, was an international bestseller except in Great Britain, where the government banned it because it revealed MI5's bungling and reputedly illegal activities. His residence in Cygnet and the success of Duloe Arabian horses put the village on the map.

Becky took a liking to Kristin and had been teaching her horse care.

In the peaceful Cygnet Farm neighborhood, our children roamed in much the same way as our resident grazers, minus the confines of paddock fences. When Kristin wasn't at home, we could always find her at the horse stud. However, I hadn't expected to find her there in the dark during a storm.

From that night on, Sunny took up residence in front of the dining room heater and became an alcoholic.

He had contracted a cold from his near drowning. Seeing the poor little guy shivering and wheezing, Ruth rang our former neighbor, Marie Jefferson, for advice. Marie swore by warm oats laced with whiskey. Sunny recovered from the cold, but not from his addiction.

Whether surrounded by diaper-wearing lamb and goat kid orphans or solo, Sunny's cardboard box nest was sacred—no shared chicken shed accommodation for the male prima donna.

The cocky little bantam took over Pecker's rooster duties. He hung out with the hens during the day, his golden, iridescent feathers glowing in the sun, just as Becky had said. His looks lured the hens to him, but when a hen squatted, positioning herself for Sunny to bring it on, he ran at full gallop to hop aboard—and fell off nine times out of ten. The hens were too big for poor little Sunny. He rarely consummated a relationship. Instead, he wandered off undeterred, clucking and scouting for his next attempt at conquest.

Our flock expanded because of Sunny's occasional success, but the chicken sizes shrunk. As the elderly hens in the original flock died of old age or mishap, the young bantam-size chickens supplied us with bantam-size eggs instead of the extra-large eggs produced by the geriatric flock. The miniature hens improved Sunny's score, and in no time, our flock became Lilliputian.

Each evening at sundown, without fail, we heard a repeated pecking at the backdoor, prompting one of us to open it. Sunny would hop into the house on his feathered feet, strut over to the heater, and wait for his bowl of warm oats and whiskey. After dining, he hopped into his wool-lined box and slept until an hour before sunrise, when he woke the household with a crow.

His early crows were scratchy, not rooster-like, and annoying. As he aged, his ill-timed crows deepened and grew louder, and more annoying. Sunny became a household fixture and an unwanted alarm clock. I think we put up with the annoyance because, like us, he was different. Who else would voluntarily live with an audacious, whiskey-swilling rooster?

As for Sunny's ownership, that was a fuzzy topic. Throughout her childhood and past her teens, Kristin swore that Lois, the stud's owner and Becky's boss, gifted Sunny to her. We took her at her word and never checked. Well into her adulthood and long past Sunny's, Peter's, and Lois's passings, Kristin confessed she had absconded with Sunny on that stormy night. The plan was devious. She had picked a time when no adults would be around, and knew I would pass by after catching the bus to Cygnet. She positioned herself with her back to the stable lights and hoped I would see her silhouette and stop.

At age six, she had pulled off her first sting.

30. GUM WEAVES

Our next business venture—the crazy one I alluded to earlier—caught us by surprise.

Ruth let her fiber arts classmates know we wanted to buy a secondhand wool carding machine. With some leftover cash in our pocket from the magazine contest win, monies from Bret's use of our pastures, and a sliver of my salary, we thought we could find a deal on an old machine and make Ruth's wool processing business a reality. Word came back that Waverley Woolen Mills in Launceston was auctioning off surplus equipment. The century-old weaving mill listed a carding machine in the sales brochure.

Our anticipation was high when we arrived early on auction day, confident we would win the bid since, we reasoned, there would be little demand for such a machine. A carder would finally be ours.

We toured the facility and discovered that, in addition to equipment, the mill was auctioning off thousands of blankets and yarn skeins. Interesting, but our sole focus was on the carding machine.

Shock set in when we entered the floor where the machine resided. The carder was at least thirty-feet long, over eight-feet wide, and six-feet high. Built in Great Britain of cast iron, it had to weigh at least ten tons. Bolted together in sections, I thought I could reassemble it in our apple shed, but how would we move the parts and pieces to our farm? And what about all the hay we had stacked there? We would need the entire shed floor, meaning we would have to move hundreds of bales into the barn and the pickers hut—no small task.

I said to Ruth, "What do you think?"

"It's scary-big. We could card a year's worth of fleeces in an hour."

"I doubt the shed floor and foundation will support it."

"But I want it."

I knew there was no way to dissuade her from buying the carder. If we won the bid, I would have to take up residence in the apple shed for the next six months.

We joined the other attendees, taking first row seats in front of the auctioneer. A scruffy-looking hippie dropped into the seat beside me and offered his hand.

"Alistair."

I shook his hand and said, "Dick. This is my wife, Ruth."

Ruth said, "Pleased to meet you, Alistair. Where are you from?"

"Scotland. Now South Bruny Island. You?"

His brogue was easy on the ear.

"America. Now Cygnet. We're starting a fiber business. We're here to buy the carder. You?"

"A wee bit o' yarn. I'm a weaver. Come from a line of Scottish weavers and opened my shop nigh five year ago."

The auctioneer stepped to the podium and tapped the mike.

Ruth said, "Good luck, Alistair."

"Aye. You, too."

The auctioneer said, "Ladies and gentlemen. Welcome to the Waverley Woolen Mills clearing sale. I am honored to oversee this first ever inventory reduction sale since Peter Buhlman established this historic weaving mill in 1874."

I thought: "And the first-ever time Yanks are here to buy an ancient carding machine."

He continued, "However, before we begin, I must inform you the owners have stricken the carding machine from the sale. Now let's begin."

We looked at each other. Ruth scowled. I tried to hide my relief. I could continue living in the house.

Alistair offered, "Sorry, mate."

The auction began with bids for wool blankets, piles of them, all tartans. I scarcely paid attention to the bidding, thinking we came all this way for nothing. A nudge from Ruth brought me back to reality.

She whispered, "Maybe we should buy yarns, the finished product. If the price is right, I could market them to weavers. Okay with you?"

I thought about it for a millisecond, then turned to Alistair. "Alistair. When you said you planned to buy a wee bit of yarn, how much is a wee bit?"

"A truckload. I borrowed a mate's truck. Parked outside."

I looked at Ruth, and she nodded.

"Alistair. Any chance you could do two runs if we bought a truckload of yarn? We'd pay for your time, gas, and the truck rental."

He offered his hand again and said, "Aye."

We were off on a different tack.

After the blanket bidding finished, bins filled with hundreds of skeins of wool yarns came up for auction. Alistair bid nonstop.

Ruth whispered, "They're going for pennies on the dollar. Much less than what we could have produced them for had we carded, dyed, and spun the wool ourselves."

We held off bidding until Alistair finished. He won twenty bins, by my count, much more than any pickup truck could hold.

"Alistair. How big is your friend's truck?"

"Eighteen-foot box."

That was a lot more truck than I expected.

I said to Ruth, "How many bins do you want?"

"Same as Alistair."

I would have to move a heap of hay to accommodate that many bins.

We bid and won, bid and won, on and on, until we hit twenty bins. I had no clue whether we had made a wise investment. Ruth and Alistair assured me the bins were the deal of a lifetime.

***

Two days later, Alistair and his wife, Yvette, delivered our yarns. In the interim, I had moved several stacks of hay bales to the other outbuildings to clear the way for the heavy wooden bins.

Unfortunately, the height of the apple shed's loading dock exceeded that of the truck bed by several feet. We needed a forklift we didn't have. With Alistair's, Yvette's, and our neighbor Cath's help, we unloaded the truck one skein at a time. When done, we had a mountain of yarn.

The last ferry to Bruny Island had sailed by the time we finished. Alistair and Yvette were stuck for the night on what they viewed as the Big Island. We offered our newfound friends evening tea and the living room couch and floor, and they accepted.

We all stood back and marveled at the yarn mountain we had built.

I said, "Alistair, you'll weave all of your yarn over the years, but I'm not sure we'll be able to sell all of this in our lifetime."

Ruth said, "I have an idea."

Whenever Ruth utters that sentence, it translates to work for me.

"I'm hesitant to ask, but what's your idea?"

"Except for the hay stored there, the upper level of the barn is empty. I could turn that space into a yarn store. All it would need is for you to move the hay to the pickers hut and replace the sliding barn door with a new door with windowpanes. We had already planned for you to set up the loom there. I could teach and demonstrate weaving, which would help sell the yarn."

Not only would I have to move hay bales again and replace an entire barn door, but I would also have to assemble and fine-tune her loom. The barn was the only place it would fit. Busy with farm chores and tons of firewood to split, I had aimed to avoid the loom project for as long as possible.

We kicked Ruth's idea around that evening and, outnumbered when Alistair and Yvette took Ruth's side, I caved. After too much food and drink, I went to bed, defeated. I deserved a Sunday morning lie-in.

Danelle tapping my shoulder and whispering brought me out of my slumber. "Dad. Your friends are walking around naked."

"What? Naked?"

Ruth woke at the sound of my voice and echoed my response. "Naked?"

Danelle nodded.

I said, "I'll take care of it. Sweetheart, go to your room and close the door. I'll let you know when it's okay for you guys to come out."

She left, and I threw on some clothes.

Alistair and Yvette were in the living room dressing when I greeted them with an Aussie accented, "Good morning, maties. Goin' to be a cracker of a day!"

They stopped and stared at me. I believe they wanted to correct my butchering of the native language, but instead, Yvette said, "Our apologies if we shocked your daughter. We hadn't planned to spend the night, so no pajamas. Not that we're used to wearing clothes, anyway."

Her comment conjured up the image of naked Napoleon, the nudist replacement engineer in Warrego, and Bea, the cheeky secretary. My discomfort made me realize I must have some remnants of Puritan blood coursing through my veins. By Australian standards, I was a prude. I reminded myself not to judge other people's behavior based on my culture and upbringing. This couple was kind and decent.

Offering our sincere thanks, Alistair and Yvette headed off to their smaller island homestead. I remained skeptical about the wisdom of our decision to purchase the Waverley yarn in bulk, but it was too late now.

It took three weekends and the evenings in between to convert the barn into a yarn shop. When we finished, I had to admit that Ruth's window dressing skills made the shop look impressive in the rustic setting, with yarn stacked to the ceiling along the walls. She even put the now-empty steamer trunks to good use, storing and displaying the colorful skeins. And since we did not have a carding machine to process our wool and mohair, she put bagged fleeces on display for sale by the kilo.

Ruth registered her first business, *Gum Weaves*. She worked with a graphic artist to design a logo: two back-to-back swans with interlaced tail feathers. With winter hedging on spring, she opened her shop. Word spread via her fiber-arts friends and the Cygnet bush telegraph. The weekends drew a near-continuous string of shoppers and curious folk. We were still in the market for a used carder to process our current and future fleece inventories, but until then, my salary and Gum Weaves were our lifelines.

***

An upper Woodstock Road Thanksgiving dinner, a gift-laden Christmas, and an olive orchard were the most significant benefits of our increased cash flow.

Ruth stood by her word and invited the neighbors to join us for a traditional American Thanksgiving. We pre-ordered an American-size turkey from Janus, the butcher, to the tune of over $100. Ruth prepared our traditional celebratory meal: stuffed turkey, secret recipe cranberry sauce, mashed potatoes and gravy, and a pumpkin pie made from an orange pumpkin. Our close neighbors, who had become our close friends, were thankful for letting them live an experience they had only seen on TV.

We had not let Matilda into the house before, but Ruth had her trained so well that we started a new family tradition by inviting her in for the Thanksgiving dinner blessing. With the upper Woodstock Road neighbors seated and ready to feast, Ruth let Matilda in. This was not the best plan because Matilda sidetracked into the kitchen and, in attempting to salvage food crumbs she smelled beneath the oven, used her snout to tilt the oven where our expensive turkey was roasting. It took all of Ruth's control to get Matilda to stop and exit.

Matilda's behavior notwithstanding, the dinner was a success. All the guests were thankful and asked to be invited again, provided we excluded Matilda. The Cygnet bush telegraph was abuzz for days afterward.

***

We lied to our children that year, throwing Santa's visit off by one day to give us time to hide presents around the property and sleep in on the actual Christmas morning. When we woke the kids to tell them we had made a mistake and that today was Christmas and not the next day, they rushed to the Christmas tree in the living room only to discover a boxed set of the

Encyclopedia Britannica. The gift label from Santa listed their names and explained this was a gift to be shared by the Reese family scholars-to-be.

Danelle burst into tears, followed by Kristin. Ryan pulled out twenty volumes from the decorative *Britannica* wooden crate and flipped through "Volume 1: A–Bayes." While his sisters wailed inconsolably and we looked on, waiting for the big reveal, Ryan skimmed "Volume 2: Bayeu–Ceanothus." When he opened "Volume 3: Ceara - Deluc" he discovered and read the note sticking out of the "Christmas" description page.

"Fooled you! Ryan, go to the dairy. Danelle, go to the barn. Kristin, go to the apple shed. All of you, check the pickers hut." It was signed Santa.

Ruth and I had gone all out to reward them with a memorable Christmas. Shortchanged on other Christmases, this was our makeup year.

They ran from building to building, and besides the present they discovered at each, another Santa directive awaited, pointing to other locations where they found bikes, Barbies, clothes, a computer, and video games. For the first Christmas in many, they were happy and had an encyclopedia they could use as a reference for their homework, which was sorely needed in the days before the internet.

***

A drawback of our increased income was higher income taxes in two countries. I had prepared and filed our taxes until this point, but with the risk of jail time for my tax law ignorance, I broke down and hired an accountant to help us wade through the complexities of filing taxes in two countries.

The accountant told me I had overpaid the IRS for two years. I knew we had to declare foreign-earned income to the IRS, but I had not deducted the income taxes we had paid to the Australian Tax Office (ATO) when I filed our US returns.

The complexities of filing in two countries with fiscal years that differ by six months didn't help.

After cleaning up our returns and preparing our filings for both countries, the accountant recommended investing more in our farm and writing off the expenses. The yarn purchases helped, but invest in what else? A carding machine? We hadn't saved enough for that, assuming we could even find one.

Ruth to the rescue.

She had been reading that mainland Australians viewed olives as invasive, similar to pampas grass and rabbits. We knew from our California experience that olives are a lucrative crop. So far, we had only seen one small olive orchard, a young one, growing not far from Cygnet. We contacted the owner and coincidentally, he and his wife were Matilda groupies. We had met them when they came to feed and massage Matilda. Of Italian extraction, Arturo and Louisa befriended us and taught us more than we could retain about olives. Following their advice, we purchased and planted over fifty olive trees of four varieties—California Mission, two California hybrid varieties, and Sevillano. Trialing the different types would allow us to see which produced more fruit in the Cygnet Farm microclimate.

Trees were expensive, and preparing a paddock for planting was even costlier. The resulting tax write-off helped.

As with all our other farm-related endeavors, there was a downside. Our agricultural ignorance was going to really hurt this time—at a time when my salary was about to take a hit.

31. SHEEP DOG AND RAT CAT

Nearly three years after I began working at the consultancy, Andrew received his long-awaited promotion to Sydney headquarters as a reward for completing a lucrative project. It was my job to complete several smaller designs and develop new business. I was game to do that until I met the regional manager, Zagan, the fellow Andrew reported to before his promotion.

Andrew had warned me about the company's unethical business practices over my first Guinness. However, until Andrew's departure, I had not had to deal with those practices directly. Now, although he expressed it in a roundabout way, Zagan clarified the company's business philosophy for me. In exchange for a pay raise, I was expected to screw over clients to increase billable hours for senior staff.

The only upside to working with Zagan was that he was in Sydney, far away from me and my Tassie clients. Out of sight, out of mind, would work in my favor for a couple of months until the dip in receivables caught up. My time to jump ship had arrived, but where to?

The Hydro-Electric Commission (HEC) had lifted its hiring freeze, and I applied for the first position to open up. It was not in my area of expertise, and I would have to take a twenty percent pay cut. They must have been as desperate as I was because they hired me. Three months after Andrew's departure, I exchanged goodbyes with my friend Bea, that posh vixen, and slotted into the agency that had drawn us to Tasmania.

Although my reduced salary hurt the Cygnet Farm bottom line, I cashed out my consultancy superannuation—similar to an American 401(k) plan, but with greater employer contributions and no early withdrawal penalty. It was surprisingly large. It was like getting paid to leave. Those funds helped retire some of our accumulating debt caused by an accelerated influx of pets, including the latest: Ralff and Smoochball.

Our neighbor Arlene asked if she could borrow Kristin for an hour. Arlene's dog, Peggy, had produced two pups a few days earlier. Arlene recovered one. The other pup remained under the raised floor of their house, too weak to leave the nest where Peggy gave birth. Inaccessible and abandoned, the puppy needed to nurse from Peggy. As the youngest and smallest, Kristin was the best bet to crawl under the house and retrieve the skinny little ball of curly black fur. As a reward, Arlene offered Kristin the pup, a male. Once weaned, our sheepdog entered the menagerie.

Aidan, the local vet, was the first stop for pup vaccinations. I recounted how the little fellow came to be with us. As Aidan examined him, he said, "What's his name?"

We had arrived at the letter R in the alphabet of names. Since Kristin brought us the pup, she had the naming rights.

I said, "My daughter named him Ralph."

"Aye. It's a fine name, but common. He's a special lad, this one. Least we can do is fancy up his name. Let's spell it R-a-l-f-f. No other dog, man, boy, or beast I've come across spells his name that way."

"He is special. By all rights, he should've died where he was born. But now Ralff's destined to be our sheepdog."

"Aye, he doesn't lack for vigor and he has a bit of Australian Sheperd in him. The rest is a mixed cocktail. He could have the makings of a great sheepdog, or he could be the worst. I look forward to hearing how Ralff turns out."

Ralff turned out to be worst at first. He chased anything that moved: chickens, peafowl, sheep, goats, horses, pig, cows. His forte was tossing chickens high in the air and watching them flap their wings and squawk as they belly flopped on the lawn. The world was his playground. The situation didn't please the livestock or us.

As he aged, his behavior improved, and his sheepdog training began. It was frustrating. Despite the entire family's concerted efforts, Ralff didn't grasp the concept of herding, no matter how hard we tried or what approach we took. . . until he did.

Our shearing days provided free biannual entertainment for the neighbors. Word went out when they spied Angus's ute heading up Woodstock Road. By the time he set up, a gaggle of onlookers lined the fence beside the barn. This provided the perfect vantage point for the show the Yanks at the end of the road put on. If we had charged admission, we could have made more than the ever-growing wool and mohair stockpile earned us.

Ralff should have received an Oscar the first time he demonstrated his herding skills to the audience. He tried to be the dog we wanted him to be, but instead of rounding up a herd and running them toward the barn, he forced them into the farthest corners of the paddock. I believe Ralff thought his job was to protect us by keeping the woolly beings as far from us as possible. No amount of hat-waving and shouting changed his mind. It wasn't clicking with Ralff.

He left us no choice. Armed with feed buckets, we ran up, down, and across the paddock, hoping for a hairy beast to follow. That's when the miracle happened. Something finally clicked. His maneuvers became textbook sheepdog. Barking and yipping, he forced the herds toward the barn.

We relaxed and joined the audience.

Waiting at the holding yard gate below the barn, Angus called up to us, "He's a bloody good boy, that Ralff!"

After Ralff finished rounding up our expanded herds—lots of begetting had transpired—and forced them across the creek and into the holding yard where Angus closed the gate behind them, Ralff raced back along the unnamed stream and grabbed a lamb caught in the brambles. None of us had noticed the half-drowned little tyke until Ralff dragged her by the scruff of the neck and laid her matted body on the bank. The crowd cheered when she stood up; however, the merriment was short-lived. Ralff rewarded himself by having his way with the lamb. A simultaneous "Ew!" erupted from the mouths of everyone witnessing the event. I made a mental note to schedule a neutering appointment for Ralff with Aidan.

As a reward for Ralff's herding skills, we installed a pet door, giving Ralff free rein to wander the farm. In return, he insinuated himself into every aspect of our lives. He was always by my side when I cut firewood, sitting in the Land Rover passenger seat, scouring the landscape, hoping to sight a rabbit. From time to time, he succeeded in his quest and gifted us a rabbit's head on our waterbed. What a good doggy.

Ralff was a near constant companion for our children, the neighbors, and me.

***

Not long after Ralff's arrival, another companion joined the family: Smoochball.

We had enrolled Danelle in the Friends School, a private Quaker school in Hobart and the alma mater of the infamous actor, Errol Flynn, who was born in Hobart eighty years earlier.

Although we did not practice the Quaker religion, we thought the morals and structured learning might help Danelle survive her teenage years. As Ruth aptly put it, when the clock struck one past midnight, catapulting Danelle from age twelve to thirteen, she lost half of her brain cells. She transformed into a moody woman-child, happy one moment and lost in the depths of anger and despair the next. The days of Teenybopper innocence and the family's peaceful coexistence were gone forever.

The ride to the Cygnet parking lot to catch the Hobart bus each early weekday morning did not help lessen the strain between Danelle and me—dominating father versus rebellious daughter. Our neighbor Byron and I now traveled to and from the bus stop together. Wedged between Byron and me on the Land Rover's bench seat, Danelle suffered through the indignation and taunts of other private school commuters. She didn't want to be seen with her dad, especially because of my name: "Dick." Too, she was ashamed of the Land Rover. The pickup truck's appearance was not the main issue; it was the rumble of the misfiring diesel engine and the stench of the gray exhaust cloud that lingered in the parking lot air as we trudged to the waiting bus.

Only an occasional incident brought back a glimmer of the sweet preteen Danelle.

During the winter, the Land Rover cab heater struggled to warm us during the morning commute to Cygnet. However, when the conditions were perfect, by the time we reached the bottom of Woodstock Road, the heater and our combined body heat had defrosted the cab's aluminum ceiling. The condensed dew trickled and collected in the gutter trim above the doors. The turn we made toward Cygnet caused the water to spill from the gutter and, as if by design, pour over Byron's head and run down his neck. When the icy stream hit him, he cursed worse than a sailor. Danelle's giggles brought my daughter back from her teenage gloom. The real Danelle was in there somewhere.

Boarding the commuter bus one winter evening on the return trip to Cygnet, aiming for my traditional seat next to one of only two heater vents, I passed a cluster of giggling private school girls. Danelle sat in their midst, ignoring my presence and fondling a mewing gray kitten. I thought: "That cat better not be heading our way." It was.

At evening tea, Danelle argued the case for keeping the kitty.

"Dad, we need a cat to kill the mice and rats in the sheds."

Ruth chimed in. "Honey, if we have a cat, maybe you won't need to keep replacing the wiring."

They had a point. The cold winter had turned the apple shed, where we still stored some hay, into a respite for mice and rats. The occasional mouse did not bother me, but the rats sharpened their teeth by gnawing on the electrical cable sheaths. A short circuit could spark a hay-fueled blaze.

I said, "Okay. As long as she's an outdoor cat."

Danelle said, "She would freeze. Can't we keep her inside until she gets bigger?"

"Okay. For now, keep the kitty in the laundry room, but you feed and clean up after whatever her name is."

"Smoochball."

Kristin said, "I'll take care of Smoochball, too."

I'm glad I relented. Smoochball grew into a master assassin—a hit cat. She liked to hide in the hay bales, wait for her intended prey to scurry by, and attack with a vengeance. No rat was too large.

Smoochball also behaved like Pixel, the cat I had recently read about in Robert Heinlein's novel *The Cat Who Walks through Walls*. Wherever I worked on Cygnet Farm, Smoochball appeared out of nowhere. I don't believe she traveled through alternate universes like Pixel. Still, whether I was cutting firewood high in the bush or mending a fence along Agnes Rivulet at the opposite end of the farm, I would hear Smoochball's soft meow and find her rubbing against my boots. Often, she emerged from the tall grass as if she had burrowed her way to find me. The kids described the same thing. That cat was everywhere for everyone, even for Ralff. Over time, Ralff and Smoochball formed a bond and enjoyed lying curled up by the living room heater. Best mates.

32. HORSES FOR COURSES

Unlike the woolly flocks, the horse population on Cygnet Farm didn't increase through breeding but rather through acquisition. Ruth and Kristin were the culprits.

A natural athlete, Danelle was an excellent rider; however, her interests dwelled in the arts, theater, and boys. She loved playing with all the pets and had deep compassion for them, but I could never picture her as a farmer.

It was the same for Ryan, although his interests tilted toward math and science. Ryan became our go-to guy for anything computer- or tech-related, the rare person who devours instruction manuals. Ryan was more extroverted than Danelle in some respects, but less social. He was small for his age, and we didn't know until much later that the high marks on his report card masked the pain he had suffered at the hands of bullies in high school.

Our neighbor Isaac started teaching photography at Huonville High School and alerted us that Ryan was the only student who carried a briefcase. All the other kids relied on backpacks. This made Ryan a tempting target for bullies. We and the principal encouraged Ryan to switch to a backpack, but Ryan refused, claiming he needed the briefcase, with its alphabetized file folders, to organize his work. Ultimately, his height shot up over the summer, and the bullying stopped.

We still bear the guilt for not helping him sooner, but in our defense, he never revealed what he was going through.

Kristin, in contrast, was all about horses and chickens. Too small to ride Ben or Charlie, Kristin triggered the second wave of horse acquisitions with her first pony, Rocky. Our youngest saved her allowance and any money she earned by helping Becky at the Duloe Arabian stables. For $75, she bought the shaggy gray Shetland pony that had the disposition of Bambi. Rocky, at all of eight-hands high, was rock solid but no youngster. His interests were eating and sleeping. On balmy days, I witnessed Kristin stretched out on Rocky's back, napping while he trimmed the lawn.

Soon, Ruth and Kristin spent their Sundays at the Huon Pony Club. Rain or shine, in freezing cold or scorching heat, they joined other mothers dedicated to their daughters' quests to become the world's greatest equestrian. The meets tested the mother-daughter bond under whatever skies Mother Nature painted for them.

Rocky was a good starter horse for Kristin, but she needed a greater challenge as she grew in both size and competitiveness. We literally put Rocky out to pasture where he could live out his retirement grazing with Ben and Charlie.

To my consternation, Ruth's exposure to Pony Club unleashed another flurry of pet purchases. More pets that required more care, and they did not come cheap.

With Ruth's help, Kristin bought a fiery pony, Zac. He was larger than Rocky, smaller than Ben, and only green broke—just getting trained to a saddle. Kristin and Becky turned wild Zac into a competitive event pony, a fast one.

Kristin jumped headfirst into horse racing. When Becky deemed Kristin and Zac ready, she encouraged Kristin to compete on the Pony Club racing circuit. For her maiden race, Kristin entered Zac in the annual *Bothwell Races* in Tasmania's Central Highlands, a two-hour drive from Cygnet. She learned a valuable lesson about Pony Club handicapping when she renamed her horse Hurricane Zac. The "Hurricane" prefix compelled the race handicapper to relegate Zac to starting several leagues behind the competition. Mama Pony won the race. The following year, when Kristin competed, Zac was just Zac, and they brought home the gold.

Next, Ruth bought Chess from Duloe Arabians for a hefty price. A white Arabian mare, gentle by nature and well trained by Becky, Chess was a perfect fit for Ruth's riding ability.

***

I'll admit some equestrian fervor rubbed off on me.

Ruth invited me to accompany her on a trail ride one cool and misty afternoon. After Chess arrived, Ruth no longer rode Ben, so he became my mount on the rare occasions I found time for trail riding.

About halfway along Ruth's chosen trail, we stopped for a break—for the horses and us. When we resumed, Ruth mounted Chess as usual, but some macho streak overrode my common sense. I couldn't halt this overwhelming urge to show off for Ruth by vaulting onto Ben's back, like a cowboy in a classic TV western. I cinched my Akubra cowboy hat, and with my oilskin coat billowing behind like Zorro's cape, I ran full pelt toward Ben's flank and sprung. My plan was to jump high enough to land on his back with poise. Instead, my rib cage met his with a resounding pop of a rib—mine, not his.

I found myself on my back, staring into dull gray clouds.

Ben swung his head around and looked down at my prone form, no doubt confused.

Ruth cried, "Honey, are you okay?"

I answered from where I lay on the soggy ground, "Yup. Just dandy."

Ruth cracked up. "That was hilarious!"

With my ego and rib cage dented, but my spirits high, I recovered and tried again. This time, I gained enough elevation to pop the rib below the one I cracked on the first try.

Sprawled on my back for the second time, I felt the pain from two cracked ribs that would keep me from taking a full breath for the next few months.

After the unfortunate event, I realized that two-years of dining on down-on-the-farm home-cooked meals had transformed my body shape from slim to doughy, and that I'm poor at riding but good at complaining.

***

With justifications I can no longer recall, Ruth purchased Finney, Sky, and Madeline in quick succession. Kristin added Shady, an experienced show jumper twice Zac's size.

Finney, three-quarters Clydesdale and one-quarter Arabian, and almost as big as Charlie, did not take kindly to me. Whenever I came near, she ran away or turned her back, posturing for a swift and deadly kick. We shared a mutual distrust and had many run-ins and calamities.

Sky, born of a long line of Australian World War I war horses called Walers, was naughty when she could get away with it. On one trail ride, Sky bucked Ruth off. Ruth survived unscathed, but Sky bolted and tumbled upside down into a deep drainage ditch. Ruth had to coax and cajole Sky upright while avoiding thrashing hooves. This was not Sky's worst behavior. Several dozen moons later, Sky almost sent Ruth's spirit skyward.

Madeline, a Morgan mare with an ebony coat, stood about Ben's height. I don't know where she came from or why because by this time, not only were we caring for our original horses (Ben, Charlie, Rocky) and our newer horses (Zac, Chess, Finney, Sky, Shady), but friends and friends of friends had turned their horses loose in our paddocks. At one point, our land and hay were supporting eighteen horses.

On the weekends, I opened up a vacant paddock to accommodate parking for cars and trailer-towing pickup trucks. It was pandemonium, with some horses carted off to events before sunrise and not returned until after sunset. Other equestrians rode their horses into the bush, finding and following long-abandoned apple cart pathways.

Besides introducing Kristin to track racing, Becky kindled Kristin's fascination with endurance riding, which entailed steeds clopping at a trot for long distances, typically thirty miles; however, some circuits went as long as sixty miles. Cygnet Farm became part of an endurance trail route. Trail markings appeared throughout the bush, and even more riders came and went on the weekends.

***

I should explain that we first met Becky, a remarkable woman who played a key role in our lives, under rather inauspicious circumstances.

Sarah had warned me that no fence could contain Charlie if he got a whiff of a mare in season. We learned the truth of that caution when one of Duloe's prized Arabian mares came into season. Unbeknownst to us, Charlie shoved his enormous rump against a steel paddock gate and popped it off its hinges before galloping a mile to pay an amorous visit.

I was on my day off when Becky called in a panic. She explained she was fending off Charlie, but holding off over eighteen hands of Clydesdale was more than a one person task, so could we please hurry?

Buyers for the Duloe stud progeny came from wealthy families around the globe, many backed by Saudi oil wealth. If Charlie impregnated the mare, the reparation would break us.

With that foreboding hanging over us, Ruth and I arrived within minutes, armed with a harness and a bag of apples. Charlie paced back and forth along the wooden corral fence line while Becky kept pace with him inside the corral, cracking a whip over his head. We had to get over a ton of testosterone-fueled Clydesdale under control before he breached the castle walls—in this case, the weatherworn split rail fence.

Whenever I worked in a paddock where Charlie grazed, I would start at the rush of warm horse breath on my neck when he poked his yard-long head over my shoulder to inspect what I was doing. Sometimes, I carried apple bits in a plastic bag to spoil him. His curiosity led to a lot of handling. He, along with Ralff and Smoochball, became my paddock mates.

Since we didn't have a saddle large enough to fit him, I rode Charlie bareback. He was easy to handle, and being the gentle giant he usually was, Charlie never tried to buck me off.

After watching the farrier, I taught myself how to trim Charlie's dinner-plate-size hooves. It took me at least a half hour to nip and file each hoof, and I came away drenched in sweat, even in winter. To his credit, he never kicked me; if he had, I wouldn't be here to write this memoir.

In short, I controlled Charlie in the same way Ruth controlled Matilda. Otherwise, he wouldn't have let me lead him home, away from the mare. The apples helped, too, with Ruth walking ahead and offering him his favorite snack.

Despite the episode with Charlie, Becky became a close friend of the family, particularly of Kristin. She was a regular at our farm, trail riding, instructing young students, and advising us on proper horse training and care.

***

Even with Charlie's escape and blind date with an invaluable mare, I hesitated to emasculate my best equine friend, but Ruth took over and had the deed done while I was at work in Hobart. I came home that evening to a different Charlie.

Trimming Charlie's hind hooves from that time onward became a bruising task. He didn't trust anyone, even me, getting close to the surgical site. The giant was no longer gentle, at least when getting near his hindquarters. He broke the latch on more than one lead rope and sent me flying with the flick of a hind hoof. It was grand entertainment for visitors, but after a few near-bone-shattering bouts, I gave up and called a farrier. Sinewy and skilled, he got the job done but said, "Mate, ya might wanna call another farrier next time." I did, from the north and the south, and each one claimed Charlie was the biggest horse on their Tasmanian circuits. That helped ease my doubt about my farrier skills, and I continued trimming hooves on our other horses. I only called in a farrier for Charlie or when a horse needed to be shod, which was all too often.

Although the farriers lifted some of the horse chores off of my shoulders, with all the needs of equestrians, Gum Weaves customers, and the local rubberneckers, my schedule was still at the mercy of horses, riders, and shoppers, all the while tending to our wool-bearing flocks, maintaining the property, and holding down an eight-to-five job. With Ruth off riding, taking Kristin to riding events or Pony Club, I became the weekend tea ceremony host and shop clerk, a clerk unable to demonstrate weaving using Ruth's loom. That business dwindled along with our income.

Something had to give.

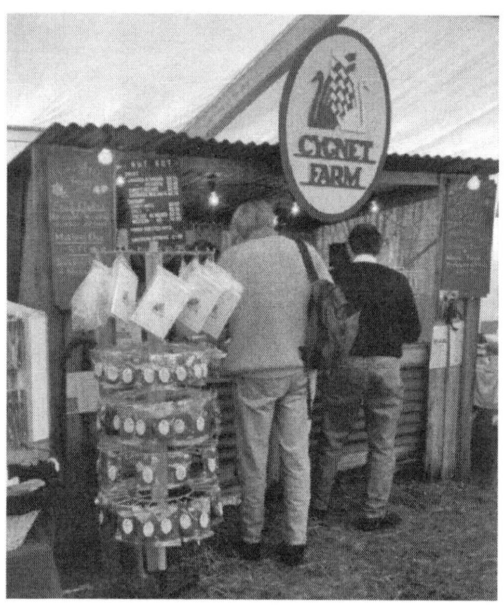

33. GOING NUTS

One evening, with the kids bedded down, Ruth and I lounged by the living room heater and came to a reckoning.

I said, “What do you want to do about the Gum Weaves business, the wool and mohair, the stacks of unsold yarn and raw wool? The horse maintenance and cost to feed all the livestock? We still don’t have a carding machine, the—”

“Stop. I get it. We need income. That’s why I’ve taken a part-time community health nurse job.”

“What?”

“Now that the kids are older and I’ve completed the fiber course, it’s time to return to work. It’s three or four days a week, and I’ll be off on the weekends.”

“Are you sure?”

“I’m the one who veered off of the wool business plan. It’s still our best option to remain solvent, but until we can buy a carder, I’ll work as a nurse.”

“What about horses? Are you planning on more?”

“I’m done, for now.”

I didn't like the "for now," but I could live with it, for now.

Ruth eased back into her profession. What began as part-time morphed into full-time and shifted from community health to hospice nursing, an area of practice I would have no stomach for, but one in which Ruth proved to be an asset to Cygnet families. Because of her involvement with local folks, the living and the dying, she recognized the need for intervention in the lives of the elderly, the lonely, and the poor. That drove her to create an enterprise she named *Henry's House*.

Henry, from Cleveland—one of three American men in Cygnet, all Ohio escapees—became a dear friend to our family and a stand-in uncle to the kids. A former monk and a gifted schoolteacher, he helped mentor Ryan and Kristin when Ruth pulled them out of school and homeschooled each one for a year—Ryan in the third grade and Kristin in the second.

Henry lived in an abandoned apple shed in the heart of Cygnet. A bachelor should not need a 2,400-square-foot home; however, in true monk style, his living quarters took up only 400-square-feet in one corner of the building. The remaining space housed his library. A dedicated scholar, he had vast interests in everything. If you were looking for a book on some obscure subject, Henry would let you borrow the relevant volume. Want to know about the history of wooden pencils? Henry would accompany you to find a two-inch thick hardbound book dedicated to that topic. His library was double the size of the Cygnet public library.

When Ruth came up with the concept of a community integration center open to all Cygnet residents—especially those facing mental or physical challenges—Henry was quick to offer his home as the weekly gathering place. Participants cooked and ate meals there while socializing and taking arts, crafts, and music classes. Henry's House provided a needed service for the isolated aged population, those with low incomes, or both.

Besides Henry, others in the community and the Huon Valley Council pitched in to make the program a success. Ruth wrote and won government funding grants, received recognition from the community, and an award from the Council. She was happy to give back to the little village she fell in love with at first sight.

***

Five years into our migration, our adopted land was feeling more like home. Comfortable with the culture and the people, we researched the ins and outs of Australian citizenship. Since our arrival on the island, the rules had changed. The government no longer required relinquishing US citizenship to qualify for Australian citizenship; we could become dual citizens. The only catch, a minor one for me but a major one for Ruth, was pledging loyalty to the Queen of England. Ruth refused.

I took the vow with my fingers crossed for the children and me. As dual citizens, the four of us could travel freely between Australia and the US using our two passports. A few years later, after the Australian government dropped the Queen loyalty edict, Ruth relented and got her Aussie passport.

However, no matter the feelings and loyalties you develop for your adopted land, there will be things from the land of your birth you cannot live without. In our family's case, it was Reese's Peanut Butter Cups—unfortunately, no relation to our surname. Although the local shops carried an amazing array of tempting Cadbury chocolates produced at the Hobart factory—my favorite was the Violet Crumble—none compared with the Reese's Peanut Butter Cups that weren't available in Tasmania.

At Ruth's request, Mary sent care packages to help us cope with our addiction. When we received the contraband, we hid it in our bedroom, where we gorged on the treats while the children slept. We got away with this for a time, but when pajama-clad Ryan strolled into our room late one night, unannounced, and spied the crumpled orange wrappers on the bedspread, he sounded the alarm. From then on, we found ourselves at war with our children. We had to keep our bedroom door locked day and night.

One night, when we believed the kids were sound asleep and, with our door bolted, we indulged in the latest shipment of tasty treats. We jumped at the pounding on the door.

Ryan yelled, "Open up! We know what you're doing in there!"

Busted.

Danelle and Kristin whined in unison, "Open up!"

Ryan said, "This isn't fair, and you know it."

He was right. We opened the door and invited them in for a late-night snack. After that, as much as it pained us, we shared the spoils with the kids.

Besides satisfying our insatiable appetite for peanut butter cups, munching on our favorite sweet inspired Ruth. What American treats might Australians like?

***

With her entrepreneurial radar at maximum power, Ruth shook me awake one night and said, "Nuts."

"What's wrong?"

"Nothing."

"Then why did you wake me and say 'nuts'?"

"Because that's what's missing. Hear me out."

"Can't this wait? I'm tired."

"No. You need to hear this now."

"If I do, will you let Ralff and me sleep?"

Ralff, lying on my side of the bed, stared at Ruth. Under the pale glow cast by our nightlight, he looked as annoyed as me.

"I'll make it short."

"Okay."

"You know my nurse-friend Lisa, who I help from time to time, cooks and sells sugar-coated almonds at markets on the weekends?"

"Yes."

"She only cooks almonds. What about candied peanuts? Zero. No savory-flavored peanuts. And where's the popcorn? Rarely have I seen anyone eating popcorn unless they're at the movies. No honey popcorn. No colored popcorn. No popcorn balls. No dried fruit strips. No brownies—I could keep going."

"You woke me up for what? Because you realized they don't have some American snack foods in Tasmania?"

"No. I woke you up to tell you we're going to buy out Lisa and rename and expand the business. I think I'll call it Cygnet Farm Nut Hut. What do you think?"

"I don't think at this hour. Let's talk when the sun is up."

Ralff and I nodded off, leaving Ruth to continue pondering.

As it transpired, Lisa had put her business up for sale and was leaving for the outback, where she planned to offer medical care to Aboriginals.

Ruth purchased Lisa's business that included cooking equipment, utensils, and a canvas-enclosed market stall enclosure.

A few days later, upon my return from work, I discovered stacks of cardboard boxes crowding the hallway. Per their labels, they contained shelled peanuts and almonds from a wholesaler in Melbourne.

My nose followed a sweet, tantalizing aroma that wafted through the house.

Ruth stood at the kitchen counter, one gloved hand gripping the handle of a jumbo steel wok. The hose from a gas bottle on the floor snaked to a burner ring under the wok. Trays overflowing with sugar-coated peanuts covered most of the remaining countertop. Focused on her task, Ruth did not hear me arrive. I watched her plaid apron sway in time with her arm's movement as she stirred the wok's contents with a long-handled wooden spatula.

I said, "I take it we're now in the nut business?"

She turned halfway toward me, smiled, and said, "The Cygnet Farm Nut Hut business."

"Let me taste-test the product."

I sampled a candied peanut and enjoyed the crunchy texture and caramelized-sugar flavor of the glazed coating on the still-warm nut. This was way beyond any other candy I had tasted, even peanut butter cups—insanely addictive.

"I was going to tease you and say how bad it tastes, but I can't tell that big a lie. I'm having a hard time holding myself back from eating them by the handful."

She turned off the burner ring flame, dumped the wok contents onto an empty tray, and said, "We'll give these a few minutes to cool, then you can tell me what you think about my candied almonds."

"Okay. Where do you intend selling?"

"Agricultural shows, craft fairs, markets. Ideally, Salamanca Market."

Salamanca Market—bright, busy, and colorful—is world famous and the best of its kind in Australia. Stretching along Hobart's waterfront, crowds of tourists and locals mob the market every Saturday. We had visited several times to shop and dine. Open year-round, rain or shine, hundreds of vendors hawk their wares. Vendor space was at a premium. Ruth had set her sights high. Why wasn't I surprised?

Initially, we sold fresh-cooked, candied peanuts and almonds in small white paper bags at any agriculture show or market we could find. It was a fun, high-profit enterprise that required minimal prep since we cooked on-site. The venues also gave us the opportunity to make new acquaintances. Word of mouth spread about the Yanks selling sweet nuts, and we soon had so many customers that we couldn't meet the demand. Turning customers away tarnished our reputation.

We needed prepackaged products to sell. Ruth began experimenting, creating recipes for all kinds of nut products. Soon, our home became a nut processing facility. The hallway served as our nut warehouse. Boxes of raw nuts stacked floor-to-ceiling forced us to sidestep between the kitchen and the bath and bedrooms.

Ruth registered the business with the government and used her Gum Weaves swan artwork as the Cygnet Farm Nut Hut product label logo. Next came thousands of cellophane bags, a bag sealer, and a gas-fired popcorn machine imported from Michigan.

***

Weeknights became work nights. After finishing our day jobs and tending to the pets and our three offspring, we downed a quick evening tea, then shifted into cooking and bagging Ruth's ever-expanding product lines: Chili Nuts, Curry Nuts, Sherried Walnuts, Honey-Roasted Cashews, Coffee-Roasted Cashews, Honey-Roasted Macadamias, Coffee-Roasted Macadamias, Garlic Almonds, Italian Almonds, Mexican Almonds, Sweet Pecans, and Spiced Pecans.

When the Hobart City Council approved the Cygnet Farm Nut Hut vendor application, Ruth landed a 10 x 14 foot Salamanca Market space at a coveted spot near, of all places, Knoppies pub. Serious money began flowing our way, building our confidence and allowing us to upgrade our enclosure to a modern, bright yellow pop-up canopy.

On top of the popular line of fresh-cooked and packaged nuts, Ruth developed a boutique line of products: decorative jars of Chili Nut Butter and gourmet dark-chocolate-coated nuts of all varieties presented in handcrafted native-wood boxes—products that appealed to the higher end of the market. Soon, barristers and politicians looking for unique gifts for friends and staff became frequent customers.

Ruth carved out time to write and publish a cookbook featuring recipes using the nuts featured at the Cygnet Farm Nut Hut as the base ingredients. We offered the book at the stall for a low price to drive up nut sales.

Continuing to experiment, Ruth introduced another American-style treat: chocolate-walnut brownies. We sold out every Saturday before noon.

Honey-coated popcorn, Honeycrunch, was another winner. And when a customer said she was curious about popcorn balls, the cellophane-wrapped treats she had seen used as Christmas tree decorations in an American romantic comedy, Ruth imported a popcorn balling tool. Popcorn balls wrapped in brightly colored cellophane became another sought-after item in the run-up to the holidays.

Ruth and I manned the Nut Hut every Saturday in the early days. We tasked Danelle and Ryan with chores on the farm while we were away. Once finished, they could play with friends as long as they watched over Kristin.

We developed friendships with other Salamanca Market stall holders, which involved good-natured ribbing. We gave as good as we got except when it came to the American tourists who flooded the market when a cruise ship docked there on a Saturday—the *boaties*. Garbed in psychedelic polyester jumpsuits that helped camouflage the excesses of cruise passenger appetites, their loud American voices reached us well before they did. As if on cue, our market neighbors started rubbing it in. "Hey, Nut Hut. I can hear some of your countrymates headed this way."

In the same way we were initially reticent to speak to Tasmanians, we held back speaking to the boaties. Our neighbors didn't help and took every opportunity to let the visitors know they had poor fellow Americans trying to eke out a living in this godforsaken outpost. On the occasions we spoke with the boaties, their response was generally: "Ya'll sound American.

What brought you to Tasmania?" And the boaties were our worst customers. I couldn't blame them. Why would you want to buy any confectionary after gorging on bottomless cruise liner cuisine?

***

Returning from the market one Saturday afternoon, our neighbor Isaac—the professional photographer and teacher who'd alerted us to Ryan's bullying predicament at Huonville High School—flagged us down at the bottom of his driveway.

I lowered my window, and he leaned on the roof to steady himself as he spoke.

"G'day. Sorry to bother you because I'm sure you're knackered, but I wanted to tell you about an incident with Kristin this morning."

I couldn't help but notice his slurred speech.

Ruth said, "I hope nothing bad happened."

"She's fine and I wouldn't call it bad, but it could have been."

Isaac described the excitement Kristin had brought into his life that day.

Danelle and Ryan had run off to play with their mates, leaving Kristin alone. With her fondness for chickens—or any member of the bird genus—she followed a peahen, Lila, and her newborn chicks through the backyard paddock along a trail leading to the upper eastern paddock.

A Tiger snake basked atop a large flat rock that blocked the peafowl family's path. The mum and her chicks hopped over the deadly serpent's head unscathed, but Kristin fretted they might not be so lucky upon their return.

She picked up a nearby rock and plunked it down on the snake's head, wedging the snake in place. Then Kristin ran the quarter-mile down Woodstock Road to Isaac's home and asked if he had a rifle. When he said he did, she convinced him to follow her.

“I thought Kristin was having me on, but there it was, the biggest bloody Tiger I’ve ever seen with its body whipping, trying to get its head unstuck.”

No doubt Ruth and I had the same thought: “We’d almost lost Kristin in the Gunns Plains Caves, and we almost lost her again today.”

“I made sure Kristin was well out of ricochet range when I flipped the top rock aside with the rifle barrel, backpedaled, and took the first shot. Did nothing more than make the bastard rise into what I’d call a snake’s standing position. With his head cupped like a cobra’s, he looked me straight in the eye. I reloaded by feel while thinking, if I didn’t hit him this time, he’d be the last snake I’ll ever see.”

I said, “Isaac, you could’ve let it go at that point.”

“No, I couldn’t. I didn’t want to let your daughter down, and that bloke had brought it on when he reared up. I popped him on the second shot. Quite proud I am, especially since that Tiger’s head was swaying side to side.”

I said, “After all that, would you like to come up and have a beer or two?”

“Thanks, mate, but I’ve already knocked back a six-pack.”

Isaac had again gone beyond being neighborly. He was our family’s hero.

How Kristin escaped death by snake bite that day was a miracle. The snake must have been sound asleep when she pinned its head down.

We had gotten careless. No more leaving our children on their own, unsupervised.

***

While on the topic of snakes, I’ll take a moment to digress.

Snakes, Tigers in particular, were a constant threat; however, not as great as we had first imagined. As much as we feared Tasmania’s snakes, the snakes feared us more. This is best exemplified by Tony the Tiger—named after my boyhood favorite frosted-flakes mascot—whose vacation home was under my workbench in the apple shed.

I believe Tony—I assumed the male gender—pre-dated our Cygnet Farm arrival. He was long, fat, and shy. Whenever I entered the shed, I could smell Tony before I could see him. It was not a pleasant odor—close to rotting flesh in nature—but a fair early warning that prompted me to shuffle my feet, signaling a human was in the neighborhood.

I rarely sighted Tony beneath the six-inch gap between the shed's concrete floor and the lowest bench shelf. When I did see him, it was only the tip of his tail as he escaped through a hole at the base of the outer wall. To view all of Tony's curled up body, I peeked around the corner of the shed where he liked to sun next to an abandoned steel water tank.

Accepting Tony's live-in arrangement resulted from our live and let live, no-kill policy and the benefit of a reduced rat population when Tony was in residence. However, since you can't tell when a snake's had a bad day, I never, ever let my Blunnies or gumboots protrude beneath the shelf.

***

Because of the need to more closely monitor the kids and the overwhelming demand for Ruth's products, Cygnet Farm Nut Hut blossomed into a family enterprise. Danelle took over making Honeycrunch. Ryan and Kristin became skilled at weighing, packaging, and labeling. Ryan had the dual role of taster. His sense of taste for sweet and savory and tolerance for sampling extra hot chili nuts made him a key asset.

Although our home felt like a sweatshop with Danelle popping and honey-coating popcorn and Ryan and Kristin packaging nuts for the upcoming market day, they learned the value of money, each in their own way. With their earnings, Danelle bought fabric and sewed stylish clothes, Kristin saved for an endurance horse, and Ryan bought practical joke gadgets. His antics included smearing fake dog poop cream on Hobart's pedestrian crosswalk pushbuttons, triggering a fart gas aerosol canister in the midst of a market crowd, and popping open a mayonnaise packet next to his face to make it look like he split his eyeball open when bumping into a door. Those were the infractions we were aware of.

Two annual shows where we sold our products, Agfest near the village of Carrick and the Craft Fair at Deloraine, both near Launceston, generated as much profit in one week as Salamanca Market produced in one year. Vendors like us set up our stalls in recently grazed sheep paddocks, complete with fresh sheep droppings underfoot. The beautiful countryside and the money compensated for the messiness.

Besides being lucrative, the shows substituted for annual vacations. Leaving Cygnet Farm in the hands of friends and neighbors for one week each year, we treated ourselves to motel stays. Unless you've experienced three-minute dribbling showers from a farm's tank water system, you may not relate to the luxury of a long, hot shower. After a day of cooking and selling nuts to hungry customers, we took turns showering. Those not in the shower spent the rest of their waking hours weighing, packaging, and labeling nuts.

Regardless of how much we worked to build up inventory before each show, we never had enough product to satisfy the appetites of the throngs. Ruth and I took turns each night cooking for the following day to replenish stock. At the shows, we set up a backroom behind a curtain where Danelle, Ryan, and Kristin, if not manning the sales counter, packaged the freshly cooked nuts. It was nuts!

Stirring a wok of candied almonds in our kitchen one evening, Ruth said, "Honey, I've been thinking about something."

"What now?"

"I haven't seen any popcorn carts. Could you build one to suit the popper?"

I pictured the classic red carts of our homeland in my mind.

"I would need a couple of spoked wheels."

"There's an antique wheelchair at the medical center they plan to send to the tip. The wheels might work."

"Bring it home and I'll have a go."

"Okay. And one other thing."

I sensed more work for me.

"Go ahead."

"We need better presentation at the shows. Could you build an enclosure that looks more farm-like?"

I was relieved of nut processing for the next two weeks to work on the new projects.

Spending evenings and weekends at my workbench in the apple shed, I fashioned the popcorn cart from plywood, metal channels, and plexiglass. With the cart body painted a glossy fire-engine red and the chrome popper visible through the transparent panels, the wheelchair wheels added the right vintage touch. We parked the cart on the side of our Salamanca Market stall each Saturday and hired Henry to bag and sell freshly popped popcorn. With the enticing smell of popcorn and candied nuts wafting through the crowd, we sold out even on blustery, bone-chilling days.

A new barn-style enclosure we could transport to the shows turned out to be the more challenging project. I bought structural steel channels and hardware. Salvaging weathered planks and faded red, corrugated metal roof panels from the pickers hut carport, I cobbled together a semi-enclosed, portable structure. The bolted-together sections fit on our trailer. Assembling the market stall on-site provided us with a replica of the pickers hut from which to sell Cygnet Farm Nut Hut products.

***

Kristin's goal to buy an endurance horse made her keener on earning and saving than her older siblings. She matured into the nut business. On Saturdays, when Ruth had other commitments, usually due to Danelle's or Ryan's extracurricular activities, Kristin would get up at five and help me at Salamanca Market. Her help would prove fortuitous for the family's livelihood in the coming years.

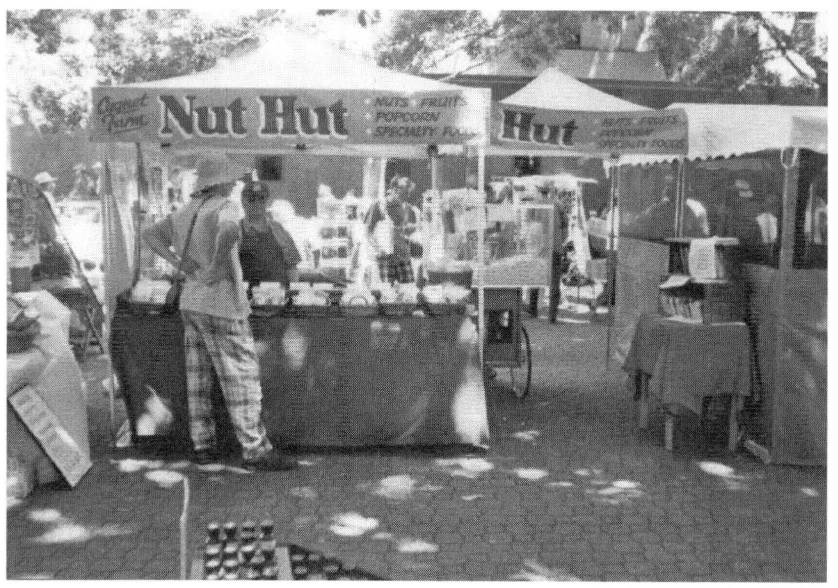

34. ACTS OF GREENNESS

In our seventh year on the island, Ruth got caught up in the horse whisperer craze. The fad gained popularity even before the release of the movie starring Robert Redford. When a renowned real-life horse whisperer toured Tassie and offered lessons, Ruth was an exuberant pupil.

I attended one lesson out of curiosity. Controlling a horse using soft-voice, pats, and leg-squeeze commands sans harness was impressive. However, the visiting whisperer repeatedly cautioned his students, "Don't go home and try this. Practice, practice, practice. Slow and easy. You jump right in and ride bareback without a harness, and you will get hurt or die or both."

It could have been worse. Ruth *only* got hurt.

Of all the horses to test her whispering skills on, Ruth chose Sky, the mare with the volatile emotions of a teenager who had flipped upside down into a drainage ditch a couple of years before.

The Cygnet football field—the *oval*—was open to riders outside of scheduled footie practices and matches. The soft, flat turf offered a safe training ground. To her credit, Ruth successfully applied the whisper technique when she controlled Sky sans halter, bridle, and saddle on the ten-minute ride to the oval. Things went south not long after arrival when Sky decided she didn't take kindly to whispers.

Becky, our family's horsey friend, happened to pass by the oval, and stopped when she spotted a riderless horse grazing on the field. Becky was shocked to find Ruth on the ground, half-paralyzed. Months of physical therapy followed a mad rush to the Cygnet Medical Center and an ambulance ride to the Royal Hobart Hospital. Recovery from spine and hip trauma would take at least one pain-filled year. For the foreseeable future, Ruth could not drive our vehicles—both had manual transmissions—tend to our children, run the Nut Hut and Gum Weaves, ride horses, or do farm work.

***

My career at the HEC ended rather abruptly when I resigned to help care for Ruth, her businesses, and our children.

I was reluctant to leave my job at the HEC since I liked the work and the people I worked with. More importantly, I had unfinished business.

When this government-owned utility took its first baby steps toward commercialization—the prequel to privatization—I was in the right place at the right time. I had weaseled my way into a higher-profile position as an Account Manager. Ivan—a colleague who would become a trusted friend—and I became the face of the HEC to their largest industrial customers. Besides catering to customer needs, backed by a team of economists, we negotiated long-term power supply agreements. I was at the forefront of setting energy rates for the pulp and paper companies, some of which were intent on despoiling Tasmania's native forests.

I had enjoyed the challenges of an engineering career and its rewards, especially keeping food on the family table. However, I was not proud of my environmental track record. Over the years, working with nuclear and coal fired power plants, I became a party by association to degrading the environment and depleting irreplaceable resources. At the HEC, for the first time, I found myself in a position to remedy an environmental wrong: wood chipping—the conversion of timber into chips—of old-growth forests to manufacture paper products in Asia.

Unsure how to wade into restructuring waters and unable to lay off or fire government employees, HEC upper management forced us to endure a one-week team-building exercise. An outside consultant led our department through a series of brainstorming sessions designed to push the HEC toward a slimmed-down, flat organizational structure, as opposed to the hierarchal structure typical of government bureaucracies.

The consultant directed each of us to explain what we did in our current position. A group critique followed to determine what changes would improve efficiency—for example, merge two positions.

Halfway through the week, our group journeyed to the Freycinet Lodge on Tasmania's East Coast, where we stayed for the remainder of the week. We regularly got together to eat, drink, hike, eat, bond, drink, and drink some more. When we returned to the office, upper management assigned new job titles and issued new business cards, and we continued to perform the same tasks we had performed before we rebuilt our team.

The consolidation of positions was not moving fast enough. No one in my group declared, "Stuff it, I'm out of here." So, the process repeated every six months. None of us liked what was happening, but the stays at various resorts were enjoyable.

I decided that if I had to put up with the restructuring and the resultant interference and delays in ongoing negotiations with the wood chipper companies, I would get some personal gains out of the process. I brought Cygnet Farm Nut Hut into the analyses as an example of a commercial enterprise the consultant could use as a business model. With a different consultant each time, only my workmates knew my ploy. They weren't all that pleased but put up with me, the pompous Yank.

I didn't care for the consultants because I didn't like what they were doing, but I valued their business acumen. I convinced them that by adopting the Nut Hut as a business model, we could exemplify business principles and practices everyone could understand (I more so than the others). Biannually, we explored Ruth's latest product concepts.

On one trip, we assessed a new Nut Hut product under consideration: organic strawberry ice cream sandwiched between two organic brownies. We brainstormed the product while on a group hike around pristine Dove Lake nestled below world-famous Cradle Mountain: target market, product differentiation, materials sourcing, price determination, profit margin, price elasticity, performance indicators, packaging, test marketing—many of the same factors that a large-scale enterprise would consider before proceeding with investment in a new product or service. It was not a precise fit with restructuring a power company, but it served its purpose for the HEC and the Nut Hut.

By the time I resigned, I had successfully negotiated several wood chipper contracts in the HEC's favor, and the HEC had assisted with a range of Ruth's product concepts like Dehydrated Organic Fruit Flakes and American Indian Fry Bread, which would become best sellers. When Ruth suffered her injury, I was the first in my department to depart. Management got what they wanted, I had more than paid for my keep, and they were one quitter closer to inevitable privatization.

Did I actually make a dent in Tasmania's logging market by gnawing off a tiny chunk of wood chippers' profits by upping their rates? I like to believe I delayed the felling or perhaps saved the life of an ancient Huon pine or two.

That said, Ruth and our children deserve the real credit. They marched through the streets of Hobart to protest the Australian government's push to build a mega-pulp and paper mill at Wesley Vale in the north of Tasmania. With the efforts of Tasmania's Green Party and other like-minded individuals, the billion-dollar project never saw the light of day.

Good on you, Ruth, Danelle, Ryan, and Kristin.

***

I would miss the comradeship at the HEC.

On my last day, my colleagues were all in for a farewell blow-out party. We kicked it off with our traditional HEC Friday lunch, which on this occasion included pint after pint of Guinness. Trying to keep up with my co-worker's penchant for the brew, I lost several hours. I woke to Ivan shaking me. My jaw rested on the pub bar.

"Dick. Wake up! Are you catching the bus?"

"What?"

"Are you catching the Cygnet bus? The one you ride with Danelle?"

I made an effort to focus on my wristwatch but couldn't.

"What time is it?"

"It's five, mate. You have fifteen minutes, and your briefcase is still at the office."

I staggered my way back to the HEC, grabbed my stuff, and wandered outside. I saw my bus in the far lane turning onto Davey Street, where it stopped at the traffic light. It had left without me.

The fear of having to call Ruth and ask her to ask a neighbor to make the one-hour drive to Hobart to retrieve her drunken, unemployed husband drove me into running into the street, dodging traffic, and pounding on the side of the bus as it pulled away. I glanced up to see Danelle's panic-stricken face framed in a window. Cars swerved around me, and horns beeped as I jogged to keep up with the bus. The brake lights lit up, and the bus screeched to a stop. I ran to the opening door on wobbly legs and willed my feet to climb the stairs.

The bus driver said, "Lucky ya had a daughter on here screaming 'Stop for my dad!'"

I dropped into the seat Danelle had saved for me and passed out until she shook me out of my stupor at the Cygnet parking lot.

With a voice like her mother's, she asked, "What did you do?"

"I drank Guinness. Too much."

It wouldn't be the last time.

35. SPLINTERING OF THE PLATOON

I wore farmer, nurse, dad, and mom hats after I left the HEC. None of them fit. The dad hat was the worst fit of all. I wasn't used to being around. The kids, teenagers Danelle and Ryan in particular, weren't used to me being on their cases and kept asking, "When are you going back to work?"

They didn't want me meddling in their lives.

They hated my cooking.

They needed their mom.

Ruth was in pain and in no shape to help. Until she recovered, the kids needed to suck it up.

Money, as always, was a concern, but a huge benefit from my HEC employment was the superannuation payout. Larger than I'd received when I cashed out from the consultancy where I worked with Andrew. This payout was enough to retire the Cygnet Farm mortgage. Losing the farm was no longer on our worries list.

Still, we weren't worry-free.

***

Finney was a mean and gigantic worry. Ruth's Clydesdale-Arab mare did not like me and, as it turned out, did not like olive trees.

One day, while attempting to move the horses into a lusher paddock, I started with Finney and Charlie. As I led Finney through our olive orchard to reach the greener pasture, with Charlie and his ever-present mate Matilda tagging along and nipping at his tail, Finney reared and broke free of my grasp on the lead rope. Galloping through our maturing olive orchard, she ripped a tree from the ground by its roots and flung it aside before ripping out another tree. Of all the trees Finney uprooted, she chose the Sevillano trees. Native to Spain, this was the variety that showed the greatest promise. How did she know that would hurt us the most?

I could not catch her as she wiped out our dream of a thriving olive business. Charlie clopped alongside Finney, trampling on a few trees while Matilda trotted behind him. I sprinted to open the gate I had intended to take them through. Whooping and waving my Akubra hat, I shooed the threesome out of the orchard. However, I hadn't counted on the influx of goats after I opened the gate.

The prized food of goats happens to be the olive tree. They love to chew on the leaves and gnaw on the bark. The result is the slow death of the skeletal remains of a ring-barked tree. In the ten minutes it took to rid the orchard of horses, a pig, and goats, I witnessed the decimation of half of our olive orchard.

I was determined to get rid of Finney, but before I could, she wreaked more havoc. But this time, it was not her fault.

Kristin continued to help man our Salamanca Market stall, which was a blessing. Without her steadfast help, we would have lost that income stream. In so doing, she saved enough to buy Fleur, her dream endurance horse. Becky helped Kristin train the Arabian mare from the Duloe stud, and all was well until

Kristin tried an experiment—she just wanted to see what would happen.

On a whim, while Fleur and Finney grazed rump-to-rump, she braided their tails together. The experiment did not bode well for either horse, especially for Fleur at fourteen hands high, while Finney was seventeen hands high—a foot taller. Finney towed Fleur backward up and down the paddock as Kristin attempted to calm Finney. Getting in between the backsides of two spooked horses to undo their knotted tails was not a good place to be. As with her other near-death experiences, again, Kristin came away unscathed. As for Fleur and Finney, they came away with shorter tails after Kristin gave them tail-cuts with her birthday gift Cashel horseman knife.

***

While Ruth continued to recover, Danelle turned sixteen and left the farm.

She graduated from the Friends School at the end of grade ten and, seeking more freedom and tired of her father's badgering, continued her education at a public college, Hobart College. Unbeknownst to us, to ensure students in rural areas have fair and ready access to higher education, the government provides a stipend to cover rent and food for young adults living fifty kilometers or more from Hobart. Much to our sorrow, Danelle took the government up on the offer and moved into a flat in Hobart with several friends.

The departure of our eldest left a gaping hole in our hearts.

Three years later, at sixteen, Ryan followed suit, insisting on moving to Hobart to attend college with his friends. We couldn't come up with a way to stop him. Again, like his sister, the government was on his side. However, since Ryan was socially immature and continually tested physical boundaries—remember the water barrel rolling and swing incidents—we demanded that he find lodging in a supervised flat. Sigrid Von Hartmansdorff, a German expat and the mother of Ryan's best geek friend, felt the same about her only son. Siggy, as she called herself, had bought a large house in Hobart, planning to rent the spare rooms to other teen students and to take on the role of full-time housemother. Before we agreed to Ryan's living arrangements, we wanted to interview her.

Siggy came to our farm for the meeting on a cloud-free summer afternoon. Ruth and I greeted her when she arrived in her silver Mercedes—what else would a German drive—and parked beside the apple shed where Woodstock Road officially ended.

The sylph-like woman with rainbow-dyed locks got out of her car and turned full circle, taking in the surroundings, before she nodded, smiled, and proclaimed in a strong German accent, "End of the road people."

Ruth and I exchanged a puzzled look that said: "Is she daft?"

Ruth said, "Thank you for coming, but what did you mean by 'end of the road people?'"

"I've met people all over our world who live at the end of roads. I know you."

Ruth and I discussed her comment later, trying to figure out what she meant. Did she mean that we're after privacy? Maybe crazy people live at the end of roads? Worse yet, were we at the end of our road, done for?

The strange assessment aside, Siggy impressed us as a no-nonsense Fräulein who would have no problem maintaining order. We released Ryan to her oversight and crossed our fingers.

Kristin remained on the farm, but her interest in horses waned in favor of boys.

The Reese platoon splintered as each child grappled with their identity while the parents struggled with the question: "What's it all about?" We had migrated to help our children, but now all we had done felt pointless. We still had Kristin, but how long would that last?

36. GONE MAUI

Ruth had not fully recovered from her horse-inflicted trauma, but she no longer needed my care and feeding. I began looking for employment.

The job market for power engineers in Australia was tight. That's why a call from a consultancy came as a surprise. Tasked with bringing the National Electricity Market (NEM) online, they needed an electrical power engineer to respond to inquiries phoned into the NEM help desk in Melbourne. The NEM was comparable to California's Enron but with pricing safeguards. The position was not in my wheelhouse, but it paid well and came with benefits: roundtrip airfares, hotel, meals, and a chauffeur.

I accepted the offer but had to reside on the mainland during the work week. It was a temporary gig, four- or five-months. However, while I enjoyed life in Melbourne, Ruth and Kristin were stuck down on the farm doing all the chores I wouldn't be doing. I still manned the Salamanca Market stall on Saturdays, with Sundays reserved for farm work.

Warrick, my contact at the NEM office, scheduled an in-person meeting in Melbourne on the Sunday evening before I started work. I arrived punctually at a lavish waterfront restaurant and found Warrick and a female companion, both dressed to the nines, seated at a table overlooking the harbor.

Neither stood to welcome me as they eyed me up and down. I was wearing a three-piece business suit, and before arriving, I had made sure I didn't have any bits of hay, straw, or fur clinging to me, compliments of Cygnet Farm.

I said, "Hey, Warrick. It's a pleasure to meet you in person."

"Likewise. This is Natalie, a partner in my firm."

"Natalie. My pleasure."

She motioned for me to sit across from them, facing away from the harbor view.

Warrick read me well because as I sat down, the waiter asked what apéritif we preferred. They ordered some French drink with a name I couldn't pronounce. I was still trying to think of a fancy drink I could order when Warrick interrupted my thoughts and said, "What kind of beer would you like?"

Did they look down on me, see me as an unrefined bogan? This job promised to be a formidable challenge, both culturally and technically. I was out of my element. Although the compensation was needed to keep us afloat, I missed the down-home feel of Tasmania and our simple farm life. And most of all, I missed Ruth.

***

While I toiled away in Melbourne, Ruth became a picker.

Tired of being the victim of her horse-whispering injuries, she joined migrant pickers and toiled through long summer days harvesting fruit at several orchards in and around Cygnet. And when the harvest season ended, she worked sorting and packing apples pulled from cool stores. Her recovery regimen was cure or kill. Ruth's can-do attitude helped her return to good health.

She also made many connections. One with an organic apple orchard owner, Seamus. Ruth was ready to introduce organically grown dried fruits and fruit leathers—she named them "Fruit Flakes"—to Nut Hut customers. To test the market, she purchased the minimum quantity of organic apples Seamus would provide. When he delivered the apples to our shed, I discovered the brimming box contained roughly 2,000 apples. That's a half ton of apples to process before they rotted.

Ruth used to dehydrate fruits and make fruit leather for school lunches using three tabletop dehydrators that were now sitting idle. I stopped doing farm chores and spent my Sundays and she spent every evening and Sunday washing, coring, peeling, and slicing apples before turning them into apple rings or flakes. The enterprise left us exhausted, and the farm neglected.

However, packaged dried apples and apple flakes were a hit. Stock sold out each Saturday. The impediments to expanding production were the peeling and coring effort and the limited capacity of the dehydrators.

My contract employment at the NEM ended, and I could get back to farm and family life. I was overjoyed, but with Danelle and Ryan living in Hobart, the farm family was down to Ruth, Kristin, and me.

Our fractured family needed to heal.

***

Ruth lured Danelle and Ryan home for the weekend by promising a big surprise. Seated around our Huon pine table and eating burgers and homegrown veggies fresh off the barbie, Ruth said, "I'm taking the family to Hawaii."

We all burst into laughter.

I said, "Honey, you can't be serious?"

The look she gave me told me she was.

"I sold my loom and bought the family tickets to Maui. Let's escape and enjoy some quality time together. Chris and Dan invited us to stay with them in Kihei by the beach."

Our closest American friends, Chris and Dan, with whom we'd grown close in Truckee years earlier, were the only friends who visited us in Tasmania. Their family, with two children similar in age to Ryan and Kristin, stayed on the farm for a week. We had a great time and were sad for weeks after they left.

I said, "What about the farm and the Nut Hut and giving up your loom?"

"I arranged for Becky to tend the farm, and the Nut Hut staff will be away on vacation for a month. As to the loom, it can be replaced."

So, our family went to Maui and re-bonded for a month, but when our vacation ended, they returned to Tasmania without me.

Since I was jobless, Dan offered me the opportunity to earn some American dollars. I became his construction company's quality control engineer with all expenses paid. For the next three months, the money I made would go into our Tasmanian bank account. Three months stretched to six. So, for longer than we had ever been apart, I worked a high-paying, low-stress job and enjoyed my free time on Hawaii's beaches. Ruth ran the farm and our businesses on her own.

Or so I thought.

37. RUTH VERSION 2.01

Ruth had kept me in the dark about Cygnet Farm happenings in our weekly phone chats while I was working (and playing) in Hawaii. She claimed she wanted to surprise me.

Upon my return, after clearing Hobart airport customs, I waited curbside, scanning the incoming traffic. I couldn't wait for Ruth to pull up in our old red Subaru. I briefly looked away to peek through the window at the Budget rental car counter. Anne was there, unaged. I thought about how far we had come since that Saturday night over a decade ago. I turned back to find a new sky-blue Peugeot sedan had stopped at the curb. The honking of the car's horn startled me. Seeing Ruth behind the wheel startled me even more.

She shouted through the open driver window, "Unless you want to try your luck hitching, best you get in, mate."

As she got out, we embraced, and I said, "So this is where my hard-earned wages went?"

"That's partly true."

Before I could delve further, she said, "You drive. But remember which country you're in."

On the ride home, she explained the Subaru had blown a head gasket, so she traded in our trusty all-purpose transport and bought the Peugeot—pure luxury compared to the Subaru. With its sleek handling and opulent leather interior, this was a car for city folk—very un-Cygnet-like and not a goat-toter. I didn't tell her that. Instead, I said, "This is a great ride. How can we continue with the Nut Hut using this car?"

"We don't. I bought a used cargo van. It even has a trailer hitch."

"Now I understand why you hinted the Peugeot took only part of my wages."

She broke eye contact, pretending to admire the passing scenery. I sensed I was in for more revelations.

She encouraged me to prattle on about the work I did for Dan. When I ran out of things to say about work, I told her about the ocean life I saw while snorkeling. I couldn't shut up for the rest of the one-hour drive home.

As I piloted the Peugeot into the driveway, I saw the cargo van Ruth had mentioned parked beside the apple shed. What she hadn't mentioned was the travel trailer parked in the remnants of the olive orchard, right where I stored the tractor and the brush hog. Where was my farm equipment? I set the question aside to ask, "You bought a trailer?"

"No. It's Julian's."

Julian, a longtime friend and Oxford-trained architect, had retired to Cygnet years before our arrival. All of five-foot-four, skinny as a whip, and a devoted chain smoker, he and his stout Eastern European wife, Ramona, were at the pinnacle of Cygnet society. We had attended several extravagant (by Cygnet standards) parties at their residence.

So why had Julian parked a trailer—a *caravan*—in our paddock?

Ruth answered my unspoken question.

"Ramona ran off with a dashing Belgian and left the country with their savings after clandestinely selling the house she and Julian jointly owned. That left Julian nearly penniless and living in a trailer less than half the size of an American mobile home. I felt sorry for him and offered a spot where he could run an extension cord into the apple shed for power. In exchange, he agreed to design and build Matilda's dream house."

"What? Matilda already has a house, well, a barrel. She seemed happy with that."

"Well, she was not. She's getting old and grumpy. And she has trouble standing up in the morning, especially when it's cold. The vet said she suffers from rheumatism. She needs a cozy house where she can stay warm and dry."

"You're kidding. An architect designed a house for a pig, and then he built it?"

"Correct."

Thinking things couldn't get crazier, I parked the Peugeot in the garage where my Land Rover should have been.

"Where's my Land Rover?"

Her jaw tightened. She crossed her arms and turned her head away. I knew what had happened. My comeuppance had arrived.

"I got rid of it."

"No. No, no, no. How could you do that? Was it because of the Volvo? Were you still upset about my trading it in?"

She turned and locked eyes with my tear-filled eyes.

"It wasn't that. Do you remember the time the Land Rover almost killed you?"

She had me.

***

Several years earlier, following the track down from the bush with a full load of firewood mounded on the bed of the Land

Rover, I stopped to open the cattle gate. We kept the gate closed to prevent livestock from roaming out of the paddock and into the bush. I commanded Ralff to sit tight in the passenger seat. After setting the parking brake, I stepped down from the cab.

I swung the gate open. Far below me, Ruth walked toward the pickers hut. We waved to each other, except Ruth wasn't just waving. She was hopping around, her arms swinging back and forth as if performing jumping jacks in gym class.

Confused, I shrugged and turned back to the Land Rover, only to find the Land Rover coming to me. My first impression was that Ralff was driving. He calmly stared at me through the windshield, sitting as I had commanded.

Then I realized we weren't in America, and Ralff was in the passenger seat. Besides, dogs don't drive!

Now, the vehicle was upon me. I gripped the roo bar and leaned into it, reasoning with some remnant of Neanderthal logic I could stop several tons of steel and firewood using brute strength. The Land Rover kept coming, accelerating, pushing me backward, my Blunnies sliding over the slippery turf.

I finally had the presence of mind to jump to the side, jog along, jerk the driver's door open, hop in, and slam on the brakes. Ralff and I slid down the slope, skidding to a stop just short of a sheer drop that would have sent us nose-first into the creek.

Ralff remained stoic, staring ahead like nothing had happened.

I composed myself, reversed back up the hill, parked on a level patch of ground in the paddock, got out, and latched the gate.

To help calm my nerves, I sang the ditty our kids learned in school when we moved from city to farm:

You gotta shut the gate, mate,
You gotta shut the gate,

Listen silly cobber, let's get something straight,
It's a simple task, don't underestimate,
You gotta shut the gate, mate,
You gotta shut the gate!

Ralff and I crept down the hill to where Ruth waited with her fists firmly planted on her hips.

I was ready for battle when I stopped. She met my gaze, her face grim, rigid, with fists still on hips.

Before she could open her mouth, I offered a reasonable explanation.

"I thought I had adjusted the parking brake shoes after I replaced them."

Pulling a Land Rover's parking brake lever clamps a set of brake shoes against a drum on the drive shaft. It's a clever design that, when properly adjusted, locks all four wheels. After replacing the shoes, I adjusted them but did not allow for wear.

"Your mistake almost cost you your life and made me a widow."

I didn't know then that her witnessing the near catastrophe caused by my poor mechanical skills would someday cost me the Land Rover. That day came while I was in Hawaii.

Many years in our future, Ruth revealed she had given my Land Rover to a friend who agreed to keep it out of my sight. Hopefully, her friend's mechanical skills were better than mine.

Women claim they don't have power like men. That may be true for women, but not for wives, at least not mine.

***

I jerked my suitcase out of the Peugeot trunk, bereaved and angry at the loss of my beloved pickup truck. Following the footpath toward the house, Ralff bounded through his dog door and about bowled me over. The joy of seeing my old friend dialed down my anger. I dropped my suitcase, stooped, and ruffled his fur. This was the first time I noticed graying on his snout.

Appearing out of nowhere, Smoochball rubbed against my leg, purred, and meowed, "Hello." The poor little thing looked scrawny, no longer the chunky ball of fur I remembered. I was petting her when I noticed a new building in the backyard paddock. It had to be Matilda's new residence.

Ruth followed me as I traipsed into the paddock, stopped, and faced the new house, somewhere in size between a Barbie doll house and our house. It was Victorian in design, clad in fresh-milled Tas Oak. Dull gray metal panels covered the steeply sloped roof. I peeked through the dormer window and saw Matilda napping. A ramp on one side of the house led to a low, open doorway covered by a burlap flap.

I walked to the other side and found a man-size door. I opened it, and Matilda offered her familiar "Humph" greeting. She looked comfortable, all six feet of wire-haired rooter stretched out on her side, nestled on a thick bed of straw. Tas Oak planks covered the walls. Fiberglass insulation batts lined the ceiling between the rafters. The one-bedroom home was cozy and just big enough for Matilda to turn full circle when she chose to. The fragrance of fresh-cut timber, the scent of straw, and Matilda's porcine aroma created a sense of calm. I had the strongest urge to sit beside Matilda and zone out.

Ruth entered behind me and said, "Do you like it?"

"I have to admit, Julian more than covered his rent."

"Let's go to the house. You can catch up with him and I'll get your bag unpacked. Too, there's someone I want you to meet."

"Where's Kristin?"

"She's not here right now. She's in Hobart with some friends."

I didn't like the sound of that, but I was too stressed to pursue the topic.

When we entered the house, I saw Julian at the Huon pine table, absorbed, playing cards with a younger fellow about Danelle's age.

I said, "G'day, Julian."

He dropped his cards and rushed over to shake hands.

After I thanked Julian for his design and building help, Ruth said, "Honey, I'd like you to meet Edwin. He's been staying with us."

Edwin came over, and I sized him up. He had a thick bandage covering his forehead. When I looked down, I saw he was wearing my bedroom slippers. My mind-voice screamed: "What the hell?"

We shook hands, and he said, "Very pleased to meet you. Your wife is an angel."

Ruth interjected, "Danelle and I were having Devonshire Tea at a Hobart café when we came across Edwin. He was in a bit of a pickle."

I said, "What kind of pickle?"

Ruth motioned me toward our bedroom.

"You can help me unpack your suitcase."

Julian and Edwin returned to their card game.

I hesitated. Something had changed in the kitchen—a lot, in fact.

The cork floor tiles used to be dull and scuffed. They were now polished to a glossy finish.

The countertops used to be Formica. They were now thick, end-grain butcher block.

The cabinets used to be white. They were now a dark walnut color that matched the countertop finish.

The sink and faucet were modern and complemented the updated space.

I looked at Ruth, questioning.

"Follow me."

Behind the closed bedroom door, Ruth began by explaining Edwin's presence.

While she and Danelle were chitchatting over tea at the Hobart café, they witnessed Edwin pass out on the sidewalk outside the window where they sat. When he fell, his head slammed into a parking meter pole. Blood spewed and pooled around him. Mother and daughter grabbed napkins and ran out the door to help him. They did what they could to stem the blood flow as he came to. Ruth told him she would call an ambulance to get him to the Royal. At that, he became agitated and said if she did that, he would go to jail because he was high on drugs. Ruth's compassion trumped common sense when she and Danelle helped him into the Peugeot, and Ruth brought him to Cygnet Farm to recuperate.

She said, "I'm sorry I didn't explain earlier and even more sorry he's wearing your slippers. He's a nice young man faced with family abuse issues. I had him stay in Ryan's bedroom. He's close to recovered. I've arranged placement for him in a halfway house in Hobart. They'll admit him next week."

Cygnet Farm now had a human sanctuary division with Edwin and Julian as the current residents.

"Okay. But what about the kitchen? Who did all the work?"

"Julian replaced the countertops. Another couple of guys you don't know refinished the floors and the cabinets."

Jet-lagged and overwhelmed by all the changes, I had to sleep.

I said, "I'm going to need some time to process everything."

"But I have other things to show you."

"Can it wait until tomorrow? I need to rest."

"Sure. You sleep. I'll ask our guests to keep it down."

As I drifted off, I realized I need not worry about Ruth surviving should I go belly up. Even with me still kicking, she had no shortage of backup men available.

***

In one of my nightmares that night, with Ralff sitting next to me, I drove the Land Rover through the open gate and down the slope toward the creek. I pulled the parking brake lever, and the pickup rolled over in my dream world as I rolled over and snapped awake in my real world, snout to snout with Ralff. It was a toss-up which was worse, the nightmare or Ralff's tongue lapping my face.

What a way to start the day, but at least I was home, partly refreshed and ready for whatever came next. And that was lucky.

Ruth rolled over to face Ralff and me.

She said, "Good morning. Would you like breakfast? Eggs and a slice of homemade bread with butter and jam?"

"Sounds wonderful, but first, tell me about Kristin. I take it she's not here?"

"I did everything I could to keep her from leaving, but she followed in Danelle's and Ryan's footsteps and lives with friends in Hobart. She works part-time as a dog groomer at a pet salon while she finishes college. It's just us and, of course, Julian. In your absence, it was comforting to have Julian around for emotional support. And Edwin helped me focus on something other than our family problems."

"How are Danelle and Ryan doing?"

"The only time I see our kids is when I make a special effort to meet them in town or on Saturdays when they help with the Nut Hut. When they can't help, Henry does. Our children may have gone astray, but we have good friends."

My unvoiced thought: "All male."

Because of her independent streak, I knew Kristin would move on at some stage, but I hoped against hope that her love of horses would be strong enough to keep her down on the farm. I was disappointed but not surprised.

After all Ruth had sacrificed to pull the family back together, much like the HEC's restructuring efforts, it was all for naught.

***

After breakfast, Ruth dropped more bombshells.

First, besides refinishing the kitchen and bathroom cork tile floors, Ruth's worker-friends had refinished all the Tas Oak floors in the house to like-new condition.

Second, a new loom awaited me in the barn shop. I needed to assemble the largest loom yet. Before that, I would need to rearrange merchandise; otherwise, shoppers wouldn't have enough room to get around the loom.

While strategizing where to move the Gum Weaves yarns and bagged fleeces, baskets filled with colorful carded wool roving caught my attention.

I picked up a basket and turned to Ruth.

"Where did the roving come from?"

"From me. We now have a carding machine. I'll show you. It's in the apple shed."

So, we finally had the carder Ruth yearned for.

Somebody had cleared the shed of hay. In place of the hay, we now had a VW-bug-size carding machine and a commercial dehydrator the size of a walk-in freezer.

We also had three antique apple peeler-corers, each twice as big as our kitchen refrigerator. The British-made peeler-corers, according to their nameplates, could each peel forty-four apples per minute, which meant they would peel and core a bin of apples in under an hour. The machines were in poor condition. Ruth explained that although we only needed one machine, she bought three, thinking I could bring one into working order by pilfering parts from the other two.

I said, "I can't believe you did all this while running the farm."

"I didn't. Have you noticed the sheep and goats are gone, all 160?"

She continued. "And we're down to two horses."

"Oh no, you didn't get rid of Charlie and Ben?"

"No. They're here."

Ruth had changed. I couldn't believe she had parted with her pets and wasn't begging me for more. And she appeared more serious and preoccupied. Ruth was at war with Kristin, isolated from our eldest children, and I had been away for six months. The stress would have been considerable.

I hoped the change in behavior was temporary, and she wasn't planning to replace me.

I said, "Now that we have the carder, we'll need raw material. What are we going to do for wool and mohair?"

"The fleece stockpile we have will carry that side of the business for years."

She had it all figured out, and I felt left out.

"Any other surprises in store?"

"No, other than the fruit flakes business is booming, the nut sales continue to do well, and we are now selling American Indian Fry Bread, prepared on-site. And once you get a peeler-corer working, we'll grow the fruit flakes business."

I recalled with fondness the guidance the HEC's consultants had contributed to our success. Ruth had put their advice into action.

Ruth continued. "The same for the Gum Weaves shop after you assemble my loom."

I later learned that Ruth developed the fry bread recipe and claimed that my Native American ancestors had passed it down from generation to generation. My parents looked like American Indians, but that was it—zero Indian in this son.

Another deception: Customers presumed we grew our nuts at Cygnet Farm because the business name was Cygnet Farm Nut Hut. In fact, we had a single walnut tree in the backyard paddock. A distributor in Melbourne continued supplying the raw nuts that Ruth worked her magic on.

***

Ruth had my future tasks mapped out for me. I felt relieved that she planned to keep me around, at least in the near term. I wasn't totally useless.

Standing in the shed with her, I admired all she had accomplished; however, something was missing. Overwhelmed by all the changes and revelations, I realized I had not spotted the Fiat.

"Where's my tractor? And the brush hog?"

When she turned to face me, her expression said it all.

"Did you know the Fiat's brakes didn't work?"

I thought I'd be taking that fact to the grave or that someday I'd get around to replacing the tractor's brake shoes.

"Yes, but I had a way to deal with that. I used the creeper gear when towing and lowered the brush hog when mowing. Stopped every time. No dramas."

"No dramas for you, but what about the guy I hired to mow the paddocks? You never told me the Fiat was brakeless, and who would've believed it, anyway? No sane person drives a tractor without brakes."

"Did he wreck the tractor or get hurt?"

"No thanks to you."

"All good then. So, where's my tractor?"

"Sold."

Although the tractor was not my first love, it came in a close second to the Land Rover. And without a brush hog, we'd have to hire out the mowing.

"Who did you sell it to?"

"Some orchardist from Huonville."

"You told him about the brakes."

"Yes, and he was just as foolish as you. He said it was no bother."

She had me again—another comeuppance.

The combined losses of the Fiat and the Land Rover were too much. I needed some alone time, so I went for a walk.

Leaving Ruth behind, and with Ralff trotting by my side, I wandered over to Ben and Charlie. The seasoned friends grazed together near the pickers hut. Older and wider, these last Cygnet Farm horses remained our favorites.

I communed with them while Ben nudged my pockets and burped his request for apples. Ralff sniffed nearby for rabbits.

"You guys have been mates for more than a dozen years. What do you reckon about all that's happened? Lots of horses, sheep, goats, and Bret's cows have come and gone. You two were the first and now the last. What comes next?"

Neither horse expressed an opinion, and with no prospect of apple treats, they returned to grass munching.

Their scents helped lower my anxiety before I trekked to the bush for solitary reflection. Ralff loped ahead, continuing the hunt for his archenemy: rabbits.

Veering off familiar bush tracks, we followed a narrow trail through the ferns to a clearing I had not visited before. I checked for Jack Jumpers on a blue gum tree older than me before squatting down and leaning back against the striated trunk.

Having completed his guard dog circles of the clearing, Ralff plopped down and laid his head on my thigh. I dug my fingers into his soft black fur. Aided by the camphoraceous scent of the tree's gum nut blossoms and the hum of the visiting bees, I drifted into contemplation.

I looked at the dispensing of the Land Rover and the tractor-with-no-brakes from Ruth's perspective. My cavalier attitude had put me, Ruth, and our children at financial risk. Having surplus males in reserve also made sense. I could appreciate her survival instincts.

I had left her alone to cope with farm and family many times, and now abandoned by her children, why wouldn't she have a change in attitude and behavior?

Still jet-lagged, I nodded off. If not for the scolding of a kookaburra signaling that night was upon us, I would've stayed longer. I think Ralff would have been happy with that, too, since we had been apart for so long, but to avoid tripping, falling, or getting lost, we navigated back onto the track that would lead us home.

***

Weeks later, lying in bed one night with Ralff between us, Ruth said, "I never want to be apart again. Too many things happened."

"Tell me everything."

"Well, as if Ron, as old as he is, didn't have enough Sheilas, he breached the fences and went looking for more. His flock followed. Calls came in at all hours from neighbors asking why our goats were roaming their land. Ralff and I had to hike to find them, and I used pellets to lure them home. As soon as I turned my back, the herd would escape again. On top of that, the last shearing was a multiday event. We had too many sheep and goats. One morning, after a late night spent rounding up our wayward Angora herd, I sold them along with the sheep. Then Kristin rebelled. That did it."

"What happened?"

"Well, I had these men remodeling the house, with Julian pitching in and building Matilda's house. I wanted to surprise you. At the same time, I was running Gum Weaves and the Nut Hut with fruit flakes and Indian fry bread added in. There were heaps of people to train and manage, so when Kristin and I went head-to-head, I reacted, probably overreacted, by selling off or loaning out the horses, including Kristin's horse, Fleur. I spared Ben and Charlie because they are easy keepers. Also, I love Ben, and I know you love Charlie, and I didn't know how Matilda would cope without Charlie. I needed my life simplified. I did not want to deal with the needs of farm animals every time I stepped outside. That's your department."

"Ralff, move so I can hug your mother."

When I nudged him, he jumped off the bed and flopped onto the floor.

Ruth and I cuddled while I tried to process what it must have been like for her. The real issue and the tipping point was Kristin, our baby, making us empty nesters before our time. We didn't expect our family's lives to unfold this way. Ruth's remodeling of our home, expanding our businesses, and removing livestock were driven by life without our children and the splintering of our family, all compounded by my foolish behavior and absence.

I felt thankful she wasn't planning to replace me with one of her backup men.

I finally broke the silence. "If I knew what you were going through, I would have come home."

"I thought I could handle it, and not having to worry about money was a pleasant change."

"You did handle it, but lesson learned. From now on, we're sticking together."

And we did.

38. PUB GRUB CLUB

Edwin left for Hobart as planned, followed by Julian to Brisbane, Queensland, where he planned to design anything except pig houses.

I completed the tasks Ruth had assigned, and she reopened the Gum Weaves shop, selling as much roving as I could produce. You read that correctly: *I*. Ruth employed friends, this time female, to help with the nut business. That left carding wool and mohair to me. Ruth claimed it was my responsibility since the machine was glitchy. I had to admit she was right. The carder required continuous monitoring and periodic resetting of drum clearances. Besides that, operating it was monotonous and hazardous. Losing concentration for a moment while feeding a fleece into the carder's mouth could cause the shredding of a hand and an arm if snagged by the opposing curved steel combs on the cylindrical drums.

But another task Ruth laid on me was more dangerous than the carder: the apple peeler-corer. You may recall my comments about how dangerous it must have been to operate the vintage equipment we saw when we toured the Apple Museum. Never did I imagine I would operate one of them.

The peeler-corer I brought back to life was rife with danger. Standing before this mechanical engineer's dream, the operator jams an apple onto a spike mounted at the tip of a steel arm. The arm swings up to a rotating corer tube and peeler blade. The peels fall onto the junk conveyor belt and drop into a trash bin. Now that the apple is free of the peels, a lever pushes the cored apple onto a second conveyor belt that leads to a stainless steel collection vat. The core goes the way of the peels. While all that is happening, a second arm swings down, waiting for the next apple. The machine was superfast. A moment of daydreaming could result in the peeling and coring of a hand.

After running the peeler-corer long enough to fill the vat, I handed off the peeled and cored apples for washing, boiling, pulverizing, dehydrating, and packaging for sale as fruit flakes.

After a few months of this monotonous and risky routine following my return from Hawaii, I'd had enough. Ruth relented and hired a friend from her apple factory days who was familiar with machinery. All I needed to do was land a job in my line of work, which proved more challenging than I expected.

The consultancy where I'd worked with Andrew and Bea had closed their Hobart office, so going back was not an option. Neither was the HEC, which continued to shrink its ranks. Besides, I preferred not to retrace my steps. I wanted something new and eventually found it at another Hobart consultancy, one that was Australian-owned and operated.

I felt at home in my new job and dropped right back into the bus-commute groove. Ruth's businesses still filled my nights and weekends, but without having to look after the herds, my life was closer to carefree.

My new engineering job presented fresh benefits and challenges: the Tea Lady, a bar, and an exclusive club.

***

At the HEC, a rather staid Tea Lady would visit mid-morning and mid-afternoon, offering hot tea and generic cookies from her cart.

The new Tea Lady was a bit on the bawdy side. And she didn't need a cart because she served tea and premium cookies to the entire male office staff from behind a bar—a fully stocked bar in the office. There was no escaping the morning and afternoon breaks. If you tried, a couple of guys would hound you until you joined. It didn't matter whether you were in the midst of a phone call with a client; they would hang up on the call for you. Employees took breaks seriously and with good reason.

The breaks provided the opportunity to take the piss out of workmates—tease them mercilessly. Each fifteen-minute session would begin with the managers, engineers, and CAD operators (draftsmen) lounging at or near the bar—a group of about twenty—mumbling or staring at their feet before someone slung an insult like, "Why do we have a bloody Wog working here? I thought we only hired the fair-skinned?"

The recipient of the jab, an engineer of Greek extraction, said, "I'm fair-skinned. It's you pale Pommy bastards who shouldn't be here."

And that would kick it off. Back and forth for the rest of the break. Everyone joined in and Tea Lady rekindled the verbal sparring, if it lulled.

Every break, a different guy would catch the flak. I tried not to fire unless fired upon, but, as the sole Yank, I was often on the receiving end of the taunts.

First, it was my sandals. Each day, when I arrived at the office, I exchanged my Clark dress shoes for a pair of open-toe Birkenstocks—with socks. That provided a lot of ammunition for ridicule.

Next came my tweed jacket. Was I trying to look like Sherlock Holmes or a Pom?

And when it came to politics, no matter the US president's name or party, they blamed me for voting the bastard in.

I shouldn't complain, as the managers bore the brunt of the abuse. They were also banned from the Pub Grub Club. This invitation-only club dedicated to drinking, eating, and discussing any topic except work met every Friday at noon at the watering hole selected by the Club's current president.

The verbal slams, slurs, and insults arrived at a rapid clip at these meetings. And if you slipped up and said anything workplace-related, you had to buy a round—*shout*—for the ten to fifteen members in attendance. Mention a word like "desk" or "pencil" and you paid the price. Refer to the name of a project, and you bought two rounds. Pub Grub meetings could be exorbitantly expensive, especially if they extended to quitting time, which they often did.

The office bar opened at 5:00 p.m. each day, with Tea Lady returning to serve at a buck a beer. My bus to Cygnet departed at 5:15 p.m. and was a ten-minute walk from the office. That provided an excuse to forego the nightly sessions. Had that not been the case, I'm certain I would now be a card-carrying AA member.

If you think a bunch of goof-offs ran these Pub Grub Club and after-hours bar sessions, you'd be mistaken. The quality of the work and the attention to detail on the projects designed in that office were far above those of any other firm I worked for. As raucous as they were, the teatime gatherings and lengthy Club meetings broke down unspoken cultural and professional barriers, and fostered bonds that went beyond friendships. I credit management for not interfering with the shenanigans.

I remained a member of the Pub Grub Club for three years but could never hold office because I was a bloody foreigner, a

Yank. Nevertheless, I exerted some crucial influence on these gatherings.

***

Before hoisting my first pint of Tassie Tiger lager at my swearing-in ceremony at the Hope and Anchor, I sprinkled enough salt over the brew to cause the foamy head to spill onto the bar before I drew a mighty pull. My fellow Club members' boisterous laughter faded into silence. Bluey—another redhead and the Club's president on that day—broke the silence with the rapping of his gavel.

He shouted in his gravelly Irish brogue, "You blokes see that? He put bloody salt in his beer!"

The eyes of the Club members and other pub patrons focused on me as I emptied the glass, slammed it down on the bar, and declared, "Now, that's how we drink our beer in 'merica!"

Bluey said, "You're having us on, mate?"

I swore on my mother's honor that I was not—which was only partly true. Where I grew up in Ohio and in my family, salting one's beer was a given. I do it to this day and probably have premature artery clogging because of the practice. But I was having them on when I declared that all Americans salt their beer.

Bluey surveyed the members who were weighing up what the Yank had revealed, and said, "Better pass me that salt, mate."

I slid the saltshaker along the bar. He caught it and tipped a dash into his pint—not enough to raise the head by much. He knocked back a mouthful and let the beer swish around, reminiscent of a sommelier, but instead of spitting, he swallowed.

"Bonzer! That's one hell of an enhancer."

The other Club members nodded their agreement as they took turns salting their beer.

From that meeting forward, if drinking any beer except Guinness, enhancing became standard practice.

***

Besides not being able to hold office in the Club, I was assigned a seat whenever we drank at Knoppies' outdoor tables. That's because there's a grassy knoll, Parliament House Gardens, between Knoppies and the wharf. Since the members knew about the Kennedy assassination grassy knoll theory, they presumed, no matter the odds, that there could be another attempt on a Yank. I had to sit with my back to the knoll and one chair away from other Club members. There was zero clemency.

On one of those warm grassy knoll days, a co-worker finally broke ranks and took pity on me when I slipped up and alluded to a design project I was working on. He handed over a key fob with a quarter-coin-size medallion etched with the Guinness harp logo.

"Show the bartender this when you shout."

"Why?"

"You'll see."

I got a ten percent discount on the two rounds.

When I returned with a tray of Guinness pints and handed the medallion back, I said, "Thanks. How can I get one of those?"

"Get a Guinness card and have it punched each time you buy a pint. After you drink 500, you qualify."

They chuckled as each of them held up a medallion.

***

I could never reach Guinness medallion status, but on my final day at the firm and as a Pub Grub Club member, I was determined to keep pace with the medallion holders.

I had decided to leave the firm a few weeks earlier. As much as I liked my fellow workers, I disliked the direction the new management was leading us. Instead of heavy power project designs for power plants and industrial clients, the company had dumbed down into commercial projects like power and lighting designs for department stores and music venues. I found myself dictated to by architects, those men of artistic vision clad in black, who spoke of their ethereal visions that I must bring to fruition. Their hubris exceeded my tolerance. Too, the realities of my personal life and the choices I had made were nudging me in a new direction.

To celebrate my resignation, everyone wore sandals to work. One of my colleagues who did not own a pair got creative and fashioned sandals out of cardboard and yarn. It was a silly-looking group of mates that trudged down to Knoppies that day.

And when they honored me with my very own salt shaker labeled "Beer Enhancer," I declared, "This is the greatest meeting ever!" At least, that's what I think I declared.

Someone must have called Ruth because it was getting dark when she helped me out of my grassy knoll chair and into the Peugeot.

I gave up. I would never be the Aussie drinker I aspired to be—maybe in the next life.

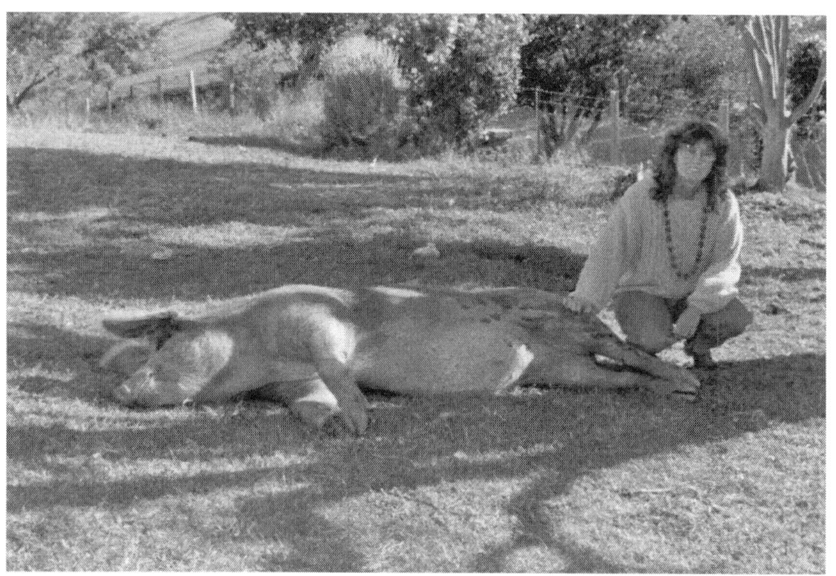

39. SAD FAREWELLS

Fifteen Christmases had passed since we left Sparks.

We had lived our dream but awoke to an alternate ending. Our family unit had crumbled. Our children had scattered like buckshot, leaving Ruth and me on our own to tend the farm and run the businesses.

Danelle had moved to Sydney, where she resided with her South African husband and our blessed two-year-old granddaughter.

Ryan remained in Hobart with his friends, enjoying a bachelor geek lifestyle.

Kristin lived and worked at an Arabian horse stud near Melbourne.

With our two daughters far away on the mainland, family get-togethers were history.

With our lives adrift in choppy seas, we felt emotionally seasick.

What happened to our Hollywood ending? I suppose we should have been happy our offspring were alive and well, but this was not how we envisioned things turning out. If any of our children had decided to return to America and attend university or go back and find work, our Tasmanian adventure could come to a close. Ruth and I would choose where to move to be near them, our granddaughter, and any future grandkids. In hindsight, we had not considered the impacts of raising our children in a foreign land during their formative years. The answer to whether they were more Yank or more Aussie was obvious.

We had left the crucial role of family support out of the equation when we moved far from home. Our dreams had clouded our judgment.

We expected that Ruth's sister, Mary, and her family would visit at some stage; however, we had not thought it through. Their allotted annual two-week vacation boiled down to one week when flight durations and jet lag recovery times were factored in. Too, living on the same financial plateau as us, spending thousands of dollars for what would effectively be a one-week vacation was out of the question.

The visit by our Maui friends, Chris and Dan, who owned a private business and could schedule longer vacations, was helpful, as was a visit from my parents (bless their souls) when they were well into their eighties.

But that was the extent of American family and friend support and influence. If we had family nearby to help raise our kids, maybe we would have had our Hollywood ending.

***

I was approaching early retirement age, with Ruth not far behind. The repercussions of the rough-and-tumble farm lifestyle we had adopted greeted our bodies every morning. Although Ruth never acknowledged it, we were getting old, as were the pets that remained in our care.

Mother Nature has a dark side when it comes to the lifespans of dogs and cats. Ralff and Smoochball did not have many years ahead of them. It wasn't fair.

Ben might make it another ten years.

A pig's natural life expectancy averages a dozen years.

Charlie could look forward to a few more decades of lazy grazing, but his mate, Matilda, would be long gone. They still roamed the farm together, but only after I helped Matilda get on her feet each morning. And every morning played out the same—think of the *Ground Hog Day* movie—with Ruth standing in the open doorway of Matilda's house, cautioning me. "Be careful Matilda doesn't roll on you!"

My help consisted of pulling and pushing a 400-pound pig up to her four-legged stance. Once she was standing, I urged her to shuffle through her low door and onto the ramp. After she limped to her feed trough to slurp down the warm breakfast Ruth had prepared for her, I was free to go.

Aidan, our veterinarian and friend, visited a week earlier, and left Ruth in tears. He attempted to administer painkillers to Matilda via a shot and discovered Matilda was needle-averse. Although not steady on her feet, she ran away like a piglet when Aidan got as far as pricking her on the rump. He recommended putting Matilda down. Ruth assured him that would never happen.

Aged farmers with aged pets and adult children determined not to return—the time to revise our life plan had arrived.

As much as we loved Tassie and the adventure we had lived, we both missed our families back home, and since our children showed no interest in returning to Cygnet Farm, we plotted a fresh course through the choppy emotional seas.

***

The first question: Where should we go? Mary, Ruth's only sibling, still lived in California, which was the big draw; however, if we moved near her, visits from our children would be unlikely. We fell in love with Maui during our Hawaii vacation. Hawaii felt right. And who doesn't want a Hawaii vacation? If we moved there, that might entice our children, Mary, and other family members and friends to visit.

The second question: Where would we receive the best medical care as we aged? Although Australian insurance coverage was comprehensive and the health care system provided a high-quality level of care, there could come a time when we needed family support to weather a health crisis. Again, Hawaii felt right.

The third question: What do we do with the remaining pets at Cygnet Farm? There was no easy answer. Ben, Ralff, Smoochball, and Matilda didn't have much time left. Charlie was okay, but we couldn't abandon him. What to do with our old friends? Do we stay until they die of old age? We set those dilemmas aside for the moment.

The fourth question: What do we do with Cygnet Farm? If we thought one of our adult children might return and take over the farm and the businesses, we definitely wouldn't sell. But there was no interest. Maybe we should rent the farm out for the time being? Bret continued to agist his cows on our land, keeping the grasses and weeds at bay, so the paddocks would be fine if we left, but someone had to maintain the house and yard. We set aside the sell or rent dilemma, too.

I put the fifth and final question to Ruth. "Are you prepared to sell all the businesses? Get rid of everything you worked so hard to create and all the equipment? The Nut Hut recipes, business name, stock, stall enclosures, the van? Dump the remaining yarn stockpile, the carder, the fleeces, your loom? Cash-out?"

The answer was instantaneous. "Yes. As long as we can live closer to Mary."

On the presumption that Hawaii was our destination, I applied for every relevant job opening, finally hitting pay dirt for a management position at a consulting firm in Hilo on the Big Island.

Over a cuppa with Becky, we confided we might move back to America, but we didn't know whether we could abandon our pets.

She said, "Are you interested in selling your farm?"

Ruth said, "We're up in the air about selling or renting, if we leave."

"I just sold my property, and I'm looking for a place to land for a few years. Would you consider renting to me?"

Ruth and I exchanged a look. We trusted Becky like she was family. She was the substitute auntie who helped guide Kristin through her childhood and tumultuous teen years.

I said, "I'm sure we could work something out, but we still have the old animals to deal with. Could you look after them?"

Becky rubbed her chin before she answered.

"With one exception, I could do that if you cover their food and vet expenses or deduct the costs from the rent."

Ruth said with trepidation, "What exception?"

"Matilda. I ran into Aidan, and he asked if I could talk some sense into those bloody Yanks at the end of the road."

Aidan had the best interests of his patients at heart.

Tears welled up in Ruth's eyes again.

I said, "Becky, can you give us a day or two to consider your kind offer?"

"Certainly."

After Becky left, I did my best to comfort Ruth, but she was inconsolable and went to bed to cry.

When she returned to herself, she said, “I know Aidan is right, but I can’t bring myself to agree to send Matilda to the other side.”

“You want me to handle it?”

The answer was a given.

“I can’t be around. I’ll go away when it happens.”

What choice did I have? Matilda had to go whether we moved or not. But how could I put Matilda out of her misery? She was my friend too. I loathed the death side of farming.

***

I chatted with Aidan, and we scheduled Matilda’s end-of-life for the following evening. When I informed Ruth, she left for a hotel stay on the East Coast. She would return when I let her know this coast was clear.

Plan A was to lure Matilda to a suitable disposal site and ply her with grog until she was fall-down drunk. At that point, Aidan would inject her with a lethal cocktail. Matilda would peacefully cross over the rainbow bridge. I would deal with the disposal of her body afterward.

I knew Matilda liked beer—loved it. She could knock back beer faster than any, even faster than Guinness medallion holders. She proved it when a friend offered a batch of homebrew that was not to his liking, but thought I might like it since he suspected it tasted like Budweiser. I can’t complain about the stereotyping. Before moving to Australia, we thought the Aussies preferred Fosters.

When I dumped a slab’s worth of the homebrew into a bucket and set it in front of Matilda, she vacuumed it down like a living sump pump, belched, and followed me around, waiting for me to offer another round. There was no sign of inebriation, which meant I would need a stronger numbing agent to make Plan A successful.

I visited my old friend Max and came away with a slab of his cheapest beer—Matilda wasn’t picky—and three bottles of vodka. Although I had not previously tempted her with the hard stuff, I suspected Matilda would drink any booze I put in front of her.

***

The night before Matilda's last day in this world, I dropped by her home for a chat, as I had done many times in the past. Ensconced in her Victorian abode, she rested in five-star luxury compared to her previous one-star water tank home.

This would be our last meetup. I quietly entered through the human's door and found her stretched out on her straw bed, lost in piggy dreams.

I don't know why, but I had kept my visits secret from Ruth and the kids. When asked about the nights they couldn't find me, I claimed I was tinkering with this or that in an outbuilding. On those chilly nights, I recalled Ruth shouting her last command of the day—less than a hundred feet away from Matilda's home—from the back porch, "Honey, don't forget to cover the pig."

Her voice hung in the frigid night air, echoing off the gums.

"Honey!"

I stayed silent and held my breath.

Ruth would wait for what felt like an interminable time before the back door slammed, signaling her return indoors.

As on those visits, moonlight bathed Matilda's form, filtered by the cobwebs stretched across the dormer window above my head. Having gobbled down her last supper, she reclined across the room from me, half buried in loose straw. A tattered army-surplus wool blanket stretched to cover her six-foot torso.

Hunkered down opposite the old girl, with my back leaning against an insulated wall, I waited for her body heat to warm her home. With each exhale, thin wisps of vapor rose from the edges of her blanket.

Some might find the smell in Matilda's home unpleasant. For me, it brought back fond childhood memories of my short-lived farm life. That said, the pigs on the Ohio farm didn't have a guardian like Ruth. They had to endure freezing Ohio winters and sweltering summers until the Grim Butcher paid a visit. Matilda has lived a charmed life by comparison. No pig I have ever heard of got tucked in at night.

For years, I refused to have anything to do with Ruth's pig, but somewhere along the way, we became friends.

I pulled an apple from my pocket and commanded, "OPEN."

Matilda snapped awake. Her massive head lifted and swiveled toward me.

Her lower jaw dropped, and I popped the apple into the gaping maw, careful not to let my fingers get too close. Ruth routinely put her hand in Matilda's mouth, but I wasn't that brave or trusting.

Two chomps and the apple vanished.

I displayed my open palms and firmly stated, "ALL GONE."

Satisfied I wasn't holding out, her head dropped back onto her straw pillow.

The rising room temperature and her rhythmic breathing lulled me into a meditative state.

"Matilda. Do you remember the time the Tiger snake got trapped in your ceiling? Scared Kristin out of her wits when she came in looking for rogue hen eggs."

"Humph."

That was her usual crisp response to my questions when she was awake enough to listen to my jabbering. Sometimes, she would contribute a consoling grunt. No rash words, harsh judgments, or unsolicited comments, just that occasional "humph" I can take to mean anything I want.

The blanket shifted, and I pulled it back over four exposed cloven hooves. I know the discomfort I feel when my feet escape the blankets on a cold winter night.

"Matilda. Do you remember the TV reporters who filmed and interviewed you?"

"Humph."

"I'll take that as a 'yes.'"

She can be so agreeable.

"I'll always remember our chats and trust they helped you as much as they helped me. Goodnight, old girl."

"Humph."

I checked her blanket one last time before leaving.

You'd be justified in questioning my grip on reality, especially if you're a city dweller. However, reminiscing over past visits with Matilda, I realized the meetings were convened during periods of high stress. In this final get-together, I faced hastening the death of a pet that had become an integral part of our family's life. This last visit was the most stressful ever.

***

The following morning, without the aid of Ruth's safety warnings, I helped Matilda into a standing position. I fed my friend her usual warm breakfast and turned her loose to roam with Charlie for the day.

At dusk, after Aidan arrived and before Matilda bedded down, she followed a bucket of beer to a piece of level ground near the apple shed. She sucked the brew down in record time.

Rather than risk wasting all the vodka, I dumped one bottle into her bucket. She knocked it back like a career boozer, so I followed with the other fifths. Again, it was no surprise that the contents vanished in two gulps.

I spread her trusted blanket and commanded her to lie down. Kneeling beside her, I scratched her belly until she nodded off.

To give the alcohol more time to work, Aidan and I strolled to the house and had a cuppa.

"Aidan, we're considering moving back home. If we do, can we put you on a retainer to care for the animals we leave behind?"

He paused and frowned.

"I'm sorry, but I can't make that commitment."

His response surprised me. Our friendship went back to Ralff's inaugural visit.

"My apologies if I've offended you."

"Nothing like that at all. My reticence is more of a personal nature."

Night had fallen when we wandered down to Matilda. Under the light cast by a full moon, we found her sound asleep. The alcohol had done its job.

While Aidan loaded a syringe, I squatted beside Matilda's head and whispered my goodbyes.

Aidan waited behind her, ready to administer the shot.

I nodded my okay, but when Aidan inserted the needle, Matilda jumped up, knocked me out of the way, and scooted across the paddock. Her squeals of discontent echoed around the farm.

Aidan said, "Aye. Plan B then?"

"Unfortunately, yes. I'll get a pail of pellets and lure her back."

"I'll pack up my ute."

"Once I get her back and she's eating, I'll wait at the house."

"Aye. Will let you know when it's done."

Back in the kitchen, I poured another cuppa and waited.

The crack of a rifle shot broke the night's stillness. Sadly, Matilda got the quarter ounce of lead behind her ear.

I couldn't bear to leave the kitchen until a knock at the door forced me to move.

I opened the door, and Aidan said, "She's on the blanket."

"Thank you."

"She'll be right, mate."

That was the last time I saw Aidan. Two months later, he died from a rare form of cancer. That explained his reluctance to commit to taking care of our pets. Aidan was a Cygnet fixture and a beloved friend to all who knew him. I'm sorry we parted on such a sad note.

***

I had no stomach for my last chore.

Relative to other members of her species, Matilda had lived a long and pampered pig life at Cygnet Farm. Loved by family and friends, she would be dearly missed.

I found her on her favorite blanket in peaceful repose. She appeared to be smiling. I hoped she was happy and her soul was free of her physical form I was about to incinerate.

I carted enough firewood from the woodpile to encircle her body. After setting it alight, I stood back and witnessed the flames engulf what was once our happy pig friend.

I watched TV to take my mind off of the deed I had done, then trudged back to her funeral pyre. The firewood had burned down to coals, but the flames had only blackened Matilda's frame. Aside from singeing Matilda's wiry coat, the only thing the fire had accomplished was to permeate the air with the tantalizing smell of bacon.

I carted and stacked more wood around her and watched the coals set the new fuel alight. I returned to the TV until the evening.

After calling Ruth to give her the all-clear to return the following day, I checked on the cremation process. When I opened the back door, I breathed in bacon scented air.

Red coals glowed in the night, shedding enough light for me to see that Matilda's carcass remained intact. I wondered whether Bret's method only worked on cows.

I piled all the firewood we had around and on top of Matilda and watched it flare twenty feet toward the starlit sky. This had to do the job.

I rose early the following day, expecting to see a few embers and a pile of ashes in place of Matilda. The last thing I needed was for Ruth to return and find the unburned remains of her favorite pet.

The bulk of Matilda's body remained. I rang Bret.

"G'day, Bret. We had to put Matilda down. I tried to cremate her, but it's not working. She won't burn."

"That's why all of Cygnet's craving bacon. The three butchers have had a run. Ya won't find a bacon slice for sale this side of the Huon."

"I've been craving it myself. I guess this morning's offshore breeze wafted the smell into town."

"Spot on, but tell me how you built the fire."

I explained the procedure I had followed, the unacceptable results, and that I had depleted our woodpile.

"Mate, that pig was too thin. If she had some fat on her, like me cattle, she would have popped and sizzled down to nothing. Ruth fed her well."

I believe Bret was right. Ruth raised Matilda on a weight watcher's diet. Matilda's BMI would have been dangerously low if there was a comparable scale for pigs.

I needed a heap more firewood, but I had no way to get it without the Landrover or the Subaru. Thanks, Honey.

"Bret. You know anyone selling firewood?"

"Go see Snag. He lives at the other end of Woodstock Road."

"Snag?"

"Yup. Can tell him I sent ya."

"Okay."

I took the cargo van in search of some bloke named Snag.

We passed his place every time we traveled to Cygnet, but I never knew who lived there.

A dwarf-size fella was pulling split firewood from a pile and tossing it onto a trailer.

I got out of the van and said, "Bret sent me this way to buy firewood. Looking for a bloke goes by the name of Snag."

"That'd be me, mate."

"Yeah, I live up at the Whitbread property. I need firewood. Today."

He removed a leather glove, and we shook hands.

"What's the rush, mate? Weather's warming up."

I told him my predicament, and when he finished laughing, he said, "I reckon that's why I been smellin' bacon and why me missus said we run out and couldn't buy no more."

Janus, the butcher, owed me a commission.

"Well, you think you could drop off a ton of split wood at my place today?"

"No worries, mate. See ya by noon. Cash to hand."

True to his word, Snag—I had no wish to know how he came by that moniker—delivered. He tipped the load off his dump trailer close to Matilda, and I forked over the cash.

I covered Matilda's body in dry firewood, sprinkled a cup of gasoline over the lot, and threw a lit match at it. The fire whooshed to life, forcing me to backpedal. Ruth would be home soon. I didn't know what I'd do if this fire didn't erase Matilda's remains.

What I did was repeatedly apologize to Ruth and continue piling on firewood for three more days until Matilda was a mound of ashes and the smell of bacon was no more. After Ruth recovered enough to face life again, we spread Matilda's ashes over her truffle-hunting hillside.

Our venture into farming came to an abrupt close. We were done.

***

In quick succession, an American family, newly arrived in Cygnet, adopted Ben. Charlie went to live with a local family headed by a younger Australian version of me. He planned to put Charlie to work hauling logs out of the bush.

We had multiple offers for the Nut Hut, the popcorn cart, and Gum Weaves, including the loom, the carder, and all the inventory. The proceeds allowed us to get off to a start in a new old land—Hawaii.

It was time to close our Tasmanian chapter and open a new one. We had reached the end of our road in Tasmania.

My Hawaii employer arranged travel and accommodations for Ruth and me and, at the last minute, for Ryan, who decided he could live the geek life in Hawaii as easily as he could in Tasmania.

We boxed up our personal items and stored them in the barn. Everything else stayed with the house and the outbuildings.

Becky moved in as soon as we departed. Although her familiarity and friendship with our pets helped ease the pain of leaving Ralff and Smoochball behind like we had done with our dog, Molly, fifteen years earlier, it was heartbreaking. Leaving the farm that fulfilled our dream was no easier. The memories we made will drift through our minds until we are no more. And in case there's no Heaven, and even with all the downs and the ups on Cygnet Farm, we had lived our version of Heaven.

Did we do the right thing?

Did we move for the right reasons?

Did we regret our decision?

In his hit "My Way," Frank Sinatra expressed it best when he crooned: "Regrets, I've had a few, but then again, too few to mention."

I agree with Frank.

Next stop Hawaii! From Cheers to Aloha—volcanoes, beaches, and da kine!

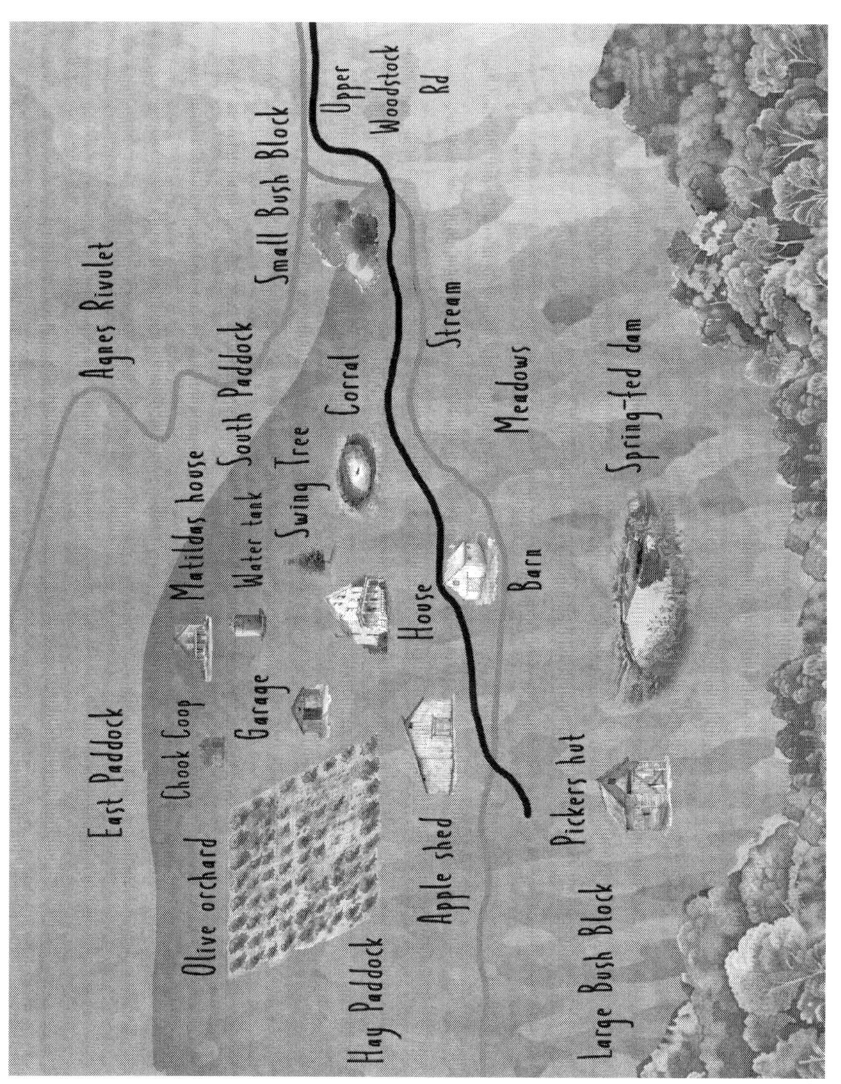
Agnes Rivulet
East Paddock
Chook Coop
Matildas house
South Paddock
Small Bush Block
Olive orchard
Garage
Water tank
Swing Tree
Corral
Upper
Woodstock
Rd
Hay Paddock
Apple shed
House
Stream
Meadows
Barn
Pickers hut
Large Bush Block
Spring-fed dam

CYGNET FARM

ACKNOWLEDGEMENTS

A special thanks to Ruth, the love of my life soulmate; Danelle, Ryan and Kristin, our three offspring; Mary, Ruth's sister; Ed and Dorothy, my spirit parents; Edie Jarolim, the amazing editor; Karen Phillips, cover designer; best friends, Chris and Dan of Hawaii; DJ Grummer, author-mentor and friend; the Beta readers; and all the Cygnet neighbors, friends, and natives who put up with the obnoxious Yanks at the end of the road.

AUTHOR BIO

Dick Reese, a born storyteller, was trapped in an engineering career until a win in a short story writing competition inspired the creation of his debut memoir about an American family migrating to farm life in Tasmania, Australia's island state—Down Under Down Under. He currently lives a citified life in northern California with his wife, Ruth, and Chiweenie sidekick, Frodo.

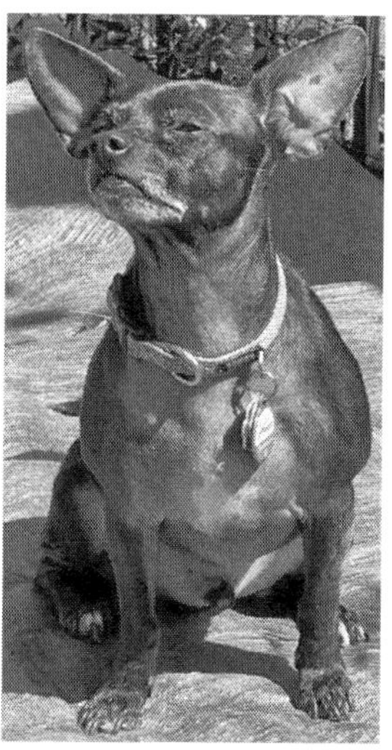

NOTE: For Memoir bonus material, photos, and a glossary, visit rdrrpublishing.com. Email: books@rdrrpublishing.com

Made in the USA
Middletown, DE
06 February 2025